BRITISH LEYLAND
THE CARS, 1968–1986

AUSTIN
ALLEGRO

TR7
TR 7

BRITISH LEYLAND
THE CARS, 1968–1986

JAMES TAYLOR

THE CROWOOD PRESS

First published in 2018 by
The Crowood Press Ltd
Ramsbury, Marlborough
Wiltshire SN8 2HR

enquiries@crowood.com

www.crowood.com

This impression 2023

British Library Cataloguing-in-Publication Data
A catalogue record for this book is available from the British Library.

ISBN 978 1 78500 391 2

Designed and typeset by Guy Croton Publishing Services, West Malling, Kent

Printed and bound in India by Thomson Press India Ltd.

CONTENTS

INTRODUCTION AND ACKNOWLEDGEMENTS

The story of British Leyland is a vast one, and already there have been many books and monographs that have tackled aspects of it. There are many different ways of looking at the story, but this book deliberately focuses on the cars and car-derived commercial products. The story of the company's evolution in the first section is designed to provide essential background to those products, and is not in any sense intended as an in-depth study of what is an enormously complicated piece of British social, economic and political history.

Surprisingly perhaps, defining exactly what was a British Leyland product and what was not is by no means straightforward. The approach taken here is a logical one, which separates the products into two groups: those that were inherited at the formation of BLMC in 1968, and those that were developed or reached the showrooms during the British Leyland era.

Inevitably these groups are complicated by the fact that some inherited products were further developed under British Leyland; the Mini, as an extreme example, was inherited, but survived right through the British Leyland era and beyond. The solution I have chosen is to discuss the further development of 'inherited' models in the chapter devoted to them, but to treat any major change as the creation of a new model, therefore including it in the British Leyland chapter. So, to follow the example of the Mini, the story of the 'inherited' Mk II models is in the earlier chapter, but from the point where they became Mk III models with Leyland badges, they are in the later chapter.

As for a cut-off point, I have chosen 1986 because this was the year that the old British Leyland ceased to exist, and what was left of the car and light commercial business was renamed the Rover Group. Inevitably, some new models appeared right on the cusp of the changeover – a notable example being the Rover 800. However, even though these were developed under British Leyland, they were not sold during that company's lifetime and are therefore not included in this book.

Vitally important in the British Leyland story is the question of exports. Listing all the countries to which each individual model was exported would be tedious and probably not very enlightening. So would the full story of all the overseas assembly plants that built BL models from CKD. However, where overseas plants developed distinctively different models, I have guessed that their story might be of more interest, and so have included these in a further chapter.

Next, British Leyland used an enormous and potentially confusing variety of engines in its car and car-derived commercial ranges in this period. To avoid complicating the main text, and to avoid a degree of repetition, I have put the details of all these engines in an Appendix. Finally, British Leyland inherited a large number of factories, and another Appendix provides a ready reference to these.

Throughout this book, every effort has been made to ensure technical accuracy. I have drawn on a large number of sources for the information in it, and I have also tapped into the knowledge and the memories of a very large number of people. To all those who contributed their thoughts and ideas, here is my chance to say thank you, and to apologise if I have misunderstood what you tried to tell me.

James Taylor
Oxfordshire, 2017

VANDEN PLAS

I AN OVERVIEW OF BRITISH LEYLAND

THE STORY OF BRITISH LEYLAND is an enormously complicated one, and the purpose of this section is simply to provide a framework to act as background to the story of the cars it produced. Indeed, it is sometimes difficult to determine exactly when British Leyland began and when it ended; the dates chosen for this book are 1968, when the British Leyland Motor Corporation was formed, and 1986, when what was left of that grouping was formally renamed as the Rover Group.

One other point needs to be made at the start. British Leyland was a vast organization, with manufacturing interests in many areas beyond cars and light commercial vehicles. This book makes no attempt to deal with these other interests: it is purely about those cars and the light commercials that were directly derived from them.

The British Leyland Motor Corporation, 1968

BLMC formally came into being on 17 January 1968, and was the result of a merger between British Motor Holdings (BMH) and the Leyland Motor Corporation. BMH was then the largest car manufacturer in Britain, nearly twice the size of the Leyland group. It had been formed as BMC (British Motor Corporation) in 1952 by the merger of Austin and the Nuffield Organisation. In 1966 it had become BMH, when Jaguar and its Daimler subsidiary joined the fold. Leyland, meanwhile, was a long-established truck and bus manufacturer that had branched out into car manufacture by taking over Standard-Triumph in 1961.

The 1968 merger was brokered by the Industrial Reorganization Committee, which was then run by Tony Benn. It was an organization established by the Labour Government under Harold Wilson to create a more efficient British industrial base through mergers and reorganization. While the Leyland group was in a strong position, BMH was getting dangerously close to collapse, partly because many of its models were outdated.

Benn was particularly concerned that Britain had no motor industry group big enough and strong enough to counter the major groups in Europe, particularly Volkswagen. He believed that merging the two British groups would produce a group large enough to achieve this, and would also save BMH from collapse. Over the summer of 1967, he encouraged talks between the top management of both sides, and agreement was reached.

There was no doubt that the Leyland group was the stronger partner in the new alliance, and it was a Leyland man who was appointed as Chairman and Managing Director of the new British Leyland Motor Corporation. He was Sir Donald Stokes, who had made his name particularly through export sales, and he was a clear-thinking and often ruthless individual.

British Leyland used this instantly recognizable 'flying wheel' logo. The flying wheel was later used on its own without the words.

First Stages

One of the first tasks that fell to Sir Donald Stokes after the merger was to examine the future products portfolio of the companies he now controlled. He was reportedly quite shocked to find that what had once been BMC (principally Austin and Morris) had very little on the stocks. The Austin Maxi was on the way, and work was being done on a planned replacement for the Mini, called 9X. But there were no plans to replace the big-selling medium-sized models, the Morris Minor, the 1100/1300 range, or the larger 1800 saloons.

Stokes clearly thought that much of the blame for this deficit in the future product programme could be laid at the door of Alec Issigonis, the Technical Director of BMC. So he rapidly sidelined him in a management shake-up, giving him the new job of Special Developments Director. He moved Harry Webster from Triumph to replace him, now with the job title of

Architects of British Leyland's early days: Stokes is on the left, his Financial Director John Barber is in the middle, and on the right is George Turnbull, who was then Managing Director of the Austin-Morris division. ALAMY

Technical Director, Small and Medium Cars; and as Triumph's new Technical Director he appointed Spen King, who had been in charge of Rover's future model think-tank.

All this happened in and around May 1968, and on 12 June, Stokes addressed a meeting of former BMC distributors at Longbridge, promising them a completely new model policy over the next five years under the direction of Harry Webster. Webster was a very shrewd choice, as he had overseen the engineering of a company that had produced not only sports cars but also 'executive' saloons, and had experimented with front-wheel drive for its medium saloons as well.

Stokes also decided to recruit new management talent from outside BLMC in order to inject some fresh thinking into the company. One of his first appointments was John Barber, an experienced former Ford man who became BLMC's Finance Director and Stokes' right-hand man. Ford was then regarded as the best training ground in Britain for motor industry managers, and over the next few years a sizeable number of former Ford employees were recruited to BLMC. They certainly did inject some new ideas, but they also aroused a degree of suspicion among the established workforce: they were not members of the 'tribe' associated with each of the old companies, and they wanted to do things differently.

The rest of the Stokes management team was almost exclusively drawn from the Leyland side, but it would be wrong to suggest that this was favouritism. The fact was that BMH was in a bad way, which strongly suggested that new management was needed to sort it out. So its former top management was scattered: Joe Edwards, the Managing Director, was retained as a consultant, though he quickly saw which way the wind was blowing and resigned in July 1968. The new Austin-Morris division, which was really a continuation of what had once been BMC, went to George Turnbull, a Leyland man whose career had begun with Standard. And as his two deputy chairmen on the new BLMC Board, Stokes appointed Sir William Lyons of Jaguar and Lewis Whyte, who had been on the Leyland Board since 1964.

Resolving Model Clashes

Quite rightly, Stokes and his team concentrated their initial energies on the failing enterprise that had once been BMC; this was where the major problems lay, and the model clashes with the former Leyland companies could be resolved later.

It was immediately obvious that there was far too much duplication of products among the marques once owned by BMC. So as a start, the Stokes team decided that Austin and Morris would in future be more clearly distinguished: Morris badges would go on cars with conventional engineering, and Austin badges would be reserved for cars with the advanced front-wheel-drive layout and other innovations that had been Alec Issigonis' speciality. Some of the other former BMC marques, which only existed as 'badge-engineered' versions of Austin and Morris models, would have to go. The first that did so was Riley, which disappeared in 1969.

Most importantly, the Stokes team wanted new products. Stokes wanted BLMC to make a big splash in summer 1970 (just over two years away) with some stunning new models. So he applied pressure on Triumph to deliver their new Stag grand tourer, and on Rover to deliver their new Range Rover. Both did appear in summer 1970, although in each case the final stages of development were rushed in order to meet that tight deadline.

Meanwhile, Harry Webster's first task on taking over the Small and Medium Cars Division was to put together a crash programme for developing new models. Meeting that summer 1970 deadline was virtually impossible, but Webster tried. He drew up a conventional car that would appeal to fleet buyers and could be engineered using largely existing production components. This became the Morris Marina – but despite heroic efforts it was actually delivered later than Stokes wanted, in 1971.

A particular problem resulting from the merger of two companies that had formerly been rivals was that there were several overlaps and clashes between their product ranges (see sidebar for a list of the most obvious model clashes). So the next job for the Stokes team was to resolve those clashes and streamline the product range so that the BLMC marques would not be in competition with one another. Over the years, this would prove to be an enormous undertaking, not least because of the tribal loyalties and vested interests of those who had spent many years working for one of the companies whose identity was to be lost. It was one cause of the industrial unrest that plagued British Leyland in the 1970s – although it was far from the only one.

The Stokes team faced their first challenges in 1969 when a new sports car designed by Rover (in a departure from their usual model portfolio) threatened to clash with the Jaguar E-type. They refused funding for the Rover. A further clash with Jaguar resulted in the big Rover P8 saloon being cancelled in 1971.

Shortly after that another clash arose between Rover and Triumph. Both companies had started work on replacements for their existing saloon models of similar size, and it was clearly absurd for both to proceed. Stokes resolved that the two engineering teams should work together on a single new model from early 1971, and that car eventually wore Rover badges. In early 1972, the two marques were then formally merged as the Specialist Division of BLMC. At about the same

In the early days, when company identities were still being retained, the BL logo was often seen in tandem with the individual marque names. This one dates from 1970.

MODEL CLASHES

When BLMC was formed in 1968, an inevitable result was that there were multiple model clashes. Formerly rival companies operating in the same market sectors each had their own products, and it was obvious that a coherent new manufacturing policy could only be created by scrapping some products in favour of others.

In their attempts to do that, Stokes and Barber encountered rebellion and resentment from those whose products faced being sidelined. In some cases they chose to wait until British Leyland could replace two formerly rival products by a single new one. What follows is a rapid overview of the problems that they faced in 1968; only in the small car sector, where the Mini had no direct competition, were their decisions easy.

Medium saloons with front-wheel drive: Austin had pioneered front-wheel drive in the medium family saloon sector with its ADO16 (1100 and 1300) range, but Triumph had mounted a challenge with its own medium-sized front-wheel-drive saloon (the 1300) from 1965. Both remained in production.

Medium saloons with rear-wheel drive: All the internal competition in this sector of the market was from badge-engineered versions of the same BMC 1.6-litre design, which was available as an Austin, an MG, a Morris and a Wolseley. These were elderly models, which could be allowed to wither away.

Large saloons: Austin had the front-wheel-drive 1800, which had no direct rivals because of its sheer size, although it was priced like a medium-sized family saloon.

Executive saloons: Rover and Triumph had been rivals in the executive saloon market ever since 1963, when the Rover 2000 and Triumph 2000 had both been introduced. Both model ranges had been expanded upwards since then, but both were still competing for essentially the same group of customers.

Sports saloons: Riley and Triumph both had entries in this sector of the market, but there was no competition for the Jaguar models at the more expensive end of the sector.

Luxury saloons: There were some very obvious overlaps in the luxury saloon sector. Austin, Daimler, Jaguar, Rover and Vanden Plas were all making cars in the 3-litre-and-over class, and it was nonsensical to continue with all of them.

Sports cars: There were no fewer than four sports-car marques in the new British Leyland combine, and two of these – MG and Triumph – had been deadly rivals since the early 1950s. The third, Austin-Healey, was no less well regarded, although by 1968 it had no unique models and its only product was a badge-engineered MG (although, ironically, the design was by Austin-Healey). The fourth sports-car maker was Jaguar, which produced models that were generally much more expensive than the other three marques.

time, the old Austin-Morris teams under Harry Webster were renamed as the Volume Cars Division.

There were some anomalies in these two broad groupings. Jaguar and Daimler were theoretically part of the Specialist Division, but they always did their best to remain aloof from it. Triumph's medium-sized saloons and sports cars belonged to the Specialist Division, while MG's sports cars belonged to the Volume Cars Division. While Land Rover sat fairly comfortably in the Specialist Division with Rover, the Austin and Morris light commercials belonged to the Volume Cars side. But this reorganization was at least a step in the direction of rationalization.

However, in resolving product issues, the Stokes team neglected to deal with problems of over-manning and poor productivity. Strong unions made it difficult to tackle both, and there was no doubt that any major efforts to tackle these issues would lead to strikes. By the early 1970s, compromises that the Heath government made with unions in other industries suggested that there was a lack of political will to confront them, and this would certainly not have encouraged the Stokes team to take any bold steps that would lead to union trouble.

Productivity was indeed poor. An article in *Motor* for 29 May 1976 compared the number of cars produced per employee by various car makers during 1975, and the comparisons were quite shocking. In Japan, Toyota produced thirty-six cars per employee, and Honda produced nearly twenty-three. In Britain, British Leyland produced just over four cars per employee. Although various factors made these comparisons inexact, it was abundantly clear that the British car industry as a whole was lagging behind, and not just British Leyland. Even Ford's UK factories managed a miserable figure of just over seven cars per employee. This was a fierce condemnation of the failure of British car makers to invest in modern production processes, as well as to deal with the steadily rising power of their trades unions.

The two cars perhaps most closely identified with the British Leyland were the Morris Marina and the Austin Allegro. Both were introduced in the early 1970s, and their relative failure – for reasons explained in Chapter 3 – has become an enduring symbol of the British Leyland period. The Marina was an unexceptional and deliberately conventional model... © MAGIC CAR PICS

... while the Allegro was intended to incorporate modern technology and advanced styling.

Crisis and Nationalization, 1974–75

Unfortunately, Stokes' new models were not arriving fast enough to keep sales afloat, and industrial troubles had their effect on productivity. A boom in car sales during 1972 should have given BLMC a boost, but it had exactly the opposite effect because the company was unable to meet the increased demand. The gap was filled by Ford, who were able to boost production, and by increasing the numbers of foreign imports. The BLMC market share of UK car sales had hovered around 40 per cent for several years, but in 1972 it slid to 33.1 per cent, and then continued to fall.

BLMC's position was not healthy even by mid-1973, but the knock-out blow came as a result of the long coal miners' strike that began in November 1973 and lasted for five months. The strike cost the company an enormous amount of money – some three-quarters of a billion pounds sterling – as it generated emergency power to maintain production and air-freighted after-sales replacement parts to the UK from around the world in order to maintain limited production of new cars.

Meanwhile sales had slumped, too, in the wake of the oil crisis that had erupted that autumn. In early October, Egypt and Syria had launched a co-ordinated attack against Israel in the hope of regaining territory lost during the 1967 Arab-Israeli war. Israel had successfully fought them off, seizing even more territory than before, and a cease-fire had been declared before the end of the month. However, the Arab association of oil producers (OPEC) now tried a form of blackmail to force territorial concessions by Israel that would allow the Palestinians their own state. They put pressure on Israel's Western allies by cutting oil supplies to some and raising oil prices for others. In Britain, fuel prices escalated and car sales slowed dramatically – all at a time of serious inflation, which would reach 23 per cent by June 1975.

The BLMC Board desperately examined a multitude of options to keep the company afloat. In February 1974 it decided to close as many as possible of the company's manufacturing plants outside the UK, and to realize the assets in order to provide cash that might offset the continuing losses. Stokes is alleged to have approached the Shah of Iran during 1974 to ask for investment, and it is also said that he tried to give away the Volume Cars Division in order to stem the company's losses – but that nobody was interested.

By late 1974, the position had become critical. BLMC was facing bankruptcy, and had to go cap-in-hand to Harold Wilson's new Labour government to seek financial support. This was granted – the alternative facing the government was to see thousands of motor industry employees suddenly out of work – but on a number of conditions. One was that the government itself would become a majority shareholder in BLMC, and would have a say in its corporate future. So a new holding company was created with the name of British Leyland Ltd (almost universally known as BL) so that this could happen. Both the company's budget and, bizarrely, its decisions about future products, became subject to government scrutiny and approval.

Sadly, the collapse of British Leyland seemed to be perfectly in tune with the socio-political atmosphere of the times. The early 1970s were a period when Britain had largely lost faith in itself, and so the 1974 collapse was just another highly public British disaster in a chain of many. In such an atmosphere it was hardly surprising that domestic car buyers came to the conclusion that BL's cars were somehow sub-standard. The public feeling was that if it had been made in Britain, it could not be any good, and of course foreign manufacturers were not slow to recognize their opportunity. Within a couple of years, BL had lost so much ground that a simply massive effort would be needed to make it viable again.

That massive effort would require constant injections of government capital throughout the remaining lifetime of British Leyland and beyond.

Ryder and After, 1975–76

In effect, BLMC had been nationalized, and unsurprisingly the government immediately commissioned a report into its affairs, appointing its industrial adviser Sir Don Ryder to do the job. Ryder was the Chairman of the National Enterprise Board, which oversaw government financing of nationalized industries and large state-owned enterprises in the UK. His report was prepared in double-quick time, and was published in April 1975. It was fairly damning of BLMC's failings, and it made a number of recommendations. One of these was that the separate marques and car divisions should be merged into a single company to be called Leyland Cars. There were also several recommendations regarding future government funding to enable BLMC to get back on its feet and become competitive again.

Changes in the top management inevitably followed the Ryder Report. The report created the new role of Non-Executive Chairman, a part-time post that was given to Professor Sir Ronald Edwards, former Chairman of the Beecham Group. Ryder himself kept a close eye on developments from his position at the National Enterprise Board. Stokes was appointed President to remove him from the day-to-day running of the organization, and would remain on the British Leyland Board until 1979. Alex Park became Finance Director, replacing John Barber, who resigned.

In the mid-1970s, the British Leyland identity was suppressed in favour of the Leyland Cars identity.

Leyland Cars
British Leyland UK Limited
Grosvenor House, Redditch
Worcestershire B97 4DQ

Supercover was the brand name given to the warranty system, and the logo seen here comes from a 1977 sales brochure.

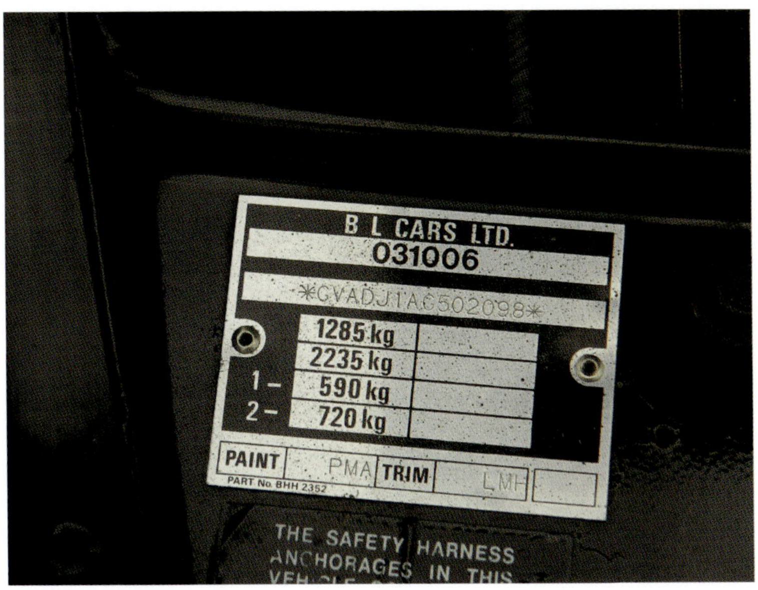

The company name also made its way on to the VIN plates displayed on the cars.

The new branding appears on a Leyland Cars all-model brochure issued in autumn 1975 for the 1976 season.

This imaginative 'motorway flyover' cover was used for the all-models catalogue of the 1978 season.

There would be two further changes at the top: Professor Sir Ronald Edwards died in January 1976, and his post was taken by Sir Richard Dobson, who had been Chairman of British American Tobacco. He remained in place until October 1977, when he was obliged to resign after making some unacceptable remarks during a speech. In fact, the NEB had already decided that British Leyland needed a full-time chairman, and had offered the job to Michael Edwardes, the CEO of the Chloride Group and a member of the NEB. Edwardes accepted and took over in late October.

The Edwardes Era, 1977–82

Edwardes was prepared to be ruthless to slim British Leyland down to a viable size, and one of his first moves was to reduce the size of the Board from thirteen members to just seven. He also swiftly recognized that some of the enthusiasm for the Ryder reforms was already waning, and in particular the idea of burying the individual car marques in the common identity of Leyland Cars.

So during 1978 he scrapped Leyland Cars, breaking it up into smaller, semi-autonomous business units. The two big ones were Austin-Morris and Jaguar-Rover-Triumph, which more or less (but not quite) corresponded to the earlier Volume Cars and Specialist Cars divisions. Key differences were that MG now belonged to what was usually known as JRT, while Land Rover was managed quite separately, and would come to belong to a new business unit called the Land Rover Group, which also had responsibility for light commercial vehicles.

Edwardes made sure that all these business units had their own management to run their-day-to-day affairs. At Austin-Morris, he appointed Ray Horrocks as Managing Director. At JRT, the Chairman was William Pratt Thompson, and Jeff Herbert was appointed Managing Director. Jaguar was a very reluctant member of this division, and always did its best to remain aloof from the Rover-Triumph and MG side; later, JRT would be split into Rover-Triumph and Jaguar Car Holdings (which included Daimler). David Abell was put in charge of a newly created division called BL

Brought in to get a grip on British Leyland, Sir Michael Edwardes did exactly that.

However, it was not all plain sailing for Edwardes. Trade unionist leader Derek Robinson – known as 'Red Robbo' – (left) was a constant thorn in his side.

Not often thought of as a British Leyland car, the Mini was introduced before the company was formed and outlasted it by several years as well. This pristine 1275 GT is fitted with a rare British Leyland tuning kit.

For a time, the light commercial vehicles were grouped together under the Freight Rover division, which had its own logo. In practice, the Freight Rover name only ever appeared on the Sherpa van, which was not a car-derived vehicle.

The chevron logo was a neat idea to link all the British Leyland brands. It later appeared in several slightly different forms, often without the brand names, and was still in use when the Maestro and Montego came on the scene in the first half of the 1980s.

For the 1979 season, the marques were being re-emphasized, and this catalogue covered Jaguar Rover Triumph.

Several British Leyland cars were assembled overseas, including the Mini. This brochure was for the Innocenti Mini Cooper 1300, which was assembled in Italy.

The flying-wheel logo has now lost its central L; this is an all-models catalogue from the 1981 season.

Reorganization yet again: this autumn 1982 catalogue was for the recently created Austin Rover Group.

Commercial Vehicles. David Andrews became Chairman of the Land Rover Group, and Mike Hodgkinson became Managing Director of Land Rover, with Tony Gilroy as Managing Director of the light commercial business, which in 1981 took on the name of Freight Rover.

Edwardes pressed on with his comprehensive restructuring plan, and implemented its final stages in 1981. Austin Rover Group became the new name for the mass-market car-manufacturing subsidiary, combining what was left of Austin-Morris and Jaguar-Rover-Triumph. The Land Rover Group and Jaguar Car Holdings remained separate. In the meantime, Edwardes drastically reduced the number of UK car dealerships, and closed a number of factories.

He had closed the Triumph factory at Speke in 1977 after an all-out strike had disrupted TR7 sports-car production, and in 1980 he closed the MG plant at Abingdon. The main Triumph plant at Canley followed, although the site survived as an administrative, engineering and design headquarters. Before long, the eight Leyland car assembly plants had been reduced to just three – Cowley (traditional home of Morris), Longbridge (traditional home of Austin) and Solihull (traditional home of Rover). And there would be more shuffling of production in 1982 as Rover cars moved out of Solihull to allow that plant to become the dedicated centre of Land Rover production.

The Honda Alliance

By the time Edwardes became British Leyland's Chairman, several reports into the company's affairs had agreed that its long-term survival could only be guaranteed by a strategic alliance with another car manufacturer. So the Edwardes team explored a number of options as a high priority. It was essential to find a partner of similar size to BL if the British company was not to end up as the junior partner.

RING IN THE NEW

Listed below are major new model introductions under British Leyland, 1968–86: these are UK-built types; overseas confections are not listed. Typically, new models were announced in the calendar year before their first model year, so that a model announced in 1970 would be for the 1971 model year. Dates given here are dates of announcement.

	Updates of existing models	All-new models
1968	Austin 1800 Mk II Jaguar E-type Series II Morris 1800 Mk II Rover 3500 Triumph Vitesse Mk 2 Triumph 1300TC Triumph 2.5 PI Wolseley 18/85 Mk II	Daimler Sovereign (XJ6) Daimler DS420 Jaguar XJ6
1969	Austin 1800S Leyland Mini Morris 1800S Triumph 2000, 2500 and 2.5 PI (Mk 2 range) Wolseley 18/85S	Austin Maxi Triumph TR6
1970	Austin Maxi 1750 Austin Sprite Rover 2000 and 3500 Mk II Triumph 1500 Triumph Spitfire Mk IV Triumph GT6 Mk 3	Range Rover Triumph Toledo Triumph Stag
1971	Austin 1100 and 1300 Mk III Jaguar E-type Series III Morris 1100 and 1300 Mk III Rover 3500S Triumph Dolomite Wolseley 1100 and 1300 Mk III Vanden Plas 1300 Mk III	Land Rover Series III Morris Marina
1972	Austin 2200 Daimler Double-Six Jaguar XJ12 Morris 2200 Wolseley Six	
1973	Daimler Sovereign and Double-Six Series 2 Jaguar XJ6 and XJ12 Series 2 MGB GT V8 Rover 2200 Triumph 1500TC Triumph Dolomite Sprint Triumph Spitfire 1500	Austin Allegro
1974	Vanden Plas 1500	
1975	Austin Allegro 2	Austin and Morris 18-22 series, and Wolseley Six, later re-named Leyland Princess Jaguar XJ-S Triumph TR7
1976	Triumph Dolomite 1300 and 1500	Rover SD1 3500
1977	Rover SD1 2300 and 2600	
1978	Leyland Princess 2	
1979	Daimler Sovereign and Double-Six Series 3 Jaguar XJ6 and XJ12 Series 3 Land Rover Stage 1 V8	
1980	Leyland Maxi 2 Triumph TR8	Austin Metro
1981	Morris Ital Morris Metro van Range Rover four-door	Triumph Acclaim
1982	Austin Ambassador MG Metro Rover SD1 facelift, 2000 and 2400 SD models	
1983	Jaguar XJ-S 3.6-litre and XJ-SC	Austin Maestro MG Maestro
1984	Austin Maestro van MG Maestro 2.0 EFi	Austin Montego MG Montego Rover 200 series
1985	Austin Metro 310 (van) MG Montego Turbo	

At the same time, BL urgently needed a replacement for the Austin Allegro, which was already dying in the market place and was not scheduled to be replaced until 1983. Its replacement, the LC10 or Austin Maestro, could not be launched any earlier because BL simply did not have the necessary engineering resources. So it became clear that BL's new partner had to be a company with a suitable car in the pipeline, and one that was prepared to share that car with BL.

Ray Horrocks at the Austin-Morris division worked with product planner Mark Snowden to draw up a list of companies that fitted the profile. Chrysler UK was at the top of that list, and Honda was number two. BL initiated talks with a wide range of European manufacturers, such as BMW, Fiat and Renault, but seem to have been pinning their hopes on discussions with Chrysler UK over the summer of 1978. Unfortunately, the Chrysler operation was in a worse state than BL's, and when Peugeot offered to take it over that year, the French company was welcomed with open arms.

So the focus switched to Honda. Talks began in August 1978 and went well; the two companies signed a Memorandum of Understanding on 15 May 1979, and in October that year the BL Board approved a draft agreement, which was later ratified under BL's 1980 Corporate Plan. In due course, a cross-holding arrangement was put in place: Honda took a 20 per cent shareholding in British Leyland, which in return took a 20 per cent shareholding in Honda UK. There would be close co-operation in the development of new models, enabling Honda to get a foothold in the European market and BL to develop new models more quickly and for less cost.

The first fruit of the agreement was that British Leyland announced the Triumph Acclaim in late 1981. Cosmetically, it replaced all the Triumph Dolomite range, but the truth was that it was a holding operation to regain buyer confidence until the planned LC10 was ready. It was simply a Honda model, built in Britain and rebadged, but it gave British Leyland the most reliable car it had built for many years. Ordinary though it was, it did exactly what was asked of it. Meanwhile, Jaguar Rover Australia (BL's Australian subsidiary) also agreed with Honda to take one of its existing models to fill a gap in its own model range.

The Acclaim was replaced during 1984 by another Honda design, this time re-engineered and restyled to some extent in Britain. In accordance with the latest branding arrangements, this became a Rover 200 series. And in the meantime, work went ahead with all speed on a proper joint project to develop a new big saloon, which would be sold as a Honda Legend and as a Rover 800 series. The introduction of that car in 1986 more or less coincided with the end of British Leyland as it took on the new name of Rover Group.

BL's Final Years

Michael Edwardes had been knighted in 1979 by a grateful British government, but he could not be persuaded to stay as the company's chairman beyond 1982. He felt that he had done what he could to set the company on the right course, and stepped down. In his place came Harold Musgrove as Chairman and Chief Executive Officer of British Leyland, and from 1984 there was also the steadying hand of Sir Austin Bide, who maintained a much lower profile than Edwardes.

By this time, however, the British government was tiring of its commitment to British Leyland, and Prime Minister Margaret Thatcher became determined to sell it off into private ownership. As a first stage, in July 1984, Jaguar Car Holdings was floated off as an independent company on the stock market, and immediately became a thriving business entity under its Chairman John Egan. As a second stage, the remaining elements of the company were renamed as the Rover Group in 1986 when Canadian-born Sir Graham Day was appointed as the new company's Chairman.

His mission would be to sell off those elements of the company that were not involved in car manufacture – the Unipart spares business and the Leyland commercial vehicles division – and to prepare the Rover Group for eventual privatization. His strategy was to move the company upmarket by focusing on the Rover and MG brands, which were perceived as the two strongest in the company's portfolio. He also wanted to give the company a younger image, and famously claimed that 'young people do not want to drive an Austin'. So another long-established British make was clearly destined for a rapid end.

And so British Leyland passed into history, perhaps a shadow of its former self, but certainly in a much better position than it had been when BLMC was formed in 1968. Sadly, in the process of that reconstruction, the heart had also been ripped out of the old British motor industry.

2 THE INHERITANCE

THIS CHAPTER DISCUSSES the models that were already in production when British Leyland was formed in 1968. A few were rapidly rationalized out of existence – which made good sense from a business perspective, even though it upset long-term enthusiasts and company employees alike. Others remained in production during the British Leyland era and, in the case of the Mini, beyond it as well.

For simplicity, the career of a variant in production at the time of the BLMC merger is discussed in its entirety here. However, where a major new variant was introduced in the BL era (as occurred, for example, with the Mini and the Triumph 2000/2500 saloon range), that later variant is discussed in Chapter 3, The British Leyland Models.

Within each marque section, sports cars precede saloons; commercials follow, but are included only where they were directly derived from cars. Models are listed in order of engine size, beginning with the smallest.

The Austin Inheritance

When BLMC was formed at the start of 1968, the Austin name stood for respectable, mainstream, everyday cars. Yet these were by no means all conventional: the company had also developed a range of innovative models that employed advanced front-wheel-drive technology, which set them apart from most of their rivals in the 1960s. Austin had been the dominant marque in the BMC partnership ever since its formation in 1952. Its traditional home was at Longbridge – although that had not stopped Austins being built elsewhere when necessary, such as at the Morris plant in Cowley.

There were eight Austin model ranges in production at the start of 1968. The smallest was the Mini, already nearly nine years old but still enormously popular. Above that came the ADO16 range of 1100 and 1300 saloons, strong sellers that incorporated much of the advanced technology pioneered in the Mini. Next up in the hierarchy was the medium-sized Austin Cambridge, the oldest design on sale and much in need of replacement. Above that came yet another modern front-wheel-drive car, the 1800, and Austin's competitor in the luxury class was the 3-litre; the A110 Westminster that it was intended to replace was still in production, but was scheduled for withdrawal that summer. Lastly, Austin also made the Gipsy four-wheel-drive light commercial vehicle, and the FX4 taxi.

All these models, except for the Westminster, the 3-litre, the Gipsy and the taxi, were also available with Morris badges, and some had Riley, Vanden Plas and Wolseley variants as well. This situation was a product of the badge-engineering policy that BMC had pursued in the 1950s and early 1960s in order to retain the loyalty of customers and dealers who had developed ties with the different marques that had made up the merged company.

During the brief British Motor Holdings period, Austin had been under the chairmanship of Sir George Harriman, with Joe Edwards as its Managing Director. Its innovative chief designer, responsible for the front-wheel-drive cars, was Alec Issigonis.

Austin Mini

The Mini was unquestionably BMC's greatest success story, and was well on the way to selling two million copies by the time Mk II models were introduced in autumn 1967, just a few months before the BLMC merger. Introduced in 1959, it

The Mini saloon looked very much as it always had, although larger tail lights, a larger rear window and a new grille distinguished the Mk II models introduced in 1967.

From the same set of press-release pictures comes this one of the Austin Mini Countryman Mk II, with its quaint but lovable wooden body battens – not structural, but applied over the metal panels.

was the first of Alec Issigonis' revolutionary designs using a transverse engine (the A-series), with the gearbox in its sump driving to the front wheels. All this saved space in order to provide the maximum possible room for passengers in the smallest possible size of car.

Just 3m (10ft) long and running on tiny 10-inch (18cm) wheels, the Mini or ADO15 really could accommodate four people, although its two-door design made rear access awkward and its steering column was at an odd angle. Since 1965 it had also had the Hydrolastic suspension pioneered on the larger ADO16 (see below). Buyers loved its handiness, as well as its handling and roadholding, and its frugal use of petrol.

Mk II Austin models came with 848cc ('850') or 998cc ('1000') engines, plus four-speed gearboxes or an optional three-speed automatic. There were saloons, sporty Cooper and Cooper S saloons, Countryman estates, vans and pick-ups – plus the Moke, a fashionable open buggy that ceased production in Britain during 1968 to find a new life in Australia. All the Mk IIs were built at Longbridge, except for the substantial quantities assembled outside the UK.

In 1969, the year that two millionth example was built, the Mini underwent a substantial redesign and re-emerged as the Leyland Mini, which is discussed later.

Austin 1100 and 1300

Like their Mini cousins, the Austin models of the ADO16 range had just been facelifted as Mk II types when BLMC was formed. They came as 48bhp 1100 models (with 1098cc A-series engines) or 58bhp 1300 models (with 1275cc A-series engines), and could be had as four-door saloons, two-door saloons, or two-door Countryman estates.

The ADO16 range had been facelifted a few months before BLMC came into being. This was the new 1968-model Mk II version of the Austin 1300.

ADO16 was the second of Issigonis' designs to incorporate his front-wheel-drive design with transverse engine and gearbox in the sump. It was the first to have Hydrolastic suspension, with fluid under pressure acting as the springing medium and interconnection between front and rear wheels evening out the ride. Front disc brakes, an eye-opener at the car's launch in the early 1960s, were still uncommon in cars of this class by 1968.

The Austin versions had arrived in 1963 but were not the first ADO16s; those were Morris versions in 1962. The neat and chiselled body design was by Pininfarina, though modified by BMC. For the Mk IIs it had been further modified, with new grilles, pared-down rear wing 'fins' and new tail-lights. The interior was disappointingly minimalist, revealing Issigonis' influence, and was one reason why these dynamically good cars were strangely characterless. They nevertheless had plenty of appeal, and were Britain's best sellers right through the 1960s.

During 1968, BLMC introduced a two-door automatic 1300 called the Austin America, with an emissions-controlled engine for the USA; however, it did not catch on and was withdrawn in 1971. Calls for better performance prompted the arrival in 1969 of a 1300GT, with sporty cosmetic changes, and the 70bhp engine from MG and Riley ADO16 derivatives. Then in 1971 came the Mk III models, distinguished mainly by a nicer dashboard.

The 1100s and 1300s were replaced by the Austin Allegro in autumn 1973, but remained on sale in Britain into 1974, and some models were still available in export markets in 1975.

Austin Cambridge

By 1968, the Austin Cambridge or A60 model was a nine-year-old design. Originally introduced in 1959 as the A55 Cambridge, it had gained a bigger 1622cc 4-cylinder engine in 1962 to become the A60. A 1489cc diesel version was also available, but was not common. There was an estate version, too, called the Countryman.

These were rear-wheel-drive cars, with quite spacious four-door bodies designed by Pinin Farina in Italy. They had monocoque construction, with independent front suspension but a leaf-sprung 'live' axle at the rear. They were attractive but strangely unexceptional cars, and were really outdated by the time BLMC was established. Their replacement, the

The lines of the Pininfarina mid-sized saloons were beginning to look dated by 1968. This is an Austin A60 Cambridge, a LHD car now preserved in Switzerland.

The ADO17 'Land Crab' was a hugely spacious family saloon. Here it is as an Austin 1800 from 1971.

Austin Maxi, was already being developed, and BLMC ended their production when that model arrived in 1969. Nevertheless, badge-engineered Morris and Wolseley counterparts remained available for two more years.

Austin 1800

Austin had hoped that the ADO17/Austin 1800 would replace the Cambridge and its badge-engineered cousins, but when it arrived in 1964 it was really too big to do that. It was another front-wheel-drive Issigonis design, with interconnected Hydrolastic suspension and simply acres of interior space. Pininfarina (all one word since 1960) had done the original body design, but Issigonis had modified it and the result was odd, though not unhappy. A notable drawback was the bus-like driving position, while performance from the transverse 1798cc B-series engine was only average. The ride quality, though, was excellent. Only minor changes were made before 1967, when power steering became a much-needed option.

During 1968, BLMC oversaw the introduction of Mk II models, with cosmetic changes, bigger (14in) wheels and an automatic option. An 1800S with more powerful twin-carburettor engine arrived in 1969 but was dropped in 1972. At that stage, Mk III models arrived with further cosmetic changes and – most importantly – a 6-cylinder option. This created the 2200 model, with a 2227cc E-series engine that had already been seen in variants of the ADO17 built in Australia.

There were Morris and Wolseley derivatives of the ADO17, and in the late 1960s the 1800 also found a niche as a rugged long-distance rally car. The whole range was replaced in 1975 by the 18-22 series, later renamed the Leyland Princess.

Austin A110 Westminster

The Austin Westminster was a traditional British luxury saloon at heart, though enlivened by attractive styling commissioned from Pinin Farina and incorporating the tail fins fashionable in the later 1950s and early 1960s. It had first appeared in A99 form in 1959, with Vanden Plas and Wolseley derivatives. The A110 arrived two years later, with a slightly longer wheelbase to give more space and better roadholding, and from 1964 smaller wheels helped further.

These were quite elegant and well-appointed cars, focused on comfort rather than performance or handling. All of them had BMC's C-series 3-litre 6-cylinder engine driving the rear wheels, and there was a choice of manual or automatic gearboxes. But by 1968 they were looking old and rather tired, and were kept in production only until the middle of the year when the replacement Austin 3-litre became available.

Austin 3-litre

The ADO61 3-litre model was announced in October 1967, but production cars were not available until the following July, by which time some changes had been made. Its role was to replace the older, big Austins, notably the Westminster, but the reality was that customers no longer wanted such cars: tastes had changed in favour of sporting executive models such as the Triumph 2500 and Rover 3500. So the 3-litre was not warmly received, and sold poorly.

Even though the 3-litre incorporated some of Alec Issigonis' innovations, such as Hydrolastic suspension, it was not one of his designs. Power came from an updated 3-litre (2912cc)

ABOVE: Pinin Farina had designed the 6-cylinder BMC saloons as well, and they were due for replacement by 1968. The essentials of the Austin A110 Westminster pictured here had not changed for several years.

BELOW: The Austin 3-litre was planned to replace the 6-cylinder Farina saloons, but it was a sales flop. © LETDORF/WIKIMEDIA COMMONS

C-series 6-cylinder engine with a fairly modest 125bhp, and the rear wheels were driven though a four-speed manual gearbox. The 3-litre's body shape was compromised by a ruling that it had to share doors with the 1800 models, and it looked so much like them as a result that buyers could see no reason to pay extra for the supposedly more prestigious car.

The standard version of the car was withdrawn in 1969, and the de luxe model in May 1971. Neither had ever aspired to leather upholstery, which was planned for Vanden Plas and Wolseley derivatives that were designed but not put into production. Fewer than 10,000 3-litres were built, and the car was not replaced under British Leyland. There were several other models that were already doing its job more competently.

Austin Gipsy

When BLMC came together, Austin was building a competitor for Rover's Land Rover, called the Gipsy. This was available with both short (2,286mm/90in) and long (2,819mm/111in) wheelbases, and with a choice of 55bhp 2199cc 4-cylinder petrol engine or 62bhp 2178cc diesel engine – both also used in the FX4 taxi.

There were also alternative suspension systems. One was a sophisticated all-independent type, using Flexitor rubber springs, and the other depended on beam axles with leaf springs. Austin had been persuaded of the value of all-independent suspension by its experience building the Champ for the British Army during the 1950s, but customers were less easily persuaded, and the leaf-sprung alternative had become available by 1965.

The Gipsy had a steel chassis frame and separate steel body with various utility configurations. However, it had never been a serious competitor for the Land Rover, and in ten years of production just 21,208 were built; by the mid-1960s, Rover was building that many Land Rovers every six months.

So the Gipsy survived only just beyond the formation of BLMC, and its production was terminated later in 1968.

Austin FX4 taxi

Badged only as an Austin, the iconic FX4 taxi was the much-loved London 'black cab'. The capital's Metropolitan Police imposed a set of unique regulations that taxis had to meet – most famously, a tight 7.6m (25ft) turning circle – and the FX4 had been introduced in 1958 to meet them.

The FX4 had a separate steel chassis and was assembled by Carbodies of Coventry, who had designed its special body. By 1968, it was still using the same 2178cc Austin diesel engine with which it had been introduced, and most were being delivered with a manual gearbox. A hire-car derivative (the FL2) was also available, as were a 2199cc petrol engine and an automatic gearbox.

Originally conceived as a rival to the Land Rover, the Austin Gipsy never became strongly established. This 1965 example belonged to the Auxiliary Fire Service. © ASTRION/ WIKIMEDIA COMMONS

The Austin FX4 taxi was a familiar sight on London streets throughout the British Leyland period and for many years afterwards, too.

A planned replacement model was cancelled, and in 1969 the FX4 was modified, most obviously taking on tail-lights from the ADO16 (Austin 1100/1300) range. From 1971 a more powerful 2520cc diesel engine was introduced, which worked well with an automatic gearbox, and this gradually became the favoured combination. The petrol option was discontinued in 1973.

Sales were consistent, but at a couple of thousand every year, not strong enough to engage British Leyland's interest. So in 1982 they sold the intellectual rights to Carbodies, and then in 1984 the FX4 was taken over by London Taxis International. From 1982–89, Land Rover diesel engines were used, and thereafter a Nissan 2.7-litre diesel. Production ended in 1996, after around 75,000 had been built.

The Austin-Healey Inheritance

Although the Austin-Healey inheritance was a big one, BLMC made little of it. The company was formed just a few months too late to inherit the 'big' Healey – the legendary 3000 that went out of production as a Mk III model in late 1967. That car had theoretically been replaced by the MGC, although few people would see the MG as in any sense an adequate replacement for the legendary sports car that Donald Healey had designed back in 1951. (For what it is worth, one final Healey 3000 was assembled in March 1968 – the only example of the breed to have been built under British Leyland.)

So the only Austin-Healey model in full production under British Leyland was the Sprite, the much smaller sports car that also had an MG clone in the shape of the Midget. The royalty agreement with Donald Healey ended in 1970, and so the model was simply dropped – although the Austin Sprite carried on for a further year.

Austin-Healey Sprite

The Sprite had entered production in 1958 as the much-liked 'frogeye' model, and had been developed ever since. Designed by Donald Healey and his team as a small sports car using BMC mechanical components, it was badge-engineered into an MG Midget for 1961 and the two cars were sold alongside one another for the next nine years.

The version that BLMC inherited at the start of 1968 was the Austin-Healey Sprite Mk IV, introduced in 1966 and capa-

The Austin-Healey Sprite represented affordable sports-car fun for two, and this 1970 model is being used for just that. MAGIC CAR PICS

ble of 153km/h (95mph) thanks to its 65bhp 1275cc A-series engine. Ironically, perhaps, it was regularly outsold by its MG Midget sister, and as the two cars were identical in almost every respect, the slower-selling model was always likely to be rationalized out of existence. For its last year in production, the Sprite was renamed Austin Sprite: now that royalties were no longer being paid to Donald Healey, there seemed no point in keeping his name on the car.

The Daimler Inheritance

Daimler had begun by licence building cars designed by the German Daimler company, but was taken over by BSA in 1910. During the 1920s and 1930s, it became one of Britain's most prestigious makes, and enjoyed a long period of royal patronage. However, the socio-economic conditions in Britain after 1945 demanded a new approach, which Daimler was slow to find. The company was on its last legs after a disastrous decade in the 1950s, and Jaguar bought it in 1961 – primarily to gain extra factory space. Daimler reached BLMC by way of BMC's 1966 purchase of Jaguar.

Despite these vicissitudes, the Daimler brand remained strong and prestigious at the start of the 1960s, and Jaguar saw the advantage of maintaining it. So there were still three Daimler models on sale when BLMC was formed in 1968. These were the V8-250 saloon and the Sovereign, both derived from Jaguar designs, and the Majestic Major, which was the last of the 'real' Daimlers.

Daimler V8-250

Among the assets that Jaguar obtained when it bought Daimler in 1960 was the company's recently introduced 2.5-litre V8 engine, at that stage only available in the GRP-bodied SP250 sports car. However, it had originally been drawn up by Edward Turner for a new Daimler saloon, which was never built, and Jaguar recognized what a superb engine it was. From 1962 they made it available in the bodyshell of their own Mk II saloon, with appropriate cosmetic and trim changes and the name of Daimler 2.5-litre V8. It sold strongly to customers who wanted a refined, medium-sized luxury saloon with the prestige of the Daimler badge.

By 1968, the model had just been renamed a Daimler V8-250, taking on the thinner bumpers and other alterations seen on the parent Jaguars at the same time. Most had an automatic gearbox, but an overdrive manual type was also available. The V8-250 remained in production until 1969, when the smaller-engined version of the new Daimler Sovereign took its place in the showrooms.

Daimler Sovereign

When Daimler dealers wanted a new model to sell in the mid-1960s, Jaguar served them up a 420 with Daimler grille, badges and interior elements. There was no denying that this was a badge-engineered Jaguar, but it was so tastefully done that nobody complained. The Daimler Sovereign was even named by one of Daimler's dealers, and appeared in 1966. Most of these 4.2-litre cars, all with an automatic gearbox, were sold in the

UK, because the Daimler name had little resonance in export markets. Production of around 2,000 cars a year was nevertheless good enough for Jaguar, who would retain the Sovereign name for the model's XJ6-based replacement in 1969.

Daimler Majestic Major

The Majestic Major could trace its lineage back to the 1951 Daimler Regency, by way of several updates and name changes. Introduced in 1960, it was a grand and formal saloon, much liked by local dignitaries and hire-car companies, and it was old-fashioned in a very pleasing sort of way. Not in the least old-fashioned, though, was its 4.5-litre V8 engine, another Edward Turner design, and related to the 2.5-litre V8 announced at the same time. With 200bhp, it drove through the standard automatic gearbox to give this huge car a top speed of 193km/h (120mph).

Unsurprisingly, Daimler developed a long-wheelbase limousine version that was known as the DR450. Both models were anachronisms by the time BLMC took over in 1968, and production of both came to an end that year. The replacement DS420 model was more of a corporate effort, drawing on both Jaguar and Vanden Plas expertise.

Daimler's V8-250 model was the final version of a long-standing model based on the Jaguar Mk 2 compact saloon.

The Daimler grille made what was essentially a Jaguar 420 look more solemn and imposing, but of course the car went just as well as its Jaguar equivalent. MAGIC CAR PICS

The Daimler Majestic Major came in two sizes, the smaller one being a four-window saloon – the one shown here belonged to Lord Brabazon.

The alternative to the Majestic Major saloon was this very grand-looking six-light limousine. © CHARLES01/ WIKIMEDIA COMMONS

The Jaguar Inheritance

Jaguar had merged with BMC in 1966 to form BMH (British Motor Holdings) before it became part of the BLMC fold. Fiercely independent before that, it had agreed to a merger only because its founder, Sir William Lyons, had no heir to take over from him.

Jaguar had started out building sidecars and special bodies for chassis such as Austin and Standard in the 1920s, moving on to making its own complete cars in the 1930s. The marque – known as SS before the 1939–45 war – always focused on sleek good looks and sporting performance, and these qualities were further emphasized in the series of superb XK sports two-seaters from 1948, in the marque's bigger saloons from 1950, and in its medium-sized or 'compact' sports saloons from 1955. There was never any doubt that Jaguar was going to be the premier sporting marque within BLMC, and so it proved.

Jaguar E-Type

The Jaguar E-type replaced the XK150 sports models in 1961 and was immediately widely acclaimed. Stunning good looks plus a claimed 150mph (241km/h) top speed, all at Jaguar's traditional value-for-money prices, made it a legend in its own lifetime. Calling it the E-type – a name that followed on from the D-type competition model – was another inspired decision, although for the USA it was renamed as an XK-E to reinforce the link to earlier sports Jaguars.

Bigger engines and additional body styles followed, and the E-types on sale when BLMC was formed in 1968 consisted of roadster and coupé models, plus a long-wheelbase 2+2 fixed-head coupé. All had the same 265bhp 4.2-litre XK engine, and an automatic gearbox was available as an alternative to the more sporting manual-plus-overdrive that was the favourite.

Jaguar had been redeveloping the E-type to meet a set of new emissions and safety regulations that would arrive for 1969, and at the end of 1968 introduced Series II models. These had exposed headlamps and a bigger air intake, the options of disc wheels and power steering, and some interior changes. Then from March 1971, the Series III E-type combined the long wheelbase of the 2+2 models with Jaguar's brand-new 272bhp V12 engine. In this guise, now sold only as a roadster and a 2+2 coupé, the E-type remained on sale until 1975. Its replacement was the XJ-S, a very different type of Jaguar.

Jaguar 240 and 340

The original 'compact' Jaguar saloon of 1955 was heavily revised in 1959 and renamed a Mk 2 saloon. It retained its monocoque bodyshell – Jaguar's first – and the original 2.4-litre and 3.4-litre engines were joined by a 3.8-litre type.

Jaguar's E-type was still a sensational-looking car by 1968, although the design was then seven years old. This is a 1966 4.2-litre roadster model.

The Jaguar Mk 2 now came as a 240 or a 340, either model recognizable by its slimline bumpers. This is a 240.

The cars epitomised the British concept of a sports saloon in the 1960s, combining enough room for four people (five at a pinch) with excellent acceleration and handling; they were also luxuriously equipped with wood trim and leather upholstery. Above all, they followed the Jaguar principle of being excellent value for money.

The earlier compacts (now known as 'Mk 1' types) had established a formidable international reputation in competition, and the Mk 2s followed. This helped to give them a reputation unlike that of their later descendants, which were more biased towards refinement and luxury. By the time BLMC was formed, the Mk 2s had been downgraded to some extent to protect sales of the S-types and 420s. Renamed 240 and 340 models (the 3.8-litre engine was dropped, but available to special order), they also had slimmer bumpers inspired by those on the S-types, and upholstery was now in Ambla PVC. The 240 and 340 remained available into 1969 while the new XJ6 established itself in the market, but were then dropped.

Jaguar S-Type

Jaguar created a new model above the Mk 2 saloons in their hierarchy by modifying the bodyshell to take their latest independent rear suspension and giving it distinctive front and rear treatments. The result appeared in 1963 with a choice of 3.4-litre and 3.8-litre engines, but it was never uni-

The main differences between the Mk 2 and S-type Jaguars were at the rear, where the S-type had a longer boot line and, less visibly, independent suspension.

versally liked: the visual mismatch between modified front and all-new rear ends was a rare misjudgement by Jaguar's Sir William Lyons.

Even so, the S-type was a strong seller, and was an essential step on the way to the ultimate compact Jaguar, the 420 of 1966. Its independent rear end gave it ride and handling qualities that the Mk 2s completely lacked. S-types were still available in the showrooms for a few months after the formation of BLMC in 1968, but their production ended that year to make way for the new XJ6 saloons.

Jaguar 420

Jaguar created the 420 by fitting their 4.2-litre engine into the S-type shell and redesigning the front end to resemble the much more stylish type on the big Mk X saloon. The result, introduced in 1966, was a compact, luxury saloon with excellent performance and handling – arguably the real ancestor of the thinking that would later deliver the acclaimed XJ models. Both manual (with overdrive) and automatic transmission options could be had.

The 420 was matched by a Daimler Sovereign clone from the beginning. However, it predeceased the Sovereign by one year, production ending in 1968 to make way in Jaguar showrooms for the new XJ6.

Jaguar 420G

Jaguar's big saloons had reached the Mk IX designation before being replaced by an all-new monocoque design called the Mk X in 1962. This was a gargantuan car by British standards, heavily influenced by US expectations of size. From 1966, it was renamed a 420G in accordance with Jaguar's new naming policy: for some reason, 420G (G for Grand) was thought to prevent confusion with the new, smaller Jaguar 420.

In practice, the 420G was the same as the Mk X, still with a 265bhp 4.2-litre XK engine but now boasting bright side trim, new hubcaps and a few interior alterations. Too big and too heavy to suit many Jaguar customers, it remained available until 1970, by which time the 4.2-litre XJ6 had secured its market share and more. The 420G platform would be used for many more years as the basis of the Daimler DS420 limousine.

The Jaguar 420 had the rear end of the S-type with a much prettier four-headlamp front end derived from the big Mk X/420G models.

American in dimensions, the 420G was Jaguar's big saloon in 1968, but it was just about to be replaced. Most had single-tone paint.

The Station Wagon body on the short-wheelbase Land Rover chassis had seats for seven people, although comfort was not its strongest suit.

The Land Rover Inheritance

At the time of the British Leyland merger, the Land Rover was still essentially a range of commercial vehicles built by the Rover Company. It shared components, mainly powertrains, with Rover cars, and even though the Land Rovers actually far outsold the cars, the Land Rover was considered within the company as very much a secondary product.

All that was because the original Land Rover in 1948 had been designed and put into production very quickly to give the Rover Company an exportable product. It needed one badly at a time when the British Government was rationing supplies of sheet steel according to export performance, because its saloon cars were not selling well outside the UK.

The Land Rover became a huge success and soon developed a life of its own. By the time of British Leyland's formation it was available in multiple different versions, of which the major ones are described below. Not only a commercial vehicle beloved of farmers and military authorities, it was also available in passenger-carrying Station Wagon form – a version closely associated in the public mind with expedition and adventure. Few people at the time used one for everyday transport in the way that would become common from the 1980s onwards. By 1968, most models in production were Series IIA types.

Land Rover 88in

The short-wheelbase Land Rover was the direct descendant of the original 1948 model. Its construction was what would now be called modular, in that different bodies could be built up on the same chassis by mixing and matching components. Some had full-length canvas soft tops, some had metal 'truck cabs', and most shared the same rear body tub, on to which further metal bodywork could be built to create van ('hard-top') or windowed Station Wagon versions. Another option was to have a canvas tilt over the pick-up tub in tandem with a truck cab. Chassis-cabs were available, too, for special after-market bodywork.

There were two engine options, both based on the same 4-cylinder design of 2286cc: one was a 77bhp petrol, and the other a 62bhp diesel. The four-speed gearbox was a long-standing design derived from a Rover car original, and a two-speed transfer gearbox allied to selectable four-wheel-drive gave the Land Rover its legendary rough-terrain ability.

Land Rover 109in

The long-wheelbase Land Rover shared all the key characteristics of its short-wheelbase counterpart, but added a much longer load-carrying body. The basic body variations were created in the same way as with the 88in models. These mod-

In theory, there was room for twelve people in the long-wheelbase Land Rover Station Wagon, but this was a Purchase Tax dodge. Outside the UK they were more realistically configured to seat just ten people.

els were favourites with military authorities world-wide, and there were several special variants to meet special military requirements. The Station Wagon models could be configured to carry ten passengers, although in the UK, tax regulations meant they were configured as rather uncomfortable twelve-seaters.

The engine and transmission options were the same as for the 88in models, although the long-wheelbase models could also be had with a 2625cc 6-cylinder petrol engine, which added some refinement but not a lot of extra performance.

Land Rover Forward Control

The forward control model was the load-lugger of the range, with a 1,524kg (30cwt) payload. In standard form, it came as a small dropside truck, but large numbers were supplied as chassis-cabs for special bodywork. Essentially, it was a 109in model with the cab pushed forwards and up over the engine to give more room behind within the same chassis 'footprint'. A reinforcing frame above the rear chassis helped cope with the additional payloads. Much taller than the normal control models, the forward controls were less stable on some types of rough terrain.

Engine choices were the same as for the normal control 109s, but the transfer gearbox had lower gearing to cope with the extra payload. There were also larger tyres. For reasons that would complicate this story unnecessarily, the forward controls were known by this stage as Series IIB types and had a 110-inch wheelbase. They remained in production until 1972, without significant alteration.

The forward control Land Rover was related to the normal control types by design, but was not usually bodied as a passenger carrier. This is a Series IIB 110in model.

The MGC looked too much like an MGB for comfort, and the bonnet bulge was the only obvious recognition feature. This was the GT version; the model could also be had as a roadster.

MGC

When BMC took the Austin-Healey 3000 out of production in 1967, they knew they would have to find a replacement for this archetypal hairy-chested British roadster. The cheap – and on the face of it, sensible – solution was to drop an engine of the same 3-litre capacity into the MGB shell. The MGC had just become available, as both roadster and GT, by the time British Leyland was created. A bonnet bulge was the easiest way of distinguishing it, but the rest of it was very much unadulterated MGB. Unfortunately, the heavy engine did nothing for the handling, and the car simply lacked distinction. It was certainly not an adequate replacement for the big Healey, and was withdrawn in 1969 because of slow sales.

MG 1100 and 1300

Along with the Riley Kestrel, the MG 1100 provided a sporting version of BMC's ubiquitous ADO16 front-wheel-drive family saloon. The 1100 (1098cc) model barely limped into 1968 and the BLMC era, but from 1967 the larger-engined 1300 (1275cc) was introduced and would take over completely. The MG 1300 was less well equipped than the equivalent Riley, and sold more strongly. So it remained in production after the Riley was withdrawn in 1969, finally disappearing in 1971.

BELOW: The supposedly sporty 1300 version of the ADO16 saloon range came with just two doors and MG badges.

The MG version of the mid-range Farina saloons had the same basic shape as all the others, and used the established Magnette name. MAGIC CAR PICS

MG Magnette

The Magnette was MG's version of the medium-sized BMC Farina saloons, a badge-engineered Austin Cambridge/Morris Oxford (and so on) with a little more performance thanks to twin carburettors on its 1622cc 4-cylinder engine. By the time of BLMC, the model had been a Magnette IV since 1961 with very little change, and was long overdue for replacement. It hung on until 1969, but was long dead by the time the Austin Maxi replaced its Austin and Morris cousins, and so had no real successor.

The Morris Inheritance

What Morris brought to the BLMC party was its substantial presence in the everyday family saloon market; at one time in its long existence, the Morris marque, as produced by the company, accounted for nearly half of Britain's entire annual car output. Founded in 1910 by former bicycle manufacturer William Morris, the company had been the core of his Nuffield Organisation and a major force in car manufacture before merging with its main rival to form BMC in 1952. Since then, badge engineering had gradually eroded the distinctive Morris character, but the public perception of Morris cars was still that they were no-nonsense, affordable and reliable cars for everyman.

Morris Mini

BMC's badge-engineering policy had ensured that Morris also made a version of the hugely successful Mini. By the time BLMC took over, it had become a Mk II, and could be had with the same 848cc ('850') and 1098cc ('1000') engines as its Austin counterpart. Although Mk I Minis had been built at Morris's traditional home in Cowley, all the Mk II Minis were built at the Austin plant in Longbridge. Like the Austin models,

The ubiquitous Mini came with Morris badges as well, when it looked just like the Austin version – give or take grille and badge differences.
© DEFACTO/WIKIMEDIA COMMONS

they came as saloons, sporty Cooper and Cooper S saloons, Traveller estates, vans and pick-ups. However, Morris-badged Minis would disappear in 1969, when the car was revised to become a Leyland Mini. During 1968 there were also Longbridge-built, Morris-badged versions of the Mini-Moke (see under Austin), but their production was then transferred to Australia.

Morris Minor

More than any other car on sale as BLMC took over, the Minor embodied the spirit of the Morris name. First sold in 1948, it had been a revolutionary design (by Alec Issigonis, who would later design the Mini) that delivered practicality, affordability and most acceptable handling qualities to the small saloon sector of the market. In 1960, it became the first British car to sell a million examples. It was also the only distinctively Morris design then still on sale.

Although it had evolved in many ways, by 1968 the Minor was still recognizable as a descendant of the twenty-year-old original. Now called a Minor 1000 (though with a 1098cc engine), it came as a saloon with either two or four doors, a Traveller estate with distinctive wooden rear body framing, or a two-door convertible ('tourer'). There were van and pick-up versions, too. However, despite its continuing popularity, BLMC determined to replace this old design as soon as possible. The tourers finished in 1969, the saloons in 1970, and the Travellers in 1971. The Minor was replaced by the smaller-engined versions of the Morris Marina.

The British public seemed unwilling to let go of the Morris Minor. These are 1970 models, by which time the convertible had gone out of production.

Van versions of the Morris Minor were also popular, and this one was snapped up by a classic car specialist business in Switzerland.

On its launch in 1961, the Elf had been advertised as the 'most luxurious small car in the world'. It did have leather upholstery and a wooden dashboard, plus more sound-deadening than mainstream Minis. That helped to give it appeal to female drivers, at a time when a 'second car for the wife' was becoming popular. However, its appeal gradually waned, and by 1968 it was clear that viable sales would not continue much longer.

Riley Kestrel

There was a Riley version of the best-selling ADO16 range, too, its name taken from a sporting Riley of the 1930s. In late 1967, the original 1098cc '1100' model was supplemented by a single-carburettor 1275cc Kestrel, available with manual or automatic gearbox. Supplies were limited in the beginning, and BLMC inherited waiting lists for this Riley.

Under BLMC – although planned in advance – the 1275cc engine took on twin carburettors from June 1968. However, from October that year the Kestrel name was dropped and the cars were renamed Riley 1300 types. It appears that there were objections by die-hard Riley owners to the use of the Kestrel name – although if that were true they had taken a very long time to get their point across, because the Kestrel version of the ADO16 had been introduced in 1965. The Riley 1300 was the slowest-selling ADO16 saloon during the 1969 model year, and it didn't offer much that couldn't be had from the cheaper MG model, or indeed from the new 1300GT saloons that wore Austin and Morris badges. So few people can have been surprised when BLMC announced its demise.

Riley 4/72

The Riley 4/72 that was in production at the start of 1968 had barely changed from the time of its introduction in 1961. It was a badge-engineered version of the Pinin Farina-designed BMC mid-sized saloons that had originally been launched in 1959. At that stage, the Riley was a less powerful 4/68 model, but it was nonetheless the most expensive of these Farina saloons.

The 4/72 had a 68bhp twin-carburettor version of the 1622cc B-series engine, normally driving the rear wheels through a four-speed manual gearbox, but also available with a three-speed automatic. In that guise it was scarcely in the sporting Riley tradition, although leather upholstery with wood trim made it feel more up-market than other versions of the same design.

Its 81mph (130km/h) top speed was looking rather feeble by 1968, but the car could not have taken more power without substantial changes, as braking and handling were not among its strong suits. Sales had reduced to a trickle by BLMC's time, and the 4/72 disappeared along with the other Rileys in 1969.

The distinctive front end and two-tone paint mark this out as the Riley Kestrel, a sporty four-door version of the ADO16 range. By 1968 it was close to being dropped from production.

The Riley derivative of the mid-range Farina saloons had become a 4/72 model by the time of BLMC, but it would not remain available for much longer. MAGIC CAR PICS

The Rover Inheritance

The British public knew exactly what Rover stood for at the time of the BLMC takeover: it was a company with a strong traditional streak, building cars that were slightly old-fashioned, but elegant, dependable and prestigious. This side of its output was very much aimed at the upper middle classes – and yet it was not a company that was mired in tradition, because its biggest seller was the thoroughly modern Rover 2000, introduced in 1963 with a wealth of technically advanced features. Rovers were respectable and aspirational, and they set comfort and elegance above performance.

Rover was an independent company until the end of 1966, when it sought shelter with the Leyland Motor Company, which already owned Standard-Triumph. The catalyst for change was BMC's purchase of Pressed Steel, who made Rover's bodies; Rover management was concerned that their requirements for bodies would become subordinate to those of the BMC marques, which were of course direct rivals in some product areas. The thinking was that an alliance with Leyland would give Rover access to a more fair-minded allocation of body-making resources.

Leyland did not interfere with Rover in the period between the merger and the establishment of BLMC in May 1968. However, there was an important change in the management at Rover, when long-standing Chairman Spencer (SB) Wilks retired and was made the company's Life President. The new Chairman was George Farmer, the financial man on the Rover Board and a key figure in the merger with Leyland. One major product event also occurred in autumn 1967, and that was the introduction of Rover's new 3.5-litre light-alloy V8 engine, originally designed by General Motors' Buick division in the USA, but now built under licence and further developed by Rover.

Rover 2000 (P6)

Introduced in 1963, the Rover 2000 was the company's volume seller. By the time of the BLMC merger it was available as a 2000SC (single carburettor), 2000SC Automatic, and 2000TC (twin carburettors). In addition there was a version of the car with the 3.5-litre V8 engine badged as a 3500 but called the Three Thousand Five (see below).

The Rover 2000 was technologically advanced when it was introduced, with an ohc 4-cylinder engine of 2-litre capacity (actually 1978cc), all-round disc brakes, and a De Dion rear suspension. It had base-unit construction with unstressed body panels, and a curious front suspension in which the coil springs acted horizontally against the bulkhead; this had been designed to make a wider engine bay for a planned gas turbine-engined version that was never commercialized.

The 2000 range, or P6 to Rover, was highly respected in the market place as a well-equipped, executive-class saloon with excellent handling. Like the P5B models, it never car-

Rover's 2000 was seen as an advanced and safe family saloon, although rear-seat passengers needed short legs to be comfortable.

ried any British Leyland identification. All three models were face-lifted in autumn 1970 as Mk II types, gaining a bonnet with power bulges, a new grille, vinyl-covered rear pillars, side-trim strips and new wheel trims, among other items. They remained available until 1973, when they were replaced by re-engined 2200 cars.

Rover 3.5-litre (P5B)

Rover's grand luxury model of the mid-1960s dated back to 1958, when it was introduced with a 6-cylinder engine as the Rover 3-litre. A more rakish roofline created the companion model 3-litre Coupé in 1962, and saloon and Coupé sold steadily but not spectacularly as the top models in the Rover range up to 1967. They were always expensive prestige cars, built in low volumes but highly respected as some of the last examples of a dying breed of British luxury car. Rover knew them as P5 types; the name probably denoted them as the fifth post-war Rover design, although that derivation is uncertain.

In autumn 1967, the P5 saloon and Coupé became the first Rovers to take on the new V8 engine. Within the company, the revised cars were known as P5B types (the B stood for Buick, originators of the engine), and to the public they were known as the Rover 3.5-litre saloon and Rover 3.5-litre Coupé. A year or so later, in an attempt to avoid confusion with the newly released P6B models described below, the name was changed to Rover Three and a Half Litre, although the original badges remained unchanged, and so did the confusion.

The V8's lighter weight improved the handling, while its additional power and torque improved the performance. All the P5Bs had Borg Warner automatic transmission, which had dominated 3-litre sales. The P5B saloons soon became Britain's favourite 'official' cars, as they took the place of the discontinued big Humbers in government and military car pools. Many were bought for chauffeur-driven duties, but the majority were probably owner-driven – and with some pride.

The V8 engine was intended to keep the big Rovers viable until the new P8 model (see sidebar) was ready in 1971. However, when that new model was cancelled by British Leyland, the P5B's life was extended by a further two years. Between 1971 and 1973 it retained its position as a much respected, old-style British luxury saloon, but there was never any doubt that it was selling to a dwindling customer base, as newer designs from rival luxury car makers stole the limelight. Under British Leyland, only running changes were made, and the cars never carried any British Leyland identification – although the flying wheel symbol did appear in Rover advertising and sales literature.

Production of the P5B models ended in 1973, just as new European emissions legislation would have demanded power-sapping engine changes. The assembly line space they vacated was claimed a year or so later by the lines for Rover's new military-only Land Rover 101 one-tonne forward-control model.

The big Rover had recently been re-engined with the ex-Buick V8 engine, which gave this stately model an unexpected new lease of life.

The Triumph Spitfire had reached its Mk III incarnation by 1968, although the main difference from earlier models was the higher position of the front bumper, needed to meet US regulations. MAGIC CAR PICS

The Triumph Inheritance

Triumph brought a quite wide model range to BLMC in 1968, and the Spitfire and TR5 roadsters, the GT6 coupé, and the 2000/2500 executive saloons represented the sporting heritage of the company. However, there were also two ranges of medium-sized saloons, the Herald and Vitesse with rear-wheel drive, and the more modern 1300 with front-wheel drive. The Herald, Vitesse, Spitfire and GT6 all shared a common chassis, while the medium saloons shared 4-cylinder engines and the TR5, GT6, Vitesse and 2000/2500 saloons shared 6-cylinder engines.

All these models had been developed under Harry Webster as Triumph's Chief Engineer, and all had body styling by the Italian design house of Michelotti. They were built at the Triumph factory in Canley, near Coventry. The Triumph marque was well established in many overseas markets, especially North America, and BLMC had no reason not to continue with it.

Triumph Spitfire

The Triumph Spitfire was a two-seat sports car built on the chassis of the Herald saloon, and by the time of the BLMC merger was being built in Mk III form. This had been introduced in January 1967, and had the 1296cc 4-cylinder engine also seen in the Herald 13/60 and the Triumph 1300.

The Spitfire had been introduced in 1962 as a direct competitor for the Austin-Healey Sprite and MG Midget in the cheap sports car market. A Mk II model brought more power in 1965, and the Mk III added a folding convertible top, a 75bhp twin-carburettor engine, and other improvements. All these Spitfires were major export earners for Triumph, especially in the USA. From 1969, Mk IIIs destined for the USA had engine and interior changes to comply with new emissions and safety legislation, and there were other minor changes for all markets.

BLMC was happy to approve the replacement Spitfire Mk IV that was introduced in 1970 with a new squared-off rear end that deliberately resembled those of the revised 2000 models and the new Stag. The optional hardtop was redesigned with rear quarter-lights, and engine power was down to 63bhp – and less in the USA. Welcome improvements were rear suspension changes (although the swing-axle design was retained) and an all-synchromesh gearbox.

The Spitfire's final incarnation arrived in 1973 for North America, and December 1974 for everywhere else. The new model was called the Spitfire 1500, and had Triumph's longer-stroke 1493cc 4-cylinder engine to help compensate for losses caused by emissions-control equipment. There were several detail changes during 1500 production, and weight gradually increased in this period, too. North American Spitfire 1500s were blessed with ungainly black plastic over-riders before mid-1978, when large all-black safety bumpers replaced them.

The Spitfire was given squarer, supposedly more modern lines in 1970, and emerged as a Spitfire Mk IV. In this picture it is wearing the optional hardtop

The last Spitfire of all was built at Canley in August 1980, just before the factory was closed for good under BL's reorganization plan.

Triumph GT6

The Triumph GT6 was essentially a fixed-head Spitfire, with a fastback coupé body and the 2-litre 6-cylinder engine. The first cars, in 1966, had 95bhp and the old swing-axle rear suspension. However, the 104bhp engine and redesigned rear suspension were fitted at the same time as these reached the Vitesse, and the revised models were called GT6 Mk 2 types. North America took a model called the GT6 Plus instead, with emissions-controlled 95bhp engine and the new rear suspension.

The final versions of the GT6 were Mk 3 types, introduced in 1970. These had a version of the new tail developed for the Spitfire 1500, a reprofiled roof, different road wheels and several smaller cosmetic differences. Most cars had the 104bhp

This was how the Mk 2 version of the Triumph GT6 was promoted to the public. It was more powerful than before, and had a much improved rear suspension.
MAGIC CAR PICS

The Mk 3 GT6 shared its new front and rear details with the contemporary Spitfire Mk IV. MAGIC CAR PICS

engine, but Mk 3s for North America had to settle for 90bhp on 1971 models, and a miserable 79bhp on 1972 and 1973 cars. Sales were sliding by this time, and further tightening emissions regulations would have robbed the North American cars of what little performance they had left. So BLMC finally had the GT6 taken out of production in 1973, and it was not directly replaced.

6-cylinder power, plus fuel injection in most countries, created the Triumph TR5 sports car. MAGIC CAR PICS

Triumph TR5 and TR250

Triumph's line of sports roadsters had begun with the TR2 in 1952, and they had always had a separate body and chassis. The version in use for the TR5 had independent rear suspension, and could trace its ancestry back to the TR4A of 1965. The TR5, however, new in October 1967, was the first of the TR range with a 6-cylinder engine; its 2498cc unit was shared with the bigger Triumph saloons, and for most markets came with the Lucas injection system used on the 2.5PI model. However, Triumph could not tune that injection system to meet the latest US exhaust emissions legislation, and so there was a special carburettor version of the engine for North America; for that market the TR5 was renamed TR250.

Both TR5 and TR250 had the same two-seat roadster body. They had a four-speed, all-synchromesh gearbox with an overdrive option; steering was by rack and pinion, and the brakes were discs at the front and drums at the rear with servo assistance as standard.

A rugged sports car it may have been, but the wooden dashboard lent an air of class to the interior of the TR5. MAGIC CAR PICS

These were the 'big' Triumph sports cars, and they remained in production until 1969, when they were replaced by the TR6. They were much liked by enthusiasts of such machines, especially in the USA.

Triumph Herald and Vitesse

The Herald was central to the range of smaller Triumphs because it was the car for which their common chassis had originally been designed. By the time of BLMC, it was available as a 1200 or 13/60 saloon, convertible and estate, all with two doors.

The 1200 had an 1147cc 4-cylinder engine with just 39bhp, and dated back to 1961; the 13/60 shared its 1296cc engine with the Triumph 1300, and had been added to the range in autumn 1967. The 13 approximated to its engine size; the 60 represented its power output of 61bhp. The two cars had different front ends, that of the 13/60 being a single headlamp version of the 'slant-eyed' design originally seen on the related Vitesse. The rest of the body was shared, and retained the original sharp-edged design by Michelotti. All models had an old-fashioned swing-axle rear suspension, with a single transverse leaf spring, although steering was by rack and pinion, and the front suspension used wishbones and coils.

The 1200 and the 13/60 saloon went out of production at the end of 1970, but the convertible and estate versions of the 13/60 remained in production until May 1971. Sadly, the Herald's labour-intensive method of construction meant that even continuing strong sales could not save it, because it was actually selling at a loss.

Meanwhile Triumph had tackled the market for a small sporting saloon by putting a 6-cylinder engine into the Herald saloon, adding a four-headlamp nose, and giving it the name of Vitesse. The original 1962 car had a 1.6-litre engine, but from 1966 the Vitesse had the 95bhp 2-litre (1998cc) engine from the bigger Triumph 2000 saloon and other improvements. This was available in saloon and convertible forms when BLMC was formed, and from July 1968 was further improved as the Vitesse Mk 2 with a redesigned rear suspension and 104bhp engine. Vitesse models remained in production under BL until July 1971.

By 1968, the Triumph Herald came as a 13/60 model with 1296cc and this stylish headlight arrangement. MAGIC CAR PICS

The Herald estate was a popular variant of the small Triumph model. MAGIC CAR PICS

The Herald 13/60 range was completed by a convertible model. MAGIC CAR PICS

Triumph's Vitesse model was essentially a Herald with a 2-litre, 6-cylinder engine and twin headlamps. This is a Mk 2 version, in convertible guise. MAGIC CAR PICS

Triumph 1300

Encouraged by Leyland to deliver a rival for the hugely successful BMC 1100 (ADO16) front-wheel-drive cars, Triumph came up with the 1300 in 1965. At the time it was intended as an eventual replacement for the Herald, but it was given a generally higher specification level to help justify its additional cost and also to distance it from the older car.

Triumph's FWD layout differed from BMC's, partly so that they could use their existing north-south engines. The gearbox was located under the engine, which made the whole assembly rather tall. This height was well concealed by the Michelotti-designed four-door body, which was drawn up with a deliberate resemblance to the larger 2000 saloons. There was twin-wishbone front suspension, and an independent rear end with semi-trailing arms and coil springs, as on the 2000.

This, then, was the car in production at the time of the BLMC merger. In autumn 1968, the 61bhp 1300 was supplemented by a 75bhp 1300TC that used the twin-carburettor engine from the Spitfire and could attain a maximum of over 145km/h (90mph). These two models remained in production until August 1970, but by that stage Triumph had become rather disillusioned with front-wheel drive, and they were replaced by two different but related cars, a front-wheel-drive 1500 and a rear-wheel-drive 1500TC.

The Triumph 1300 was a neat little saloon with Michelotti styling and front-wheel drive.
MAGIC CAR PICS

The dashboard of the Triumph 1300 made clear that this car was intended to be a cut above similarly sized front-wheel-drive designs from BMC.
MAGIC CAR PICS

Triumph 2000

As BLMC came together in 1968, Triumph's biggest saloon was the 6-cylinder 2000, which had an estate derivative that was built from part-completed saloons by Carbodies in Coventry. The 2000 had been designed as a replacement for the Standard Vanguard, but was developed along new lines; however, Triumph and Rover found they were both tackling the same market sector with their 2-litre 'executive' saloons, which were intended to add traditional luxury car qualities and equipment to a more affordable modern design.

As introduced in 1963, the 2000 had an uprated version of the old Vanguard 6-cylinder engine, now with twin carburettors and 90bhp. It was designed as a monocoque, with all-round independent coil-spring suspension and front disc brakes. Four-speed, overdrive, and automatic models were all made available. The car was always very highly rated, but by mid-decade Triumph foresaw the need for more power and began to work on a long-stroke (2498cc) engine with Lucas fuel injection.

Meanwhile, Triumph had wanted a second 2000 derivative alongside the saloon, perhaps not least to give them an edge on Rover. They hesitated for a time between a five-door fastback called the 2000GT and a more conventional estate, but eventually settled on the estate. This was introduced in autumn 1965 and was built by Carbodies as a conversion of the saloon. The 2000 estate had become a strong seller by the time of the BLMC merger.

The fuel-injected car arrived in October 1968, after the merger, and was called the 2.5PI. With 132bhp it was much quicker than the 2000, although the injection system notoriously gave trouble. However, heavily revised versions of both cars were already in development, and would be released in October 1969. Those models are discussed in Chapter 3 as British Leyland types.

The Triumph 2000 was directly competitive with Rover's 2000 and was released at the same time. Triumph relied on a 6-cylinder engine. MAGIC CAR PICS

The estate version of the Triumph 2000 was constructed by Carbodies from part-completed saloon shells. It was a capacious and attractive holdall. MAGIC CAR PICS

Based on the old Austin A135 chassis, the Vanden Plas Princess 4-litre limousine was an elderly yet elegant design. The man in the street could have been forgiven for thinking it was a Bentley – and that was largely the point. MAGIC CAR PICS

Vanden Plas Princess 4-litre Limousine

The Austin Princess had been introduced as long ago as 1952, and the Vanden Plas Princess 4-litre Limousine in production at the start of 1968 was the same car, renamed in 1960. This was a formal limousine much liked by mayors and funeral directors, its body hand-built at Kingsbury on a separate chassis with a huge 3,353mm (132in) wheelbase. The whole car was nearly 5.5m (18ft) long, and did well to achieve a top speed of 75mph (121km/h). Its engine was not the Rolls-Royce 6-cylinder, despite the coincidence of nominal size, but rather the much older BMC D-series 6-cylinder with 120bhp from 3993cc. Both manual and automatic gearboxes were available.

The Vanden Plas Princess had become something of an anachronism by the mid-1960s, and Vanden Plas were working on its replacement when BMC and Jaguar-Daimler joined forces during 1966. Jaguar was planning a large Daimler limousine based on the platform and running gear of its Mk X saloon, and it was clearly nonsensical to go ahead with both new models. So the new Princess was scrapped in favour of the Daimler DS420, which would be built at Kingsbury from 1968. The old Vanden Plas Princess, which had been built in quantities of 250 to 300 a year, ceased production to make way for it.

The Wolseley Inheritance

Like Riley, Wolseley was a much diminished marque by the time of the BLMC merger in 1968. Early in the century it had developed a reputation as a luxury car maker, but it was then bought by William Morris of Morris Motors, and from the mid-1930s it became little more than a badge on more expensive and better equipped versions of Morris cars.

Even so, there was still genuine respect for the Wolseley marque by 1968. Wolseleys came with luxury touches such as leather and wood trim, and had always kept their delightfully idiosyncratic radiator emblem that lit up with the car's sidelights. By the late 1960s, many police forces were still using the Wolseley 6/110 as a patrol car, which added to public respect for the name.

Wolseley came into BLMC with a full if entirely badge-engineered model range. The smallest was the Hornet, the company's Mini derivative. Above this came versions of the BMC 1100 and 1300, and the mid-sized saloon was the 16/60 derivative of the Farina range. Recently introduced was an 18/85 derivative of the Austin-Morris ADO17 1800, and right at the top came the 'big Farina' 6/110.

Adding a boot and Wolseley front-end details to the Mini saloon created the Wolseley Hornet, a likeable little car but not one that would last for long under British Leyland.

Wolseley Hornet

Like the Riley Elf, the Wolseley Hornet was a 'booted' derivative of the BMC Mini, with higher levels of equipment. By 1968 it came in Mk III form with winding windows, concealed door hinges, leather upholstery and some token wood on the instrument panel. The engine was a 38bhp 998c A-series, the four-speed gearbox had a remote change, and the suspension was Hydrolastic.

Sales, though, were slow. In fact with just 28,455 sold, the Hornet had the distinction of being the rarest of the UK-built Mini derivatives. It was taken out of production under BLMC in 1969, along with the Riley Elf.

Two-tone paint and a Wolseley front end created a sort of small luxury model out of the ADO16. This was how the Wolseley 1300 looked when BLMC was formed.

Wolseley 1100 and 1300

There had been Wolseley 1100 derivatives of the ADO16 range since October 1965, and a Wolseley 1300 arrived in October 1967, with the Mk II cosmetic changes and bringing the option of an automatic gearbox to the Wolseley ADO16s for the first time. Automatic models had a 60bhp single-carburettor engine; manual cars had a 65bhp twin-carburettor version. Both 1100 and 1300 remained in production when BLMC was born, but the situation would soon change.

ABOVE: The Wolseley 1300 would not change dramatically before production ended five years later – although, as this picture shows, the final models lost the two-tone paint option and gained a British Leyland badge on the front wing.

LEFT: The Wolseley version of the medium-sized Farina saloon, a 16/60 by 1968, always looked good with two-tone paintwork and that Wolseley grille. MAGIC CAR PICS

Sales were already declining during 1967, and although they picked up again with the arrival of the Mk IIs, BLMC decided that the 1100 model should go in spring 1968. Like other ADO16s, the 1300 took on an all-synchromesh gearbox later that year.

Two-tone paint was common on these early Wolseley models, but was no longer available on the Mk III 1300 introduced in September 1971. It was clear that BL were trying to save money here, a fact reinforced by their withdrawal of the Wolseley from export markets at the same time. Home-market cars were distinguished by a rectangular British Leyland badge on the left-hand front wing, but BL's hold on the Wolseley marque was by now half-hearted. Production of the 1300 was halted in April 1973, and the model was not directly replaced.

Wolseley 16/60

When BMC introduced its new medium-sized 'Farina' saloons, the Wolseley version was actually the first to be made public, in December 1958. That first version was called a Wolseley 15/60 (15 for the 1.5-litre engine and 60 as an optimistic estimate of the brake horsepower). From 1961 it was upgraded with a 1622cc engine, as were its badge-engineered cousins, and became a Wolseley 16/60. This time the '60' was a closer approximation of the 61bhp actually available.

The role of the Wolseley was to provide a luxurious derivative of the Farina range, and to that end it had leather upholstery with wood trim, and, usually, two-tone paintwork in discreet colours. An automatic option was available, but there was no estate version of the Wolseley. Grille and up-market interior apart, there was nothing to distinguish the 16/60 from the contemporary Morris Oxford, but demand was sufficient for BLMC to keep it in their line-up until April 1971.

Wolseley 18/85

It was an inevitable result of the BMC badge engineering policy that Wolseley badges should appear on a version of the ADO17 'Land Crab'. They did so in March 1967, and the model was called an 18/85 – 18 for the 1.8-litre engine and 85bhp as an accurate reflection of its brake horsepower. A Mk II model was developed quite quickly, mainly to match changes for other ADO16s, and was launched under BLMC in May 1968. With it came a twin-carburettor 18/85 S model, boasting 96bhp.

When the Austin and Morris ADO16s gained a 6-cylinder option in 1972, so did the Wolseley, although in this case the Wolseley Six completely replaced the smaller-engined model. It remained the most luxurious version of the ADO16 family until 1975, when it was replaced by a Wolseley-badged version of the new corporate wedge-shaped medium saloon.

Wolseley 6/110

The big Wolseley in 1968 was the 6-cylinder 6/110 (6 cylinders and 110bhp, although in practice its C-series engine developed 120bhp). It was descended from the 6/99 of 1959, and carried the same Pinin Farina-designed coachwork. Two-tone paint (an option), a Wolseley grille, auxiliary lamps recessed into the front panel, and a wood-and-leather interior distinguished it from the Austin A110 Westminster that was effectively the same car. It also had a more distant relative in the Vanden Plas Princess 4-litre R.

Priced just a little below the mainstream luxury saloon market, the 6/110 was a well regarded if somewhat old-fashioned car. Normally equipped with a four-speed manual gearbox, it could also be had with a three-speed automatic, and in both cases came with disc front brakes to help stop its considerable weight. However, it had no role in a company where Jaguars and Rovers were to provide the big luxury saloons, and BLMC took it out of production during 1968.

Wolseley's big saloon in 1968 was the 6/110, which lasted less than a year after BLMC took over.

The Wolseley front end on the ADO17 'Land Crab' created a rather handsome car. This was the 4-cylinder 18/85 model.

3 THE BRITISH LEYLAND MODELS

THIS CHAPTER LOOKS AT the models that can fairly be described as British Leyland types. For the most part they were designed under the aegis of BLMC or British Leyland, rather than inherited from its constituent companies. Some of them were nevertheless major revisions of models that had been inherited, where these revisions were initiated under British Leyland management.

Within each marque section, models are listed in order of their introduction. Light commercial derivatives are listed immediately following the entry for the cars on which they were based.

AUSTIN-BADGED MODELS

Under British Leyland, Austin remained a maker of everyday saloon cars, but Austin badges were mostly reserved for models that incorporated advanced engineering. BMC's advanced front-wheel-drive cars had all been designed at the Austin works in Longbridge under Alec Issigonis, even if their origins were obscured by the multiple brand names under which they appeared. So this was a logical development.

Austin Maxi (1969–81)

The Maxi's job was to replace the old Farina-styled 1.6-litre saloons in the BMC range, and it was a fourth Issigonis-designed car that was intended to fit in between the 1100/1300 and 1800 ranges, to give BMC a full house of front-wheel-drive models. However, things did not quite work out as planned: delays in development meant that the car was not released until after the BLMC merger, and although this was a BMC design, it became the first all-new model to be released by British Leyland. It would also be the last production car designed by Issigonis.

Work started on the project, coded ADO14, in 1964–65. A major influence from early on was the Renault 16, which won the European Car of the Year award in 1965, and BMC decided to copy its practical hatchback configuration. Otherwise, the design was fairly typical of Issigonis, with a spacious long-wheelbase monocoque shell, front-mounted transverse engine, gearbox in the sump, and front-wheel drive. Suspension was again pure Issigonis, with interlinked Hydrolastic units acting as the springing medium, and wishbones at the front with trailing arms at the rear. Disc front brakes and rack-and-pinion steering were part of the package.

BMC decided to save costs by insisting that the body should share its side doors with the Austin-Morris 1800 models. Those doors restricted what the designers could do with the side profile, with the result that the car looked taller and

The Austin Maxi was an immensely practical car, although its looks were distinctly average. This is a 1978 model.

Minor cosmetic changes were made over the Maxi's life, such as the new wheel trims seen on this 1980 model 1750HLS.

The folding rear seat and large hatchback made the Maxi a versatile load carrier.

dumpier than it might otherwise have done. They also rooted the car's shape firmly in the 1960s at a time when other makers were just about to introduce more stylish 'coke-bottle' shapes – the 1970 Hillman Avenger and 1971 Ford Cortina Mk III being examples.

BMC's existing 1.5-litre engines (which had already been stretched up to 1.8 litres) had been designed in the early 1950s, and a decision was made not to use one of these but instead to design a new engine. This became known as the E series, and featured a more modern overhead camshaft design, but without the inbuilt 'stretchability' that would allow larger-capacity versions to be made later. (The reasons for this are explained in Appendix I.) For these new engines, BMC constructed a new engine factory at Cofton Hackett, close to Longbridge, and the E series would be further developed and would later be used in several other cars from British Leyland. In addition, BMC designed for ADO14 a new five-speed gearbox with overdrive top gear, which was advanced thinking for the time.

At the time of the BLMC merger, the new hatchback model was intended to enter production as an Austin 1500, and there were plans for a four-door saloon model to follow, badged as a Morris 1500. However, BLMC had other ideas. The plan for a four-door saloon version was scrapped, perhaps because adding a boot made the car uncomfortably close in size to the existing 1800 models. As much of the tooling for the new 1.5-litre hatchback had already been ordered, there was little further impact that BLMC could have on the ADO14 before production began. They did, however, change its name.

Lord Stokes himself is said to have chosen the name of Maxi as a happy analogy with the existing name of Mini. Very noticeable was that it was made available only as an Austin. There would be no Morris derivative because BLMC management had decided to give the two marques clearer identities: Austin would in future stand for the advanced technology such as that pioneered by the Issigonis designs, while the Morris name would be applied to cars with more conventional engineering. Although this sounded very logical, there was inevitably a delightful inconsistency about it: the new Maxi would always be assembled at the old Morris plant in Cowley rather than the Austin plant at Longbridge.

The Austin Maxi was introduced in April 1969, at a press ride-and-drive exercise in Oporto, Portugal. Although it did replace the Austin A60 Cambridge models, taking over their assembly space at the Cowley works, it did not replace the Morris Oxford, which soldiered on for another two years. British Leyland did not give it the best possible start in life by making clear in public that it had not been their design; the implication was that it might have been better if it had been!

The Maxi remained in production for a total of twelve years, but never came close to its projected sales targets. For most of its life it was generally known as 'the Maxi', so there was no more than a ripple of recognition when the Austin name was dropped in 1977 and the car became a Leyland Maxi. Besides, the naming policy was inconsistent: in several countries outside the UK, the car would always be known as an Austin Maxi.

Just over 1,000 cars were assembled outside the UK from CKD kits shipped out from Cowley. From 1970, the Yugoslavian company IMV (Industrija Motornih Vozil – Industry of Motor Vehicles) began to assemble Maxi 1500s at its plant in Novo Mesto, following these with Maxi 1750s during 1971. Yugoslavian Maxi assembly ended in 1972 when IMV signed a new assembly contract with Renault. The exact figures (quoted from the web site AROnline) were 897 1500s in 1970 and 1971, plus 193 1750s in 1971 and 1972, making a grand total of 1,090 cars.

Perhaps the saddest part about the Maxi story was not its failings as a car, but the fact that British Leyland decided that, for marketing reasons, it should be the only hatchback in the range. That decision prevented a hatchback design being used on any other models for many years, and most importantly left British Leyland without a credible competitor for the new small hatchbacks from continental European makers in the mid-1970s. And yet... British Leyland was quite happy to approve hatchback developments of the 1100 and 1300 range as long as they were only sold outside the UK. The logic is hard to see.

Austin Maxi, 1969–70; Austin Maxi 1500, 1970–79

The Maxi was introduced in 1.5-litre form, its transversely mounted 4-cylinder engine delivering 74bhp and a maximum speed of around 86mph (138km/h). Fuel consumption worked out at around 24mpg (11.8ltr/100km). So although the car was no ball of fire, it had respectable performance for a large family saloon, and its running costs were reasonable. The earliest cars, however, had a cable-operated gearchange that was very much disliked. Not only did it feel horribly imprecise, but the cable was also prone to stretching, which made that imprecision worse. Early cars were also criticised for being noisy, and some found them under-powered.

The interior certainly was spacious, thanks largely to that long wheelbase and the flat floor that went with front-wheel drive. The front seats reclined fully, and the back of the rear seat folded forwards to increase the boot space, or backwards to line up with fully reclined front seats to make a quite tolerable bed. All that was very positive. Less so was the fact that the interior was horribly plain and dull, with a flat dashboard containing the main dials in 'tunnels' ahead of the driver. The steering wheel, too, was over-large, and the driving position altogether too similar to the bus-like one that had been so criticised in the 1800 range. It seemed that BMC's designers had not learned from customer feedback.

The earliest cars also suffered from poor build quality, and British Leyland set about making improvements as fast as it could. So the 1971 models that were introduced in October 1970 had a new rod-operated gear change, a more attractive (though still quite plainly styled) wooden facia, a smaller steering wheel, and generally improved interior trim with new expanded vinyl seat facings. Now called Maxi 1500 models to distinguish them from the bigger-engined Maxi 1750 types that were introduced at the same time, the 1971 cars also had a new radiator grille with a central badge, and body side strips to make the side elevation look less plain.

Only small cosmetic updates followed over the next few years. As noted above, in 1977 the car officially became a Leyland Maxi in the UK and some export territories. From 1978, its Hydrolastic suspension was replaced by the Hydragas system first seen in the 1973 Austin Allegro – broadly similar in principle to Hydrolastic, but using gas instead of fluid as the springing medium. The Maxi 1500 in all its forms was then discontinued in December 1979.

Austin Maxi 1750, 1970–80

When the original 1.5-litre Maxi was joined by a larger-engined companion model called the Maxi 1750 in October 1970, British Leyland publicity was able to make it look like a response to criticism of the first car's performance. It was nothing of the sort: a larger engine had been planned for some time.

The new '1750' (1748cc) engine was a long-stroke version of the E-series 4-cylinder, now developing 72bhp and capable of taking the Maxi 1750 almost to 90mph (145km). Much more important, though, was the additional torque generated by that longer stroke. Accompanied by some gearing changes, it made the car feel much more responsive, although its 0–60mph sprint times were not that much improved. Slightly better fuel consumption was another bonus.

Right from the start, the Maxi 1750 came with all the 1971 model-year improvements introduced for the Maxi 1500. It was also distinguished by its own tailgate badge and by a new grille. There were then two important upgrades in 1972 for the 1973 season: one was the option of an automatic gearbox, which was never made available on the smaller-engined models; and the other was the introduction of a third model called the 1750HL. HL stood for High Line, and the extra features that this name implied included a 91bhp twin-carburettor engine for more performance, fatter tyres, a distinctive black-and-chrome radiator grille, front under-riders, and special badges. On the inside, the dashboard gained a padded face, and there was a new steering wheel with three drilled spokes.

Like its sister car the Maxi 1500, the Maxi 1750 became a Leyland model in 1977, and switched to Hydragas suspension in 1978. Cars for the UK and some other countries gained dual-circuit brakes in 1977, and in 1978 there were additional changes for the 1750HL, which lost its distinctive three-spoke steering wheel and took on a walnut dashboard in place of the padded type.

There was then a range realignment in May 1979. The top model was now called the Maxi 1750HLS, and came with the twin-carburettor engine, while the 1750HL had the single-carburettor engine; automatic was now a 1750HL option. Both models took on more luxurious fabric upholstery in place of the basket-weave PVC 'leatherette'. Thus revised, the Maxi carried on for just over a year before there were more changes.

Leyland Maxi 2, 1980–81

The final iteration of the Maxi arrived in August 1980 with the new name of Maxi 2. That 2 was designed to reinforce the impression that this was a heavily revised car; BL had done the same in 1975 for the Allegro 2, and then again in late 1979 for the Allegro 3.

The 1981 model Maxi 2 came in three versions, called 1750L, 1750HL and 1750HLS. By this stage, only the single-carburettor 1750HL was available for export, and in many left-hand-drive markets the car was still sold as an Austin. It certainly did look different from the Maxis that had gone before, with new bumpers, full-width plastic wheel trims, relocated side indicator repeaters and fatter side moulding inserts. There were changes to the dashboard and controls, too.

One further and final change was made in 1981, when the chrome bumpers were replaced by matt black types. However, production was brought to an end in July 1981, and the very last Maxi (a 1750L model, colour 'Champagne') was handed over to the BMIHT collection at Gaydon. It would be two years before the Maxi's real successor arrived, in the shape of the Austin Maestro. In the meantime, its place in the British Leyland product range was held by the new Triumph Acclaim, which also replaced it on the assembly lines at Cowley.

IF YOU WANT ONE....

The Maxi has been somewhat neglected by the classic car movement, but its virtues are gradually becoming appreciated – though too late, sadly, for the majority of those built. The Austin Maxi Owners' Club caters for enthusiasts, and at the time of writing, could be contacted through its web site, www.austinmaxiclub.org.

Key purchasing points:
- Look for rust in the front wings and doors, and the front ends of the sills
- Front sub-frames rot from the inside, and rear suspension mounts rust
- Hydragas suspension displacers (from 1975) can fail, and new front ones are not available
- Listen for clicking CV joints
- Windscreens, front bumpers, early interior trim parts, window mechanisms and late exhausts are all hard to find

MAXI: FACTS AND FIGURES

Pressed steel monocoque with hatchback tail door; five seats. Transversely mounted front engine driving front wheels.

Engine	1500: 1485cc E-series in-line 4-cylinder, with 68bhp at 5,500rpm 1750: 1748cc E-series in-line 4-cylinder, with 72bhp at 4,900rpm (single carburettor), or 91bhp at 5,250rpm (twin carburettor)
Gearbox	Five-speed manual, mounted in engine sump. From late 1972, on 1750 only, optional automatic; automatic available on 1750HL model from 1979
Length	4,021mm (158.3in)
Wheelbase	2,641mm (104in)
Width	1,628mm (64.1in)
Height	1,405mm (55.3in)
Kerb weight	1,000kg approx (2,204lb) (1500 and 1750) 1,005kg approx (2,216lb) (1750HL)

Austin Maxi: Statistics

0–60mph	16.4sec (1500) 15.3sec (1750)
Max. speed	87mph (140km/h) (1500) 91mph (146km/h) (1750)
Fuel consumption	26mpg (10.9ltr/100km) (1500) 27mpg (10.5ltr/100km) (1750)
Production numbers	472,098 (all models)

Only a very close look will reveal that this 1971 model is an Austin Sprite and not an MG Midget or the earlier Austin-Healey Sprite.

Austin Sprite (1970–71)

The Austin Sprite is a little known car for the very good reason that not many were built. When the royalty agreement between British Leyland (as inheritors of the BMC agreement) and Donald Healey expired in 1970, the Austin-Healey Sprite was promptly withdrawn from the market. There was no need for it in the British Leyland overall plan, because the better selling MG Midget was already filling its role in the market, and the two cars were identical except for their badges.

Nevertheless, the Austin-Healey brand may have been dropped in 1970, but the old Austin-Healey Sprite was not. Rebadged as an Austin Sprite but otherwise unchanged, it remained available for a further year. Just 1,022 examples were built.

The MG Midget meanwhile remained in production and carried on until 1979.

IF YOU WANT ONE....

The Sprite belongs to a family of much liked, affordable sports cars, collectively known as Spridgets (Sprites and Midgets), and is greatly appreciated as a usable classic today. Few people know (and fewer still probably care) that it is such a rarity. Several clubs cater for the cars, including the Midget and Sprite Club (www.midgetand-spriteclub.com) and the Midget Register of the MG Car Club (www.midgetregister.com).

For key purchasing points, please see the entry for the MG Midget later in this book.

Austin Allegro (1973–82)

The Austin Allegro was perhaps the most crucial of all British Leyland's new models because it was drawn up to replace the corporation's best-selling product, the Austin, Morris (and other) 1100 and 1300 range. Its failure to sell in anything like the numbers of the models it replaced was undoubtedly a major factor in British Leyland's collapse in the mid-1970s. Industrial action and poor build quality certainly played their part in the Allegro's failure, but so did a badly compromised design.

The Allegro, then known as ADO67, was to replace a range of family saloons and estates that had incorporated advanced technology, and so it, too, would have to incorporate advanced technology. That ensured it would become an Austin under the BL scheme of things, contrasting with the conventional Morris Marina. Although the project began in 1968, there was

The Allegro's somewhat dumpy looks contrasted with its promise of the latest technology.

The Allegro estate at least showed a little styling flair, with its kicked-up rear window line.

still plenty of life in the ADO16 range, and so there was less urgency than with the Marina, and introduction was scheduled for 1973.

The design brief was to improve on the 1100s and 1300s, and to that end ADO67 was drawn up with the familiar Austin front-wheel-drive mechanical layout but more boot space, better under-bonnet access, and a better driving position. To save weight, its monocoque body would dispense with the sub-frames that the old 1100s and 1300s had needed. ADO67 would also be the first car to have the new Hydragas suspension designed by Alex Moulton, which used gas as the springing medium instead of the fluid in the earlier Hydrolastic system.

Styling was by Harris Mann in the Longbridge studio, and his original 1969 proposal was for a low-slung and stylish three-box saloon. However, the ADO67 project then suffered from what is today known as 'mission creep'. In addition to the 1100 and 1300 engines originally planned, BL decided that the car should also be made available with larger engines to spread its market appeal. The choice fell upon the 1500 and 1750 E-series engines originally developed for the Austin Maxi, and part of the plan was to increase production at the under-utilized Cofton Hackett engine plant where they were being built.

This decision immediately introduced problems for the design because the E-series engines were taller than the A-series types around which the design had originally been done. A further complication was a decision to use the big new heater unit designed for the Marina. To accommodate these changes, the bonnet line had to rise, and Harris Mann's sleek lines suddenly began to look dumpy rather than sleek, not helped by the slit-like grille design at the front end. The problem would later be compounded by errors at Pressed Steel, who over-corrected for the 'spring' in the car's curved panels. The redesign also made the cars heavier than their predecessors had been.

This fatally compromised design proceeded to production, accompanied by the doubts of its original designer, Harris Mann. At its launch in May 1973, in two-door and four-door saloon forms, it was sold under the slogan 'the new driving force from Austin'. This rang hollow to those who had attended the press ride-and-drive exercise in Spain, where poor build quality was immediately apparent, and the car seemed strangely characterless. Although the bigger-engined cars showed promise, the 1100 and 1300 models were distinctly underpowered because of the extra weight they had put on during the redesign. Meanwhile, the supposedly sporting 1750SS with twin-carburettor engine was just not sporting enough.

Furthermore, nobody liked the new 'quartic' steering wheel. Rectangular with rounded sides, it was supposedly an advanced design that gave more thigh room and a better view of the instruments. In fact it had been cribbed from a David Bache proposal for the aborted Rover P8 saloon that George Turnbull had seen and liked.

British Leyland priced the cars at 10 per cent more than their ADO16 predecessors (of which some variants would remain on sale into 1974), and bullishly anticipated production of 5,000 cars a week. But demand for the Allegro never came near to justifying such a figure. Production reached 2,500 a week in 1974, but had collapsed to 1,000 a week by 1978. By contrast (a point made in Chris Cowin's book British Leyland: Chronicle of a Car Crash 1968–1978), the Volkswagen Golf, which was aimed at much the same group of family car buyers, was being turned out at a rate of more than 10,000 a week to meet demand during the mid-1970s.

Three of the launch models that had proved slow sellers were dropped in early 1974, and the 'quartic' steering wheel was also quietly abandoned that autumn. The ADO67 programme then proceeded as planned, with the introduction of a Vanden Plas derivative in autumn 1974 (see the section Vanden Plas 1500) and the arrival of estate variants in April 1975. These certainly had the right idea, with a distinctively shaped rearmost side pillar.

That October, British Leyland tried to make amends for the problems of the early cars with revised Allegro 2 models that had additional rear legroom, a new grille, and reversing lights as standard on most models. Estates were made to look longer by means of a coachline on each side. Most of the Allegro's teething troubles were cured with changes to the engine mounts, drive shafts, suspension and brakes.

But the damage to the Allegro's reputation had already been done. A motoring magazine had nicknamed it the 'All-Aggro' ('aggro' was a fashionable term for aggravation or trouble in the mid-1970s), and there were tales of wheels falling off – which they did if the wheel bearings were not correctly adjusted – and windscreens popping out as the body twisted when it was jacked up.

Despite its desperate shortage of capital in the later 1970s, British Leyland managed to find a budget for some further Allegro improvements. These began in 1979 with the Allegro Equipe, a supposedly sporty two-door 1750 model that was intended to rival the Ford Escort RS and Volkswagen Golf GT models. Despite its red and orange side stripes and alloy wheels, it missed the mark and sold poorly. Just three weeks later, the 1980-season Allegro 3 models were announced. These had several cosmetic changes, including a new grille with the revised Leyland badge, larger bumpers and additional side indicators. The more expensive models had a four-headlamp installation that had been tried earlier on some Allegros built at the Belgian plant in Seneffe, and

AUSTIN ALLEGRO: FACTS AND FIGURES

Pressed steel monocoque with two or four doors on saloons, or two doors plus additional tail door on estates; five seats. Transversely mounted front engine driving front wheels.

Engine	1.0: 998cc A-plus in-line 4-cylinder, with 44bhp at 5,250rpm 1100: 1098cc A-series in-line 4-cylinder, with 49bhp at 5,250rpm (1973–75); 45bhp at 5,250rpm (1975–80) 1300, 1973–80: 1275cc A-series in-line 4-cylinder, with 59bhp at 5,300rpm 1300, 1980–82: 1275cc A-plus in-line 4-cylinder, with 62bhp at 5,600rpm 1500: 1485cc E-series in-line 4-cylinder, with 69bhp at 5,600rpm (single carburettor), or 77PS at 5,000rpm (twin carburettors) 1750: 1748cc E-series in-line 4-cylinder, with 76bhp at 5,000rpm (single carburettor), or 90bhp at 5,000rpm (twin carburettor)
Gearbox	Four-speed manual (1100 and 1300) or five-speed manual (1500 and 1750); optional three-speed automatic

Dimensions

Length	3,861mm (152in)
Wheelbase	2,438mm (96in)
Width	1,600mm (63in)
Height	1,397mm (55in)
Kerb weight	800kg (1,784lb) (1100) 880kg (1,940lb) (1750HL)

Austin Allegro: Statistics

Performance	0–60mph in 22.0sec (1100) 0–60mph in 16.7sec (1500) 0–60mph in 11.3sec (1750HL)
Max. speed	78mph (126km/h) (1100) 99mph (159km/h) (1750)
Fuel consumption	31mpg (9.1ltr/100km) (1100) 26mpg (10.9ltr/100km) (1750)
Production numbers	667,192

IF YOU WANT ONE....

The Allegro spent a long time being unloved before being rediscovered by the classic car fraternity, and vast numbers had already been scrapped. Interest is still limited at the time of writing, and some spares can be hard to find. Make sure you join the Allegro Club International (www.allegroclubint.org.uk), formed in 1990, if you are serious about these cars.

Key purchasing points:

- Rust at the bottom of the rear wheel-arches may have spread to the sub-frame. It hides under the plastic sill covers on Series 2 models, strikes around the light units in front wings, and even a badly rusted front valance can be an MoT failure
- As always, check that the car sits level: failed suspension displacer units will be hard to replace
- The engine is heavily worn if there is blue smoke from the exhaust on start-up and on the over-run
- Clicking on full lock means worn CV joints; four-speed gearboxes are tough, but five-speeds can be baulky; autos are long-lived, but beware stretched selector cables
- Late cloth trim on Series 3s may wear badly; trim on all models can rattle and come loose

all variants benefited from a modernized interior with four-spoke steering wheel.

A year later, October 1980 brought new engines, a 998cc A-plus that replaced the 1098cc '1100', and the uprated A-plus 1300. But these simply reflected changes in engine production for the new Metro; in fact Allegro production was cut back at the same time to provide extra production capacity for the new MiniMetro at Longbridge. Not surprisingly, the Allegro dropped out of the top ten best-selling cars in Britain shortly afterwards.

By this time, work was under way on the car that would eventually replace the Allegro. Although the Maestro was delayed until 1983, Allegro production ended in March 1982, leaving dealers with sufficient stock of unsold models to cover the gap. But the Allegro's failure to sell better was an important factor in the ultimate collapse of British Leyland, even though it was in the top ten of best selling cars in Britain for a decade. As Chris Cowin rightly points out in British Leyland: Chronicle of a Car Crash, total Allegro sales of 667,192 in nine years gives an average of 74,132 a year. Its predecessor, the 1100/1300 family of cars, sold 2,151,007 in twelve years, which gives an annual average of 179,250.

The quartic steering wheel in the first Allegros was not much liked. JOHN ROBERT SHEPHERD/WIKIMEDIA COMMONS

The Allegro's dashboard always looked very plasticky. By the time of this Allegro 2, the infamous quartic steering wheel had gone.

There really were some changes for the Allegro 2, although the only one apparent on this estate is the coachline at waist level.

The Allegro's last gasp: this is the sales brochure for the Allegro 3, with new bumpers, twin headlights, a vinyl roof and new wheels to give it the Super Vroom factor.

Austin 18-22 series (1975)

The ADO17 'Land Crab' models were solid, reliable cars that were much liked by their buyers – but they lacked what might best be called pizzazz. So when work started on their replacements, which were known within BLMC as ADO71 models, the aim was to add some pizzazz to an already strong formula. That was probably a key reason why the exterior design was entrusted to Harris Mann, who favoured dramatic wedge shapes – and dutifully came up with another one for the new car. He was quoted in a 1975 press release as saying, 'I set out to design tomorrow's luxury family saloon... a car that would instantly make the competition seem old-fashioned.'

Quite reasonably, the plan was to retain the basic engineering of the ADO17, but to update it. So ADO71 was designed to have a front-mounted transverse engine that drove the front wheels through a gearbox mounted in the sump. In place of Hydrolastic suspension would come the new Hydragas type, first seen on the 1973 Austin Allegro. Overall size was determined very much by the need to replace the ADO17.

Harris Mann's crisp wedge shape gave the cars great distinction, and was much praised by the media when the cars were launched in 1975. He had in fact designed the car with a hatchback – and a quick look at the shape makes this quite obvious – but had been over-ruled by a management decree that sales of the Maxi were to be protected by making it the only hatchback in the BLMC stable. Even an estate version was proposed, but did not get approval.

When these cars were being designed in the early 1970s, the plan was to make them direct replacements for the ADO17s, and so the plan was always to market separate Austin, Morris and Wolseley versions. Six months after their introduction in March 1975, the number of model variations was drastically reduced and they were all rebadged as Leyland Princess types; the change was symptomatic of the upheavals within BLMC at the time, and in this case was probably directly prompted by the rationalization recommendations within the April 1975 Ryder Report.

The new models were announced with the less-than-memorable name of 18-22 Series, those numbers representing their alternative engine options of nominal 1800cc and 2200cc sizes. There were three Austin versions, actually called the 1800, 1800HL and 2200HL: the 1800s had the B-series 4-cylinder engine, and the 2200 had the E-series 6-cylinder. All models came with a four-speed manual gearbox as standard, while a three-speed automatic was an extra-cost option. Austin versions were distinguished from others by their trapezoidal headlamps, flat bonnet and slatted grilles.

BL's 'wedge' was certainly an unusual-looking car, and here it is as an Austin, complete with Austin name on the grille.

IF YOU WANT ONE....

The 18-22 is not a common classic today, and some people might argue that this makes it all the more desirable. A good one is comfortable and very usable, although handling is rather wallowy, in 1970s fashion. The cars are welcomed by The Princess and Ambassador Owners' Club (www.princessandambassador.org.uk).

Key purchasing points:

- Bodies last quite well if decently maintained, but if mud build-up is ignored, they will rust in the wings, door bottoms and around the suspension mountings
- 6-cylinder engines can overheat, so watch the temperature gauge and check for leaks
- Hydrolastic fluid needs to be changed every five years to avoid pipes corroding and leaking; also check the front suspension bushes because worn ones can stress the Hydrolastic displacers
- Check the front footwells under the carpets for water leaking through a perished windscreen seal
- Seat backrests fade and deteriorate, and driver's seats can sag; headlinings also discolour, sag and tear

AUSTIN 18-22 SERIES: FACTS AND FIGURES

Pressed steel monocoque with four doors; five seats.
Front engine driving front wheels.

Engine	1798cc B-series in-line 4-cylinder, with 82bhp at 5,200rpm 2227cc E-series in-line 6-cylinder, with 110bhp at 5,250rpm
Gearbox	Four-speed manual or three-speed automatic

Dimensions

Length	4,445mm (175in)
Wheelbase	2,667mm (105in)
Width	1,730mm (68.1in)
Height	1,410mm (55.5in)
Kerb weight	1,160–1,179kg (2,557–2,600lb), depending on the model

Austin 18-22 Series: Statistics

0–60mph	14.9sec (1800) 13.5sec (2200)
Max. speed	96mph (154km/h) (1800) 104mph/167km/h (2200)
Fuel consumption	20.7mpg (13.7ltr/100km) (2200)

Production numbers

19,000, including Morris and Wolseley variants

Austin Metro (1980–90)

There were many ideas about how to replace the Mini during the early 1970s, but cash shortages within British Leyland ensured that none of them progressed very far. It was not a project that could be treated lightly: the Mini was a much-loved car that was also selling well, and would be very difficult indeed to replace. There was also the fundamental question of whether to replace it with a car of similar size, or with a 'supermini' that would compete with the established models of that class.

The Ryder Report in 1975 rightly emphasized the importance of a new small car, and so British Leyland gave a high priority to work on what was then still seen as a Mini replacement. By 1977 a classic British compromise decision had been reached, and work began on ADO88, a car that was slightly larger than the Mini (with an 88in wheelbase) but not as large as the superminis. Superb packaging by Issigonis meant that the car was expected to be competitive in both market sectors. Styling, however, was rather basic, and did not show up well at customer clinics: the car appeared too obviously aimed at the economy market.

The project had reached that stage when Michael Edwardes arrived at British Leyland, and he asked for a restyle. The Longbridge studios under David Bache and Harris Mann had a new design ready within weeks, and before long the project had been given the new Leyland Cars code name of LC8. Both three-box and hatchback models were envisaged, but a decision was made to abandon the three-box model and to keep the Mini in production alongside the new four-door LC8. Again, it was a classic British compromise – and one born out of caution.

Cash remained tight, and so the engineers made maximum use of existing components. The elderly A-series engines were redeveloped into A-plus types, which gave more power and better fuel economy, while the gearbox, drivetrain components and sub-frames were carried over from the Mini. Suspension would be the new Hydragas type, but without an interconnection between front and rear.

As development progressed, the Longbridge works was expanded during 1978, with a new robotized body assembly line

When first introduced, the Metro was sold as an Austin MiniMetro. This version is for the German market.

There were, of course, multiple versions of the Metro. This group consists of a 1.3S, a 1.3HLE and a top model 1.3HLS.

IF YOU WANT ONE....

The Metro is certainly not a mainstream classic, although its vital role in the survival of Britain's major carmaker during the 1980s suggests that it really should be. Perhaps it lacks excitement – of which more is to be found in the MG variants (see separate entry) than the Austins. But it has had its own club since 2009, and at the time of writing, the Metro Owners' Club (which caters for MG and Vanden Plas derivatives as well as Austins) can be found at www.metroownersclub.co.uk

Key purchasing points:

- Rust around the front jacking points and the rear subframe mountings can be serious; rust in the front wings, doors, valances and front panel is common but less serious
- Engines commonly leak oil, and rarely last beyond 160,000km (100,000 miles) without a rebuild
- Gear whine is depressingly normal, but gearboxes can also jump out of gear even on relatively low-mileage cars
- Rear radius arms will wear unless regularly greased according to the manufacturer's recommendations
- The petrol filler pipe can split, allowing water thrown up by the road wheels to get into the fuel tank

AUSTIN METRO: FACTS AND FIGURES

Pressed steel monocoque with two or four doors and hatchback; five seats. Front engine driving front wheels.

Engine	1.0: 998cc A-plus 4-cylinder, with 45bhp at 5,400rpm 1.3: 1275cc A-plus 4-cylinder, with 60bhp at 5,250rpm; 62bhp at 5,300 from 1983; 69bhp at 5,450rpm (1989 Metro GTa)
Gearbox	Four-speed manual; three-speed automatic optional on 1.3 models
Length	3,405mm (134.1in)
Wheelbase	2,250mm (88.6in)
Width	2,250mm (88.6in)
Height	1,361mm (53.6in)
Kerb weight	743–864kg (1,638–1,904lb), depending on the model

Austin Metro: Statistics

Performance	0–60mph in 18.9sec (1.0)
Max. speed	85mph (137km/h) (1.0)94mph (151km/h) (1.3)
Fuel consumption	42mpg (6.7ltr/100km) (1.0)

Production numbers

2,078,218 Metros of all types were built, including MG and Vanden Plas variants

that was capable of handling very high volumes. There were optimistic hopes that the new small car would sell 100,000 units a year in Britain alone, and the new car – called Metro after a ballot among the workforce – soon became an emblem of British Leyland's hoped-for turnaround. Mini and Allegro production at Longbridge were both cut back to devote maximum resources to the new assembly lines.

By launch time in September 1980 the car's name had been changed to MiniMetro, supposedly to mollify railway and bus makers Metro Cammell, but probably also in the hope of carrying over positive associations from the Mini. In practice, the name never caught on, and was dropped after a few years in favour of the original choice, Metro. All these first cars were two-door models with a hatchback, and clever packaging gave them excellent interior space for their size. Although the boot was small, a folding rear seat increased the available load-carrying area. The four models were the 1.0L, 1.0HLE, 1.3, and 1.3 HLS, all with a four-speed manual gearbox mounted in the engine sump, Issigonis style. There were disc brakes on the front wheels and drum brakes at the rear.

British Leyland kept a close eye on the model mix, and added a 1.3 Automatic after a time, while abandoning the early 1.3S and 1.3 HLS types. MG and Vanden Plas derivatives, plus a van that initially wore Morris badges, all followed in the early 1980s (and are dealt with as separate entries). Meanwhile, the Metro was living up to its maker's expectations, becoming British Leyland's best-selling model and helping to raise the profile of British cars in the key European markets of France, Germany and Italy. Not that it was without its flaws, of course: economy was good, but performance was only adequate, while the Metro suffered from noisy intermediate gears and a poor driving position, exactly like the Mini.

The Metro regularly figured in the top ten of best-selling cars in Britain during this period, and became the country's best-selling supermini until it was overtaken by the new second-generation Ford Fiesta in 1984. Rising to the Fiesta challenge, what was by then Austin Rover responded in October 1984 with a Mk 2 Metro. Among the many changes were the

The third iteration of Austin's 'wedge' was the Ambassador, with the hatchback that the design should have had in the beginning. This is the top model Ambassador Vanden Plas.

Not all Austin Ambassadors were as plushly trimmed as the Vanden Plas (note the VP script on the rear quarter), but this publicity picture does show the model's strengths to advantage.

there would be no 6-cylinder Ambassadors, in order to protect sales of the Rover 2300 – even though the Rover was permitted a new entry-level 4-cylinder 2000 model that brought it very close to the top of the Ambassador range. There would be an Austin Ambassador Vanden Plas derivative, too, the coachbuilder's name now subordinated to the Austin name to give the latter more prominence in the Austin Rover era.

The original idea was to turn the Princess into a hatchback, with minimal structural alteration planned, but as development proceeded so the new model became more and more different from the old. By the time the Ambassador was ready for production in 1982, the only panels retained from the older model were the two front doors. As they carried a strong styling line, that line had to be continued along the rest of the car's flanks, and that in turn made the Ambassador look much more like the Princess than it perhaps was.

There was a lot about the Ambassador that was new. The big hatchback was obvious, and blended perfectly with the car's existing lines. The roof had to be re-engineered to take its hinges, and of course the tail panel and rear lights had to be redrawn to suit the new configuration. British Leyland seized the opportunity to add new tail-lights to help the car look more different from its predecessor. Extra rear side windows were added for much the same reason, as were a new front end with a rearward-slanted radiator grille and new rectangular headlights, the latter shared with the Morris Ital. The rear seat, of course, folded forwards to create a good-sized load space in the back.

IF YOU WANT ONE....

The Ambassador is something of a specialist interest today, not least because relatively few survive. Prices are not high, and parts specialists do exist, but it would be foolhardy to try to run one of these cars without first joining the Princess and Ambassador Owners' Club (www.princessandambassador.org.uk).

Key purchasing points:

- Rust in the roof above the rearmost side windows and on the A-pillars is impossible to repair properly
- Check when the timing belt was last changed; it should be done every 77,230km (48,000 miles) on O-series engines
- Rust in the lower body panels can create headaches, but is not necessarily a reason to avoid a car
- Hydragas suspension displacers can leak, and new replacements were not available at the time of writing
- Seat facings, especially in light colours, seem to suffer from sunlight and will fade and, ultimately, weaken and tear

AUSTIN AMBASSADOR: FACTS AND FIGURES

Pressed steel monocoque with four doors and hatchback tail door; five seats. Transversely mounted front engine driving front wheels.

Engine	1.7: 1695cc O-series in-line 4-cylinder, with 88bhp at 5,200rpm 2.0: 1994cc O-series in-line 4-cylinder, with 92bhp at 4,900rpm; HLS and Vanden Plas models (with twin carburettors) with 100bhp at 5,250rpm
Gearbox	Four-speed manual; optional three-speed automatic

Dimensions

Length	4,456mm (175.4in)
Wheelbase	2,673mm (105.25in)
Width	1,730mm (68.1in)
Height	1,409mm (55.5in)
Kerb weight	1,198–1,244kg (2,639–2,741lb), depending on the model

Austin Ambassador: Statistics

Performance	0–60mph in 14.3sec (2.0)
Max. speed	98mph (158km/h) (1.7) 101mph (163km/h) (2.0)
Fuel consumption	31.2mpg (9.1ltr/100km) (2.0)

Production numbers

43,427 cars were built in all, broken down as follows:

24,989	(1.7)
18,438	(2.0, including HLS and Vanden Plas models)

Austin Maestro (1983–92)

The Austin Maestro and its Austin Montego sibling were the eventual outcome of a plan set out soon after Sir Michael Edwardes took over at the helm of British Leyland. They were the new mid-range cars, filling market positions above the Metro and below the Rover SD1, and they started out in 1977 with the project name of LC10. Before long, that project was sub-divided into two, the hatchback version of the car taking priority over the saloon version and becoming LM10. This was the car that would become the Austin Maestro in 1983.

LM10's task was to replace the Maxi and the Allegro, and the original aim was to have it ready by 1980. But there were delays, not least because British Leyland was constantly short of money. One result was that a conventional suspension with MacPherson front struts and a coil-sprung torsion-beam trailing axle replaced the expensive Hydragas of earlier models. As for engines, the latest A-plus 1.3-litre was to be accompanied by a newly developed 1.6-litre ohc 4-cylinder based on the existing E-series, but this was not ready in time and so the cars were launched in 1983 with a half-way house design called the R-series.

Even so, the approach to LM10 was certainly not conservative. Front-wheel drive was a 'given', and LM10 would be the first car from British Leyland to make full use of computer-aided design (CAD for short) and computer-aided manufacture (CAM for short). It would also be built in an expensively redeveloped Cowley plant, where the latest robot assembly techniques would be used. And it would have several new features, such as a bonded windscreen and electronic engine management systems. Controversially, it would also have a 'voice synthesis warning and information system' instead of traditional warning lights and dials. Customers disliked the speaking dashboard, and it was discontinued quite quickly.

In the beginning, two designs were under consideration, one from Harris Mann at Longbridge, and the other from Ian Beech; both men were working to David Bache. Both two-door and four-door models were planned when the project

Dramatic lighting helps here! The car is actually the economy model Austin Maestro, the 1.3HLE, but was just as good looking as its more expensive siblings.

began in the late 1970s, although only the four-door made it to production. The Beech design was chosen for further development, and incorporated a side scallop similar to that on David Bache's Rover SD1 (itself borrowed from the Ferrari Daytona). A strength of the Maestro was its good interior room, better than that of the Escort-class vehicles, which were its main rivals.

MG versions (see separate entry) of the car were planned, to give the Maestro range a sporting dimension, and so were light van derivatives. At launch in March 1983, there were five Austin Maestro models: a 1.3, a 1.6, a 1.3 HLE, a 1.6 HLS and an Austin Maestro Vanden Plas. As the letters suggested, the 1.6 HLS was the top model, but the 1.3 HLE was designed as an economy variant (hence the E) and had a four-speed gearbox with overdrive top gear. Conventional four-speeds were standard on all other models for the first year. These gearboxes were another new departure for British Leyland, as they were bought in from Volkswagen and were mounted on the end of the engine; earlier British Leyland practice had been to mount the gearbox underneath the engine, in the sump.

The R-series engines proved troublesome, and were dropped in 1984 when the new S-series engine (the one always intended for the Maestro) came on-stream. 1.3 HL and 1.6 HL models were added between the basic L and higher-specification HLS models, and both five-speed manual and three-speed automatic gearboxes became available for the 1.6 models. At the same time, Maestro vans were added to the range. The rounded Montego-style one-piece dashboard replaced the angular Maestro type, which had been constructed from multiple sections and was prone to squeaks and rattles. Then from August 1985 there were new 1.3 City and 1.3 City X variants, which were economy models with the Maestro van's steel bumpers instead of the other models' plastic bumper aprons; the X brought extra equipment.

The Maestro sold well, although not as well as its makers had hoped. The boom years were 1986 and 1987, and after that sales began to slide. Under the Rover Group, a diesel engine option was introduced, saloons getting it in 1990 but the vans in 1987. All diesel models used Honda's PG1 gearbox. From 1987 the Austin name disappeared and there were just Maestro badges. The range was cut back in 1989 as its R8 (Rover 200) replacement came on stream, and the last Maestros were built in the UK in 1992.

Nevertheless, that was not quite the end of the Maestro. There had been CKD assembly in some overseas countries, and in 1997 a store of CKD components was sold off to a UK company, which assembled them and sold them as new cars between then and 2001. The Maestro tooling, meanwhile, was sold to Etsong in China, who in 2003 resold them to First Automobile Works (FAW), and Chinese versions of the saloon and van variants were built until 2005.

IF YOU WANT ONE....

Like so many British Leyland cars, the Maestro had disappeared in vast numbers before enthusiasts became interested in it. Although it is therefore not a common car today, its relative rarity does not make it valuable, or expensive to buy. Intending owners should certainly contact the Maestro & Montego Owners' Club, which was founded in 1999 and can be found on the web at www.maestro.org.uk/

Key purchasing points:

- Check for rusting at the join between sill and rear wheel-arch, around the windscreen, and where the A-pillars join the roof, in the tailgate below the window, and around the rear suspension turrets
- The Volkswagen gearbox can become notchy, and the linkages can become detached – although the cure is an easy one. Linkages are also a weakness of the Honda PG1 gearbox
- Front wheel bearings wear and can be tricky to replace
- Early dashboards rattle, while later one-piece types can crack and distort above the instrument binnacle
- Upholstery sometimes wears badly; brown trim seems to suffer more than other colours

AUSTIN MAESTRO: FACTS AND FIGURES

Pressed steel monocoque with hatchback tail door; five seats. Transversely mounted front engine driving front wheels.

Engine	1.3: 1275cc A-Plus in-line 4-cylinder, with 68bhp at 5,600rpm; 64bhp at 5,500rpm for 1.3HLE model 1.6: 1598cc R-series in-line 4-cylinder, with 81bhp at 5,500rpm 1.6: 1598cc S-series in-line 4-cylinder, with 86bhp at 5,600rpm
Gearbox	Four-speed or five-speed manual; 1.3 HLE with overdrive four-speed; optional automatic

Dimensions

Length	4,050mm (159.5in) 4,000mm (157.5in) (1.3 base model)
Wheelbase	2,507mm (98.7in)
Width	1,687mm (66.4in)
Height	1,429mm (56.3in) 1,623mm (63.9in) (van)
Kerb weight	875–915kg (1,927–2,017lb) (1.3) 945–985kg (2,083–2,172lb) (1.6)

Austin Maestro: Statistics

0–60mph	12.5sec (1.3 HL) 12.8sec (1.6 Automatic)
Max. speed	96mph (154km/h) (1.3) 101mph (163km/h) (1.6)
Fuel consumption	36mpg (7.9ltr/100km) (1.3) 34mpg (8.3ltr/100km) (1.6)

Production numbers

605,411 (1983–92, all models including MG and Vanden Plas)

ABOVE: **With a better interior, bright wing-mirror bodies (one was standard on both sides) and swish wheel trims, the Maestro Vanden Plas was the top of the range in 1984.**

RIGHT: **In 1986, the Maestro City X became the economy derivative, complete with decals on its flanks to say so.**

Austin Maestro Van (1984–92)

Van derivatives of the Maestro were planned from early on and were introduced in October 1984 at the British Motor Show. It might have made sense to base them on the Montego estate, with which they could have shared body panels, but Austin Rover chose instead to modify the Maestro platform and to make the vans different from both car models.

The Maestro platform was modified with a longer wheelbase, and the rear end was modified with a robust chassis underneath the load area and leaf springs in place of the coil springs of the cars. In the beginning, the Maestro van came as a Maestro 500 with 500kg payload and the 1.3-litre A-Plus engine, less the electronic carburettor used on the car versions. The gearbox was Volkswagen's four-speed. The seats were trimmed in vinyl. From the start, Maestro vans had a simple black steel front bumper with plastic end caps instead of the body-coloured plastic apron used on the cars. They also had 14in wheels instead of the 13in size used on the cars. Headlamps were smaller than on the cars, and were tungsten units borrowed from the Metro City.

The range was then expanded to include a Maestro 700 van with 700kg payload and uprated suspension, and the 1.6-litre S-series engine and five-speed gearbox both became options. The 1.6 engine nevertheless remained quite rare; buyers preferred the 2.0-litre diesel that was introduced in 1987. There was also a new L specification, which brought more sound insulation, carpets, cloth seats with head restraints, and a cigar lighter, together with the five-speed gearbox. The economy nature of the Maestro 500 van was highlighted by renaming it the 500 City Diesel.

After British Leyland became the Rover Group, the Maestro van soldiered on until Maestro production ended in 1992, most sales probably going to the economical 2.0-litre diesel version (despite its reputation for excessive engine noise). During the 1980s, it was a favourite with many public companies in Britain, such as British Rail, British Telecom, the Gas Board and Royal Mail. There were also some camper van conversions with elevating roofs produced by aftermarket specialists.

BELOW AND RIGHT: Inevitably there was a Maestro van, and equally inevitably, several big fleets took multiple examples. These two show a 1987 model used by an AA patrol, and a 1986 Maestro 500 City that belonged to British Gas.

AUSTIN MAESTRO VAN: FACTS AND FIGURES

Pressed steel monocoque with two-door, two-seat cab. Front engine driving front wheels.

Engine	1.3: 1275cc A-Plus in-line 4-cylinder, with 68bhp at 5,600rpm 1.6: 1598cc S-series in-line 4-cylinder, with 86bhp at 5,600rpm
Gearbox	Five-speed manual

Dimensions

Length	4,351mm (171.3in)
Wheelbase	2,553mm (100.5in)
Width	1,704mm (67.1in)
Height	1,623mm (63.9in)
Kerb weight	960kg (2,116lb)

Austin Maestro Van: Statistics

The performance and fuel consumption of the Maestro van are broadly comparable to those of the Maestro car with the same engine.

Production numbers

No exact production figures are currently available.

Austin Montego (1984–92)

The Austin Montego was the second stage of the medium-car project that had begun life as LC10. When that sub-divided into two, the three-box saloon became the LM11 project, and that eventually became the Montego. It was also, sadly, the last all-new model to carry the Austin name. As for the name, that was chosen because it seemed to harmonize with Maestro; it came, of course, from the Jamaican port of Montego Bay.

The Montego's job for British Leyland was to replace the Morris Marina and also the Austin Ambassador. Out in the marketplace, it had to compete with the Ford Sierra and Vauxhall Cavalier – a formidably difficult task in which it was never successful. As with the Maestro, sales fell short of Austin Rover's expectations, and when the Rover Group was formed in 1986, a review of the Montego concluded that the British public found it just too ordinary.

The original plan was for LM10 and LM11 to share a centre section, but problems arose and were solved by giving LM11 a slightly longer wheelbase than its sibling, which also brought more rear legroom. By the time production began, the Montego was 16in (407mm) longer than the Maestro. It was also given a large boot, and some of the versatility of the Ambassador it was to replace was achieved by allowing the rear seat to fold down so that long or bulky items could be fed through from the boot.

The body design was essentially a conventional three-box type, which was started under David Bache. After he was replaced by Roy Axe in 1982 a number of changes were made, notably adding a distinctive rearmost side window and a front end that made the car look different from the hatchback Maestro. Even so, well over half the panels were shared between the two cars. Early models had the talking dashboard also used in the Maestro, but this was quickly

Following the Maestro, the closely related Montego offered a bigger car image and had a separate boot. The design of the rearmost side windows was quirky, but worked well.

The Montego estate was a very well resolved design. This is a 1984 model, 1.6 HL.

abandoned because of annoying faults and negative customer reactions.

As originally planned, mechanical units were mainly shared with the Maestro, so there were 1.3-litre A-Plus and 1.6-litre S-series engines, while a 2.0-litre O-series made the Montego a more convincing replacement for the Ambassador. All the manual gearboxes came from Volkswagen, except that used with the 2.0-litre engine, which was a Honda-designed five-speed. Steering, brakes and suspension were pure Maestro, except that the brake discs were ventilated.

The Montego was launched in April 1984, initially as a saloon only, by which time it had the additional job of replacing the Triumph Acclaim that had been drafted in to keep sales of British Leyland's medium saloons afloat. However, an estate derivative had always been in the plan, and that followed at the Motor Show that autumn; only 1.6-litre and 2.0-litre engine options were available, and it replaced the Morris Ital estate. The estate's proportions worked extremely well, and it was spacious, too; it even won a Design Council award. One notable option was a rearward-facing foldaway bench seat in the rear, designed for children. There were high-performance MG variants and luxurious Vanden Plas variants as well.

Like the Maestro, the Montego lost its Austin badges for good in 1987. A mild facelift (internally coded AR9) then distinguished the Mk II models introduced in 1988, which also gained a 2.0-litre diesel engine option, and a 2.0Si with the injected engine from the MG variants was intended to give the car's rather pedestrian image a boost. In fact, police forces had been able to buy just such a car for some time. GTI versions of both saloon and estate helped further, and in 1989 the 1.3 models were dropped altogether. Under the Rover Group, production of Montego saloons then continued until 1993, when the replacement Rover 600 model was introduced. CKD saloon packs continued into 1994, and the last Montegos were estate models, appropriately carrying the old Austin name of Countryman, in 1995.

IF YOU WANT ONE….

Rather like its stablemate the Maestro, the Montego makes a very practical classic, but is now not very common or valuable. Enthusiast owners join the Maestro & Montego Owners' Club, which can be found on the web at www.maestro.org.uk/

Key purchasing points:

- Check the overall condition carefully, because repair costs can easily far exceed the purchase price (and value) of the car
- The 1.3-litre engines struggle in a Montego, so 1.6-litre and 2.0-litre options are a better bet
- Check for rust in the rear wheel-arches, rear suspension towers, sills, door bottoms and metal around the windscreen
- The leading edge of the bonnet is vulnerable to stone chips, which will eventually lead to rust
- Electrical failures are quite common (central locking and electric windows are often affected), but replacement parts can be cheaply sourced from scrapyards – at the time of writing

AUSTIN MONTEGO: FACTS AND FIGURES

Pressed steel monocoque with four doors (saloon) or five doors (estate); five seats; optional rearward-facing two-seater bench in estate. Transversely mounted front engine driving front wheels.

Engine	1.3: 1275cc A-Plus in-line 4-cylinder, with 68bhp at 5,800rpm; 64bhp at 5,500rpm for 1.3HLE model 1.6: 1598cc S-series in-line 4-cylinder, with 85bhp at 5,600rpm 2.0: 1994cc O-series in-line 4-cylinder, with 117bhp at 5,500rpm
Gearbox	Four-speed or five-speed manual; 2.0 not available with four-speed; automatic optional except on 1.3 models
Dimensions	
Length	4,467mm (175.9in)
Wheelbase	2,565mm (101in)
Width	1,710mm (67.3in)
Height	1,418mm (55.8in) 1,521mm (59.9in) (estate)
Kerb weight	950kg (2,095lb) (1.3) 965–1005kg (2,130–2,215lb) (1.6) 1,020–1,065kg (2,250–2,350lb) (1.6 estate) 1,020–1,050kg (2,250–2,315lb) (2.0) 1,065–1,110kg (2,350–2,450lb) (2.0 estate)
Austin Montego: Statistics	
0–60mph	13.0sec (1.3) 9.8sec (2.0 HL)
Max speed	96mph (154km/h) (1.3) 102mph (165km/h) (1.6) 115mph (185km/h) (2.0)
Fuel consumption	38mpg (7.4ltr/100km) (1.6) 30mpg (9.4ltr/100km) (1.6 Automatic) 37mpg (7.6ltr/100km) (2.0 HL)
Production numbers	571,460 (all models)

DAIMLER-BADGED MODELS

Under British Leyland, all Daimler saloons were in fact re-badged Jaguars, with their focus on luxury and appointments rather than on the sporting performance that was central to the Jaguar marque. Nevertheless, the Daimler name was also used on a unique model that was conceived as a limousine – the DS420 that married a Jaguar 420G (Mk X) underframe to a coachbuilt body of considerable distinction.

Daimler Sovereign (1968–92)

The Daimler Sovereign was essentially a badge-engineered Jaguar XJ, but was introduced more than a year after its parent, in late 1969. It replaced the old 420-based Sovereign and would remain in production until 1992. Most of the changes to the three series of cars paralleled those on the equivalent Jaguars, but the Daimlers were always more expensive and exclusive cars, and equipment levels generally reflected that. They were much less common, too.

Apart from the radiator grille and badges, the first-series 6-cylinder Daimler Sovereigns differed from their Jaguar counterparts mainly in the interior, which was a little more plush. There was a V12-engined Daimler Double Six from July 1972, taking on the name of a 1930s V12 Daimler. However, the long-wheelbase model was held over until September 1972, when it was introduced as the Daimler Double Six Vanden Plas. British Leyland of course held the rights to the Vanden Plas name, and there was scarcely a more appropriate car on which to bestow it. These new top-model Daimlers were specially upholstered and trimmed at the Vanden Plas works. They had distinctive badges, bright bodyside strips, and a fashionable Everflex vinyl roof covering.

From April 1975, the Vanden Plas trim was made available on 6-cylinder 4.2-litre models as well. Thereafter, Daimler changes broadly followed those of their Jaguar counterparts until 1983. At that point, the Vanden Plas name was dropped from cars destined for the UK market, so every Daimler simply wore Double Six badges. Later that year, the Daimler

The 6-cylinder Daimler-badged Jaguar XJ6 was a Sovereign, but when the V12 engine was introduced, the flagship car became a Daimler Double Six. Rapid, refined and luxurious, this was a 1978 model and one of the last Series 2 cars.

Like the Jaguar, the Daimler was developed over the years. This is the Double Six in Series 3 guise, a very early example registered just before the start of the 1979 model year.

marque was withdrawn from most export markets, primarily to avoid confusion with the Daimler-Benz company, which was the parent of rival Mercedes-Benz cars.

Nevertheless, Daimler versions of the XJ range remained available right through until December 1992, though after 1987 they only came with the V12 engine, which was not available in the new Daimlers based on the Jaguar XJ40.

IF YOU WANT ONE....

Never forget that the Daimler Sovereign – and especially the V12 Double Six model – was designed as a luxury car for well heeled owners, and it will not take kindly to being maintained on a shoestring. That said, it is very much a usable classic, with room and comfort to suit a family, and plenty of support from clubs and specialists. Leading clubs for owners include the Daimler and Lanchester Owners' Club (www.dloc.org.uk), the Jaguar Drivers' Club (www.jaguardriver.co.uk) and the Jaguar Enthusiasts' Club (https://jec.org.uk) – although a trawl of the web will uncover several more.

For key purchasing points, please see the entry for the Jaguar XJ6 and XJ12 models below, and note that the Daimler variants are generally equipped to higher standards.

DAIMLER SOVEREIGN AND DOUBLE SIX, 1968–92: FACTS AND FIGURES, AND STATISTICS

For technical details of these models, please see the entry for Jaguar XJ6 and XJ12. For performance and fuel consumption figures, please see the entry for Jaguar XJ6 and XJ12.

Production numbers

Series 1:	
2.8-litre	3,233
4.2-litre SWB	11,522
4.2-litre LWB	386
Double Six SWB	534
Double Six LWB	351
Series 2:	
3.4-litre	2,341
4.2-litre SWB	2,435
4.2-litre LWB	14,352
4.2-litre Coupé	1,677
Double Six LWB	2,608
Double Six VdP LWB	1,726
Double Six Coupé	407
Series 3:	
4.2-litre	20,315
4.2 VdP	1,953
Double Six	9,628
Double Six VdP	401

Daimler DS420 Limousine, 1968–92

The Daimler DS420 limousine was conceived during the days of British Motor Holdings, when Jaguar and the former BMC marques were united but before the merger with the Leyland companies. So its function was to replace two long-serving and small-production models from within that early grouping. One was the Austin Princess 4-litre, a favourite of mayors and funeral directors, and the other was the Daimler DR450, a more expensive limousine favoured by similar customers. When it was actually announced in June 1968, the British Leyland merger had taken place, and so it is usually seen as a British Leyland car.

The DS420 was based on the platform of the big Jaguar 420G, which had started life as the Mk X saloon. That platform was extended by 533mm (21in) in the wheelbase to give the necessary interior room, but the Jaguar ancestry would remain apparent throughout the vehicle's life, as it always had the 4.2-litre XK engine with automatic gearbox, and its twin fuel tanks in the rear wings were a mid-1960s Jaguar characteristic.

On to that platform, the Vanden Plas coachworks built a grand, imposing and deliberately conservative limousine body with a bench seat for three in the rear, three occasional seats ahead of that, and a division behind the driver, who could be accompanied by one front passenger. However, this would always be a bespoke vehicle with a long options list, and there were individual variations of interior specification.

Daimler also supplied part-built DS420s to the funeral trade for conversion into hearses, and a DS420 hearse was often seen accompanied by a DS420 limousine for the mourners. Just two cars were built as landaulets, but several more were created as aftermarket conversions when these cars passed down to hire companies, which used them for weddings and other events.

For its first eleven years, the DS420 was hand-built at the Vanden Plas works in Kingsbury, but when that closed in 1979, production moved to Jaguar at Browns Lane. There were a few alterations over the years, too. From 1972 the twin-pane rear side windows became single units, the interior wood trim was reduced, and there were other minor changes. Bigger bumpers and a different rear number-plate surround arrived in 1979, and the final changes occurred just after the end of the British Leyland era, when new plastic bumpers were introduced in 1987, together with some minor interior alterations.

When the DS420 went out of production in 1992, it was the last car being built with the long-serving Jaguar XK engine. It was not directly replaced by any other model.

British Leyland's formal limousine offering was the Daimler DS420, pictured here in an appropriate setting.

IF YOU WANT ONE....

The DS420 models are not for everyone. Large, thirsty, and expensive to maintain properly, they require a dedication beyond the reach of most enthusiasts. Many have been used for wedding hire work, often with a quick respray in white and minimal maintenance. That said, they can be rewarding cars to own, and their distinctive looks will always attract attention.

Key purchasing points:

- Rust can quickly render these cars beyond economical repair, especially if they have been left parked in the open air for a long time
- The driving position was designed for a chauffeur, and may not be very comfortable; try before you buy!
- Check the engine oil pressure when hot, and whether the viscous fan has seized; fortunately, Jaguar specialists can assist with engine parts and with problems
- Steering boxes leak and can wear badly, and are unique to the DS420
- Check that the drain hoses from the two filler flaps are doing their job

DAIMLER DS420, 1968–92: FACTS AND FIGURES

Pressed steel monocoque with four doors; up to seven passenger seats. Front engine driving rear wheels.

Engine:	4235cc 6-cylinder with 245bhp at 5,500rpm
Gearbox:	Three-speed automatic

Dimensions

Length	5,740mm (226in)
Wheelbase	3,581mm (141in)
Width	1,970mm (77.56in)
Height	1,610mm (63.39in)
Kerb weight	2,133kg (4,702lb)

Daimler DS420, 1968–92: Statistics

Performance	0–50mph in 10.9sec (0–60mph not quoted)
Max speed	109mph (175km/h)
Fuel consumption	14.8mpg (19.1ltr/100km)

Production numbers

Limousines	4,146
Hearses	835 (total of part-finished cars supplied)

JAGUAR-BADGED MODELS

It is probably a little unfair to describe the cars in this section as 'Jaguar-badged' types because they were all Jaguars, real and unadulterated. Just two model families were introduced under British Leyland, the first being the XJ-series saloons, which had been developed during the years of Jaguar's alliance with BMC – but without, please note, any interference from that organization. The second was the XJ-S sports coupé.

The British Leyland part of Jaguar's history ended in August 1984 when the company became independent. It remained so until 1990, when it was bought by Ford. In 2008 it was bought by Tata, and was merged with Land Rover to create Jaguar Land Rover.

Jaguar XJ6 and XJ12 (1968–86)

BLMC fell on their feet with this one: Jaguar's world-beating new XJ6 saloons were announced at the October 1968 Motor Show, just nine months or so after BLMC had been formed. The XJ6 and its later XJ12 derivative would carry on in various forms and through three different series until 1992 – well beyond the life of British Leyland itself.

Series 1 Models

Actually, much about the XJ6 was familiar. It had a typical Jaguar front suspension (though now on a sub-frame), and the familiar and complex independent rear suspension with inboard disc brakes. However, this was the first Jaguar to have rack-and-pinion steering – power-assisted, of course – and it also came with new low-profile tyres specially designed for it by Dunlop.

This new car was intended to replace all the existing Jaguar saloons, and their Daimler equivalents. So it came with the proven 4.2-litre engine and a newly developed 2.8-litre version of the twin-cam power unit that was sized carefully to meet tax breaks in some European countries. Both came with

Although the original XJ6 looks a little heavy now, it was a revelation when first announced in 1968. This is a 1971 car, with the 4.2-litre engine and standard wheelbase. MAGIC CAR PICS

a four-speed manual gearbox as standard, with overdrive as an option; or they could be bought with a three-speed automatic, and most probably were. An entry-level 2.8-litre with various deletions was advertised, but it is doubtful whether any were sold: customers perceived the new Jaguar as a luxury saloon.

Most important of all, perhaps, was the lithe new shape, which was drawn up as always by William Lyons himself, but was unquestionably a Jaguar from every angle. In fact, the earliest models did not carry the Jaguar name anywhere at all! With stunning looks and superb performance (at least from the bigger-engined cars), these models were a huge sales success and by the end of 1970 had replaced all other Jaguar saloons in production.

From the start, the XJ had been designed to take the new all-aluminium V12 engine that Jaguar had been developing for some time, and this was introduced in July 1972. The new XJ12 saloons that had this engine delivered gigantic performance, with a maximum speed of well over 140mph (225km/h) – but the smooth V12 only came with an automatic gearbox, and was formidably thirsty when used hard. Ventilated disc brakes with twin servos were needed to stop it, and again Dunlop provided a special tyre to carry the XJ12's extra weight. XJ12s had a different radiator grille, with a V12 emblem at the top, and an XJ12 badge on the tail. They had new wheels with ventilated rims, and a few interior differences from the XJ6. Air conditioning was standard.

A long-wheelbase bodyshell was introduced for Daimler models in September 1972, and a month later became available in Jaguars as well. Only 4.2-litre XJ6 and XJ12 versions could be had, and relatively few were sold before the next evolution of the XJ reached showrooms.

Series 2

The Series 2 XJ models incorporated a series of improvements, with changes that were necessary to meet new US crash safety and emissions regulations. When they arrived in August 1973 there were only 4.2-litre XJ6 and 5.3-litre XJ12 models; the 2.8-litre car had been dropped. The emissions-control equipment had also badly affected the power of the 6-cylinder engine.

The Series 2 had raised bumpers to meet those US regulations, but this and associated cosmetic changes actually made the cars look much sleeker than the Series 1 models. Less visibly, the bodyshell had been re-engineered with a new bulkhead and side impact bars in the doors. All models now had the perforated disc wheels, too, along with ventilated front disc brakes. Inside, the cabin boasted new seats and door panels, plus a redesigned dash with better ergonomics and an improved heating and air-conditioning system.

All the XJ12s were long-wheelbase cars, and in fact the standard wheelbase 4.2-litre models were dropped after November 1974. But their floorpans remained in production for some new derivatives introduced in April 1975. These were the XJ6 and XJ12 Coupés, strikingly pretty two-door

Gentle tweaks turned the original XJ6 into a Series 2 model. This 1976 car has the long-wheelbase shell, with all the extra length in the rear door area.
MAGIC CAR PICS

The Jaguar XJs were also renowned for their classy interiors. This is the dashboard of a Series 2 6-cylinder car. MAGIC CAR PICS

models using the saloon's overall shape and all carrying a black Everflex vinyl roof covering. Promised at the Series 2 launch, they had been delayed by development and production problems, and in fact would never overcome their reputation for wind noise and water leaks. As a result they were taken out of production in November 1977.

April 1975 also brought an injection system for the V12 engines, which boosted power a little. At the same time came a new 3.4-litre XJ6, using an engine size familiar from older Jaguars but with the latest version of the 6-cylinder block. This car was deliberately aimed at fleet buyers, and was built down to a cost with cloth seats, no coachline, and other deletions. It did not sell as well as Jaguar had hoped: XJ buyers wanted luxury, not compromises.

Series 3

The rejuvenated Series 3 models that arrived in March 1979 were really intended as a holding operation until an all-new replacement was ready; however, they ended up remaining in production for thirteen years.

Readily recognizable as XJ Jaguars, they had been restyled by Pininfarina in Italy. Among the multitude of exterior differences, a raised roofline with larger glass area and differently angled front and rear screens were obvious. New, flush-fitting door handles, black energy-absorbing bumpers, and an absence of the rear wing kick-up were all obvious features. The Series 3 cars came with new stainless-steel wheel trims, or, optionally, with the Kent alloy wheels pioneered on some Series 2 models. They also had a distinctive new cabin design that incorporated a number of improvements.

There were 3.4-litre and 4.2-litre 6-cylinder XJ6s, plus the 5.3-litre XJ12. Both the sixes were quieter and gave better fuel efficiency, and the 4.2-litre now had fuel injection and much more power than before. The 6-cylinder cars also gained a new five-speed gearbox that Jaguar had found in the corporate parts store: it was the LT77 from Rover-Triumph.

In 1981, the V12 engines gained a more efficient Fireball cylinder-head design, and were rebadged as XJ12 HE types (the letters stood for High Efficiency, and indeed an extra 2mpg or so was attainable). At the same time, the automatic 6-cylinder cars switched to a Borg Warner Type 66 gearbox, although the XJ12 kept its GM 400 type.

From 1983, Daimler Sovereigns were withdrawn from most export markets, and were replaced by Jaguar Sovereigns in 4.2-litre and 5.3-litre form, distinguished by new 'pepperpot' alloy wheels. After that, only minor trim changes were made until the new 'XJ40' XJ6 arrived in 1986 – and in the meantime Jaguar had been sold out of the British Leyland group in 1984.

Production of the old XJ6 stopped in 1987, but the XJ12 remained in production. The reason was interesting: threatened with the Rover V8 in both petrol and diesel forms during the development of XJ40, the Jaguar engineers had deliberately designed its front end so that no V-configuration engine of any kind could be fitted. Once they were independent and the Rover threat no longer existed, they redesigned the front end so that their own V12 could be fitted; however, the XJ40 V12 didn't reach the showrooms until November 1991, so extending the life of the Series 3 model by four years.

Pininfarina helped modernize the styling of the XJ range to deliver the Series 3 variants. This is a 1984 4.2 Sovereign; the Sovereign name was adopted by Jaguar when Daimlers ceased production. MAGIC CAR PICS

IF YOU WANT ONE....

The XJ Jaguars set standards for comfort and handling that radically altered world perceptions of what a luxury car was all about. Although early ones are quite ponderous by modern standards, their dynamic qualities still put them far ahead of anything their contemporaries could offer. Although not the easiest of cars to work on for the home mechanic, they are nevertheless very well supported by specialists and by clubs. Enthusiasts should investigate the Jaguar Drivers' Club (www.jaguardriver.co.uk) and the Jaguar Enthusiasts' Club (https://jec.org.uk).

Key purchasing points:

- Engines were designed for high-octane leaded fuel, and high-compression types may give problems on modern unleaded fuels with a lower octane rating
- Rust can be very expensive to eradicate once it has got a hold, so assess very carefully how much remedial work might be needed; post-1983 cars are very much better in this respect
- High maintenance costs: for example, the rear suspension may need to be dropped to work on the brakes, and injection systems are best left to specialists
- Listen for bearing rattle on start-up, and make sure the oil pressure is up to scratch (40psi at 3,000rpm on a warm 6-cylinder)
- Retrimming interiors can be very expensive, so decide if second-hand parts will be acceptable

JAGUAR XJ6 AND XJ12, 1968–91: FACTS AND FIGURES

Pressed steel monocoque with four doors; five seats. Front engine driving rear wheels.

Engine: 2791cc XK 6-cylinder with 180bhp at 6,000rpm
3442cc XK 6-cylinder with 161bhp at 5,000rpm
4235cc XK 6-cylinder with 245bhp at 5,500rpm (Series 1); 170bhp at 4,500rpm (Series 2); 200bhp at 5,000rpm (Series 3, with injection)
5343cc V12 with 253bhp at 6,000rpm (carburettors); 285bhp at 5,750rpm (injection, from April 1975); 299bhp at 5,500rpm (HE type)

Gearbox: Four-speed manual with optional overdrive
Three-speed automatic (standard with V12)

Dimensions

Length	4,813mm (189.5in) (standard wheelbase)
Wheelbase	2,762mm (108.75in) (standard wheelbase) 2,864mm (112.75in) (long wheelbase)
Width	1,753mm (69in)
Height	1,372mm (54in)
Kerb weight	1,626kg (3,585lb) (2.8-litre and 3.4) 1,676kg (3,695lb) (4.2-litre, standard wheelbase, and 4.2-litre Coupé) 1,727kg (3,807lb) (4.2-litre, long wheelbase) 1,778kg (3,920lb) (V12, standard wheelbase) 1,880kg (4,145lb) (V12 Series 3)

Jaguar XJ6 and XJ12, 1968–91: Statistics

Performance	0–60mph in 11sec (2.8) 10.9sec (3.4) 8.8sec (4.2) 7.3sec (V12)
Max. speed	117mph (187km/h) (2.8 and 3.4) 124mph (198km/h) (4.2 Series 1 and 2) 128mph (206km/h) (4.2 Series 3) 140mph (225km/h) (5.3 V12 Ser 1) 147mph (236km/h) (5.3 V12 Ser 2) 148mph (238km/h) (5.3 V12 Ser 3)
Fuel consumption	17–20mpg (16.6–14ltr/100km) (2.8) 16–18mpg (17.7–15.7ltr/100km (3.4) 15–16mpg (18.8ltr–17.7ltr/100km) (4.2) 11–14mpg (25.7–20.2ltr/100km) (V12)

Production numbers

Series 1:	
2.8-litre	19,322
4.2-litre SWB	59,077
4.2-litre LWB	874
V12 SWB	2,474
V12 LWB	754
Series 2:	
2.8-litre	170
3.4-litre	6,990
4.2-litre SWB	12,147
4.2-litre LWB	57,804
4.2-litre Coupé	6,487
V12 LWB	16,010
V12 Coupé	1,855
Series 3:	
3.4-litre	5,799
4.2-litre	97,349
4.2-litre Sovereign	27,261
V12	5,408
V12 Sovereign	9,129

Jaguar XJ-S (1976–96)

Although the XJ-S replaced the legendary E-type, it was initially intended to be a standalone model. Development began in the late 1960s, with the internal code name of XJ27, and there were thoughts about calling it the XK-F – which would have followed neatly from the XK-E name that the E-type carried in the USA. However, the XJ-S was developed only as a closed 2+2 coupé, because during the early 1970s there were fears that US safety legislation would outlaw open cars and that other countries might follow suit. In practice, that did not happen, but it would be 1983 before Jaguar had a convertible version on the market.

The initial shape was by Jaguar's aerodynamics specialist Malcolm Sayer, but after Sayer's death in 1970 it was completed by a team under Doug Thorpe. The most controversial features of the production design were the 'flying buttresses' that ran from the rear of the roof to the tail of the car, leaving the rear window deeply recessed. In Germany, the authorities feared that these would restrict the driver's vision to the rear, and as a result the first cars for that country had to be individually imported and type-approved.

The XJ-S was announced in autumn 1975 as Jaguar's new grand tourer, and was powered by the 5.3-litre V12 engine with fuel injection. This was not the best time to introduce a new, large-engined sporting car because the effects of the 1973–74 oil crisis were still being felt; the car was also criticised for its styling, and its spartan (wood-free) interior. Both manual and automatic options were available, but the manual gearbox went out of production with the E-type, and was dropped as soon as supplies were exhausted. The automatic was, in any case, better suited to the XJ-S's character as a grand tourer; early cars had a Borg Warner Type 12 gearbox, but from 1977 production switched to the GM 400.

By mid-decade it was clear that the threatened US legislation was not going to materialize, and Jaguar responded to an approach from Pininfarina who planned to design a convertible model. The XJ Spider was built on a redundant prototype of the XJ-S, and had much more curvaceous lines than the original, together with that convertible roof. Shown at the Birmingham Motor Show in 1978, from 1980 it became the basis of Jaguar prototypes that carried the XJ41 (targa coupé) and XJ42 (convertible) names. They were to have delivered a model called the F-type, but sadly this never reached production.

After the second fuel crisis in 1979, Jaguar addressed its likely effects on XJ-S sales in two ways. In July 1981 they introduced a re-worked 'HE' ('high efficiency') V12 engine, with more power and better fuel economy. This was accompanied by a mild facelift that brought five-spoke alloy wheels, chrome inserts on the bumper tops, a body-colour tail panel (early ones were black), and interior wood trim. Then in 1983 came an alternative engine option, when the new 3.6-litre AJ6 engine was made available. This brought with it a bonnet bulge, and initially only came with a five-speed Getrag manual gearbox.

Jaguar also put an open variant into production that year, a targa cabriolet known as the XJ-SC, which initially could only be had with the AJ6 engine. It was not a strong seller, so a V12 XJ-SC followed in 1985. However, by this stage Jaguar had left the British Leyland fold to become an independent company.

A full convertible was next on the list, and from 1986 US buyers could order a Hess & Eisenhardt conversion that had full Jaguar approval. The company's own convertible followed in 1988 (with only two seats), as did an XJR-S model from JaguarSport, owned jointly by Jaguar and TWR, who had prepared

The XJ-S coupé was more than a little controversial when it first appeared. This 1976 car is one of the first.
MAGIC CAR PICS

Adding a convertible to the XJ-S range made the car visually a much more attractive machine. This is a 1990 model. MAGIC CAR PICS

Restyling over the years did away with some of the less liked elements of the original XJ-S, and the car remained in production into the 1990s. This is a 1994 coupé model. MAGIC CAR PICS

the racing XJ-S coupés in the mid-1980s. From May 1991 the XJ-S entered its third major period, restyled by Jaguar's Geoff Lawson with different side-window trims that minimized the 'flying buttresses' and made the windows look larger.

The AJ6 moved up to 4.0 litres in 1989, and the V12 to 6.0 litres in 1992 (there had been an earlier, different 6.0-litre V12 from JaguarSport). The convertible became a 2+2 at last, and then in 1994 the 4.0-litre engine was substantially revised as an AJ16 type. Celebration models with special features in 1995 marked sixty years of Jaguar, and the last XJ-S was built in April 1996. The model was replaced by the new XK-8 sports car.

IF YOU WANT ONE....

Jaguar's XJ-S is a grand tourer, not a sports car like the E-type and earlier XK models. That said, it has more than enough performance for most enthusiasts, and like many Jaguars, can be expensive to run and look after. The cars like to be used, not garaged. They are very well supported by specialists and by clubs, and among the latter are the Jaguar Drivers' Club (www.jaguardriver.co.uk) and the Jaguar Enthusiasts' Club (https://jec.org.uk).

Key purchasing points:

- Rust in structural areas can be very costly to deal with: check the jacking points, radius arm mountings, and belt mountings in the floorpan; the post-1991 models had better rustproofing from new
- Rust also affects more visible areas, such as the rear wheel-arches, the front wing where it joins the sill, the scuttle on post-1991 cars, and the front edge of the roof behind the finisher
- The V12 engine needs to be properly and regularly serviced, and you should particularly avoid one with overheating problems; that said, it is mostly a strong and reliable engine, and gradual improvements made the later ones even more so
- Early models feel less luxurious because of the absence of wood trim in the interior; rear seats on all models are little more than token
- 6-cylinder cars may lack the glamour of the V12s but are probably more practical for most owners

JAGUAR XJ-S, 1975–96: FACTS AND FIGURES

Pressed steel monocoque with two doors: coupé (1975–96), targa (1983–88) and full convertible (1988–96) available. Most models with 2+2 seating, but convertibles from 1988–92 with only two seats. Front engine driving rear wheels.

Engine: 5343cc V12 with 285bhp at 5,750rpm; 299bhp at 5,500rpm (HE type from July 1981)
5993cc V12 with 318bhp at 5,400rpm (from May 1992)
3590cc AJ6 6-cylinder with 223bhp at 4,750rpm
3980cc AJ6 6-cylinder, with 238bhp at 4,750rpm

Gearbox: Four-speed manual (to 1979)
Five-speed manual (3.6 models, from 1983)
Three-speed automatic (initially optional; standard on V12 from 1979)

Dimensions

Length	4,870mm (191.8in)
Wheelbase	2,590mm (102in)
Width	1,790mm (70.5in)
Height	1,270mm (50in) (coupé)
Kerb weight	1,770kg (3,902lb) (V12 coupé)

Jaguar XJ-S, 1975–96: Statistics

Performance	0–60mph in 6.7sec (V12 manual) 0–60mph in 7.5sec (V12 automatic) 0–60mph in 8.6sec (V12 with US emissions controls) 0–60mph in 7.5sec (V12 HE) 0–60mph in 8.2sec (V12 HE with US emissions controls) 0–60mph in 6.6sec (6.0-litre V12)
Max. speed	153mph (246km/h) (V12 and V12 HE) 137mph (220km/h) (V12 with US emissions controls) 140mph (225km/h) (V12 HE with US emissions controls) 141mph (227km/h) (3.6-litre) 161mph (259km/h) (6.0-litre V12)
Fuel consumption	14.0mpg (20ltr/100km) (V12) 16.3mpg (17ltr/100km) (V12 HE) 17.6mpg (16ltr/100km) (3.6-litre)

Production numbers

115,413 (total of all types, 1975–96)

LAND ROVER-BADGED MODELS

BLMC swiftly selected the Land Rover marque as the one that would provide its 4x4 models. The Austin Gipsy was despatched in 1968 and Land Rover's own engineers were allowed to examine the proposed Austin Ant light 4x4 and to influence the decision about its future. As it happens, they rather liked it and could foresee a niche for it alongside their existing models – but BLMC top management was not prepared to go down that route, and the model was cancelled.

Under the British Leyland reorganization that followed the Ryder Report in the mid-1970s, Land Rover was divided off from the remains of the old Rover Company, and in 1978 was set up as a stand-alone business within British Leyland. In the meantime it had introduced two new models, and for ordinary customers these would be its only new ones during the British Leyland period. One was the successor to its Series IIA 88 and 109 types, and was really a logical and not very adventurous progression from them. The other was a hugely important newcomer called the Range Rover.

There were also two other Land Rover models introduced during the British Leyland era, the 88 Lightweight and the 101 Forward Control. Both were designed specifically as military vehicles, and for that reason they are not discussed here. (Nevertheless, many were subsequently sold on to the civilian market, where they found a ready welcome among Land Rover enthusiasts.)

Range Rover (1970–96)

The Range Rover was among the planned new models that thrilled Sir Donald Stokes when he examined Rover's future products portfolio in 1968. By that stage only a couple of prototypes existed, and the definitive body style had not been designed. However, Stokes could see the potential for this five-seat estate car, which had originally been conceived simply as a more comfortable Land Rover station wagon.

Ideas man Spen King had flown against all Land Rover tradition by incorporating long-travel coil springs and disc brakes in his design to improve the vehicle's dynamics; he chose permanent four-wheel drive instead of a selectable system so that the engine torque could be split between lighter axles to improve the ride. Many in the company thought it could never be made to work.

However, as soon as the Range Rover was launched in June 1970 they had to eat their words: waiting lists built up rapidly, and new vehicles started changing hands for more than list price. A big factor in the vehicle's success was its use of the Rover 3.5-litre V8 engine, which gave excellent road performance even if the gearbox (shared with a new military Land Rover) was noisy and obstructive. A separate chassis followed the rugged Land Rover tradition. The vehicle came with only two doors, because with four, King thought the body would be too weak

Planned as a more comfortable passenger-carrying Land Rover, the Range Rover quickly became a runaway success. Here it is in its original two-door form, complete with vinyl interior that could be hosed out after a hard day's work.

A four-door option arrived for the Range Rover in 1981, and after that the model was steadily moved up into the luxury market. This Vogue model, with decal side stripes, was the most expensive variant available for 1985.

and also unsuitable for CKD shipping. By the time Rover realized their mistake, he had gone to Triumph as chief engineer – in fact, he had gone before Range Rover production began.

During most of the 1970s there were waiting-lists for Range Rovers, and so BL allocated only minimal development funds. Their reasoning was that the cash was needed more urgently elsewhere. However, once Land Rover became a stand-alone business unit with special government funding in 1978, development could proceed. A bought-in four-door conversion by Monteverdi held the fort from 1979 until Land Rover could get its own four-door into production from June 1981.

Improvements followed thick and fast after that: an automatic gearbox came in 1982, the five-speed LT77 manual gearbox from the Rover SD1 in 1983, much better trim on top models in 1984, and then a fuel-injected V8 with more power in 1985. Just as BL became the Rover Group in 1986, Land Rover announced an alternative diesel engine.

After that, the Range Rover remained in production for another ten years, adding air suspension and a long-wheelbase variant in 1992, and although a replacement model arrived in 1994, the original remained in production with the name of Range Rover Classic. It was one of the most influential designs of the late twentieth century – but British Leyland got (and deserved) very little credit for it. The only BL identification it ever wore was hidden away on the chassis number plate under the bonnet.

IF YOU WANT ONE....

Range Rovers started out as comfortable Land Rovers with better on-road abilities, and only became luxury cars later. So early ones are quite spartan, although they have plenty of charm. Many were used as workhorses, and after that were turned into off-road specials. Many have also been upgraded with later specification parts, or given diesel engines to reduce fuel consumption.

The owners' club is the Range Rover Register (www.rrr.co.uk), although Range Rovers are also welcomed by many other Land Rover or off-road enthusiasts' clubs.

Key purchasing points:

- Rot in the inner body shell, especially sills and inner wings, can be very expensive to eradicate
- Four-door models are more practical, but two-doors are seen as more 'collectable', and good ones will cost more
- Many have been used as workhorses, and have been correspondingly abused
- All had V8 engines in the British Leyland era. Regular oil changes are essential to the engine's health
- Check that the transfer box lever will select low as well as high range, and drive the car in both ranges

RANGE ROVER, 1970–96: FACTS AND FIGURES

Separate steel chassis; body with aluminium alloy outer panels on a steel frame; two doors (1970–94) or four doors (1981–96). Five seats. Front engine and permanent four-wheel drive.

Engine: 3528cc carburettor V8 with 130–135bhp at 5,000rpm (1970–81); 125bhp at 4,000rpm (1981–88)
3528cc injected V8 with 165bhp at 4,000rpm (1985–89)
3947cc injected V8 with 181–188bhp at 4,750rpm (1989–96)
4278cc injected V8 with 200bhp at 4,850rpm (1992–95; long-wheelbase models and some 'specials')
2495cc VM 4-cylinder turbocharged diesel with 112bhp at 4,200rpm (1986–89)
2500cc VM 4-cylinder turbocharged diesel with 119bhp at 4,200rpm (1989–92)
2495cc 4-cylinder turbocharged and intercooled diesel with 111bhp at 4,000rpm (1992–95)

Gearbox: Four-speed manual with integral transfer box (to 1983)
Five-speed manual with separate transfer box (1983–96)
Three-speed automatic with separate transfer box optional (1982–85)
Four-speed automatic with separate transfer box standard on some models and optional on others (1985–96)

Dimensions

Length	4,770mm (176in) (with 100in wheelbase)
	4,648mm (183in) (with 108in wheelbase)
Wheelbase	2,540mm (100in) (standard)
	2,743mm (108in) (long wheelbase)
Width	1,780mm (70in)
Height	1,780mm (70in)
Kerb weight	1,723kg (3,800lb) to 1,986kg (4,379lb) (with 100in wheelbase)
	2,150kg (4,739lb) (with 108in wheelbase)

Range Rover, 1970–96: Statistics

Performance	0–60mph in 14.0sec (3528cc carburettor, manual)
	0–60mph in 12.0sec (3528cc injection, manual)
	0–60mph in 16.5sec (2495cc turbodiesel)
	0–60mph in 11.0sec (3947cc and 4278cc)
	0–60mph in 15.8sec (2500cc turbodiesel)
	0–60mph in 16.8sec (2495cc intercooled turbodiesel)
Max. speed	95mph (153km/h) (3528cc carburettor)
	102mph (164km/h) (3528cc injection)
	92mph (148km/h) (2495cc turbodiesel)
	95mph (153km/h) (2500cc turbodiesel)
	94mph (151km/h) (2495cc intercooled turbodiesel)
	110mph (177km/h) (3947cc and 4278cc)
Fuel consumption	14.0mpg (20ltr/100km) (3528cc carburettor, four-speed)
	15.5mpg (18ltr/100km) (3528cc carburettor, five-speed)
	16.5mpg (17ltr/100km) (3528cc injection, automatic)
	22.5mpg (12.6ltr/100km) (2495cc turbodiesel, manual)
	15.0mpg (18.9ltr/100km) (3947cc, automatic)

Production numbers

317,615 (published total of all types, 1970–96; the real figure is nearer 326,000)

Land Rover Series III (1971–85)

During the 1960s, Rover had been content to let their Land Rover models evolve slowly. They had been able to sell every one they made without difficulty, and the constraint on selling more was that there was nowhere to make them. Most were light commercials, although a sizeable proportion were built as passenger-carrying Station Wagons.

A number of evolutionary changes were in development by the end of the 1960s, but Land Rover had no particular plans to make a big splash and introduce them in a new model. One new model – the 1970 Range Rover – was quite enough for the time being. However, it appears that the Stokes management had other ideas, and the word came down from above that a new Land Rover would be a good thing in 1971. Probably the Stokes team thought that this would add to the new model momentum they were trying to build up for British Leyland; equally, it would prevent the new Range Rover from making the long-established Land Rover look too old-fashioned.

So a series of changes was rounded up, and a Series III Land Rover specification was prepared. The key changes were a new all-synchromesh gearbox (actually introduced on some of the last Series IIAs), a stronger rear axle, a much improved heater, and a new 'safety' dashboard (the latter prepared to meet new legislation, especially in Germany). All this was wrapped up with some cosmetic changes: better seats, a new ABS plastic grille, and flatter door hinges (again, developed to meet new safety legislation).

The Series III Land Rovers were introduced in September 1971, with the same 88in and 109in wheelbase options as the Series IIAs. There were no changes in the multiple body options, and the engines remained the same: 2.25-litre petrol and diesel 4-cylinders, with a 2.6-litre petrol 6-cylinder in 109in models only. The military-only 88in Lightweight simply evolved along the same lines.

Although there would be multiple changes of detail over the next fourteen years, the Series III Land Rovers that ended production in 1985 were much the same as those introduced in 1971. The main change was that a detuned 3.5-litre V8 engine had replaced the 6-cylinder in 109in models during 1979. In 1981, the 4-cylinder engines were re-engineered with five main bearings instead of three.

These Land Rovers were effectively replaced by new coil-spring models, the long-wheelbase One Ten in 1983 and the short-wheelbase Ninety in 1984. However, only the V8-engined Series III 109 went out of production in 1983; the 4-cylinders and the 88s continued until 1985. Not once did those built in the UK carry any British Leyland identification – although Australian-assembled models did gain Leyland badges from 1975.

Emissions and safety regulations in the USA caused nightmares for the Land Rover engineers as they became tighter in the early 1970s. Making the existing petrol engines meet US regulations robbed them of so much power that performance became completely unattractive. Sales were in any case low, and British Leyland decided that the cost of keeping Land Rovers compliant was too great in the light of the returns on sales. So in 1974 Land Rovers were withdrawn from the USA altogether.

The Series III Land Rovers could be recognized by their new plastic grilles and flat door hinges, although there were other changes under the skin. This is the seven-seat Station Wagon on the 2,235mm (88in) chassis...

... and this is the Station Wagon on the 2,769mm (109in) chassis.

IF YOU WANT ONE....

The Land Rover Series III has been a popular enthusiast's purchase for many years, and both spares and expertise are readily available. However, many vehicles have been modified for off-road motorsport of various kinds, and many were simply worked into the ground. Unmolested survivors in good condition are therefore relatively rare and correspondingly pricey. However, much of the Land Rover ownership experience can be had from a well used example, as the vehicles are remarkably rugged and hard-wearing. Owners and their vehicles are welcome in the Series III and 90–110 Owners' Club (http://www.thelandroverclub.co.uk/), the Land Rover Series III Club (lrs3c.com) and in many other off-road clubs as well.

Key purchasing points:

- Rear chassis cross-member and front dumb-irons are favourite places for rust; check the condition of the leaf springs, too
- Really good 4-cylinder petrol engines are quiet and refined; 6-cylinders and V8s are thirsty; there have been many DIY diesel transplants
- Check for rust in the front bulkhead and in the detachable door tops
- Beware of stiff steering; lubrication is often neglected, and replacing a seized steering relay can be troublesome
- Vehicles used for towing may have clutch problems; synchromesh will also deteriorate over time, and the gearbox may jump out of engagement

LAND ROVER SERIES III: FACTS AND FIGURES

Steel ladder-frame chassis with predominantly aluminium alloy body; four-wheel drive with front axle disconnect (permanent four-wheel drive on V8 models).

Engine 2286cc 4-cylinder petrol with 77bhp at 4,250rpm
2286cc 4-cylinder diesel with 62bhp at 4,000rpm
2625cc 6-cylinder petrol with 85bhp at 4,500rpm (109in models only)
3528cc V8 petrol with 91bhp at 3,500rpm (109in models only)

Gearbox Four-speed manual, with separate two-speed transfer box (integral transfer box with V8 engine)

Dimensions

Length	3,617mm (142.4in) (88 models) 4,445mm (175in) (109 models)
Wheelbase	2,235mm (88in) or 2,768mm (109in)
Width	1,676mm (66in)
Height	1,968mm (77.5in) (88 models) 2,057mm (81in) (109 models)
Kerb weight	1,485–1,709kg (3,277–3,768lb), depending on model (4-cylinder and 6-cylinder types) 1,532–1,726kg (3,378–3,806lb), depending on body (V8 109)

Land Rover Series III: Statistics

Performance	0–50mph in 16.3–23.1sec (4-cylinder petrol depending on model) 0–50mph in 20.5–23.4sec (4-cylinder diesel depending on model) 0–50mph in 15.9sec (6-cylinder and V8)
Max. speed	70mph (113km/h) (4-cylinder petrol) 65mph (105km/h) (4-cylinder diesel) 75mph (121km/h) (6-cylinder) 85mph (137km/h) (V8)
Fuel consumption	18–20mpg (15.7–14ltr/100km) (4-cylinder petrol) 28–32mpg (10–8.8ltr/100km) (4-cylinder diesel) 17–20mpg (16.6–14ltr/100km) (6-cylinder) 14mpg (20ltr/100km) (V8)

Production numbers

440,000 approximately

LEYLAND-BADGED MODELS

BLMC and British Leyland were wholly inconsistent about using the Leyland name on cars. Perhaps they thought that it was too closely associated with trucks and buses in the public perception. One way or the other, they applied it to just two cars and one van. A proposal from about 1975 to call the forthcoming V8-engined Rover 3500 a Leyland Eight was quickly shot down, even though there was by that time a clearly identifiable Leyland Cars division within the company.

The first of the two cars to carry the Leyland name was a reworked version of the Mini in 1969. There was some sense in the use of the name here, as the Mini range was rationalized at the same time, and there had been very little difference between (for example) the Austin and Morris versions for some years. Nevertheless, the new name did not catch on, and the general public simply called the car a Mini. That name was so strong that, many years later and under BMW ownership, it was used to found a separate brand.

The second car range that was badged Leyland was the renamed Austin-Morris-Wolseley 18-22 series. It had been available for barely six months before all variants were renamed Leyland Princess types. The public reacted in much the same way as they had done for the Mini: the car was always called simply a Princess.

In fact, the only new British Leyland product to which the Leyland name seemed to stick was the Leyland Sherpa van, and perhaps the obvious conclusion is that the Leyland name did indeed stand for commercial vehicles in the public mind. The Sherpa was, of course, a dedicated commercial vehicle, and was not derived from any model of car, so it is not discussed here.

The Mini soldiered on with Leyland badges, and would go on to outlive British Leyland by many years. This 1976 model is readily recognizable as a derivative of the original, although the Leyland badge on the nose was a sign of the times. MAGIC CAR PICS

Not everybody liked the squared-up Clubman front end, which had been introduced to give the Mini a more modern appearance. However, it remained available for many years – this is a 1978 model.

Leyland Mini (1969–88) and Rover Mini (1988–2000)

With Issigonis out of the way so that he could not object, BL embarked on some improvements to the Mini. The Mark III model introduced in October 1969 was always built at Longbridge, and was different enough from the original to get the new internal code of ADO20. At the same time, the separate marque names all disappeared, and the model was simply called the Mini. Although it was sometimes called the Leyland

RIGHT: There were still multiple varieties of Mini: these are the Leyland-badged types available in 1973. MAGIC CAR PICS

Mini as well, the Mini name was strong enough to work as a brand in its own right.

The Mark III had bigger doors with concealed hinges and winding windows, and there was an additional model called the Clubman. Designed by Roy Haynes, this had a longer and more modern-looking nose, a more elaborate dash and better trim, and it cost extra. The Clubman shape was also used for the new 1275GT, which was intended to replace the Mini Cooper. The Clubman and 1275GT retained Hydrolastic suspension, but BL wanted to save costs, and all other Minis reverted to the original rubber cone type; in July 1971 Hydrolastic was finally withdrawn for good. At the same time, the last Mini-Cooper S was made. Estates in this period were all Clubman types.

Mini sales remained ridiculously good for a car that was more than a decade old. The two millionth was built in 1969, and in 1971 more Minis were built than ever before. Even so, BL was caught off guard by the sudden increase in demand for Minis that followed the 1973 oil crisis. Suddenly, everybody wanted a small car that used as little fuel as possible. This was no time for major production changes, although the 1275GT did change from its original 10in wheels to 12in types in 1974, to accommodate bigger front disc brakes. A larger fuel tank also became standard.

Hoping to replace the Mini in the next few years (see sidebar), BL continued to make minor changes in the mid-1970s. From October 1975, the 1098cc A-series engine became standard, except with an automatic gearbox when the 998cc size was retained. Only the light commercials and some export saloons could now be had with the 848cc engine. From May 1976 there was improved sound-deadening from new rubber sub-frame mounts; some people call these Mark IV Minis, but the name was not official. Then in August 1977, the 1275GT gained Dunlop Denovo run-flat tyres as standard. This was part of a cross-range policy by BL; the tyres were also made available on the Princess and Rover SD1 ranges, but did not catch on.

More big changes occurred in 1980. The 1098cc and 1275cc engines changed to the A-Plus types developed for the Metro that was introduced that year, and the 848cc size disappeared from saloons. The Clubman disappeared, although its front end was retained on the estate models, which were now renamed HL types. Estates, vans and pick-ups all went out of production in 1982, and with them the 848cc engine. With this reduced range, the Mini's last year among Britain's top ten best-selling cars was 1981, and it was clear that BL was trying to allow it to die in favour of the Metro.

However, the car simply refused to die, reaching five million sales in 1985. BL had recognized its longevity in 1984, standardizing the 12in wheels and bigger brakes previewed on

TRYING TO REPLACE THE MINI

While Issigonis worked in his retirement on ideas for an even more compact Mini, called 9X, BL began to look at how they might eventually replace the Mini. Many of its ideas had been adopted by other manufacturers, but the general trend was towards slightly bigger cars, and especially with a hatchback configuration. So in 1972, BL designers began work on the ADO74 'supermini' project, and also, as insurance, another one closer in size to the original Mini, which eventually became ADO88.

ADO88 was ready for production when Michael Edwardes was appointed as BL's top man in 1977. He was disappointed by reactions to the car at customer research clinics, and halted production plans. ADO88 then evolved into LC8, the supermini that was released as the MiniMetro in 1980.

IF YOU WANT ONE....

The original Mini has been an enthusiast's car for many years. Indeed, it was arguably one such from the moment it reached the showrooms in 1959. Although early ones are the most valuable, a Mini of any age will provide classic entertainment aplenty. There are many Mini specialists, and several clubs, too, such as the British Mini Club (https://britishminiclub.co.uk), the National Mini Owners' Club (www.miniownersclub.co.uk), and the Mini Cooper Register (http://www.minicooper.org).

Key purchasing points:

- The biggest Mini problem is rear sub-frame rot, both in the frame's strengthening webs and around the mounting points; fixings are often seized solid
- Structural rust affects the floorpans and boot floor, the sills, the rear of the front wheel-arch and the base of the screen pillars; cosmetic rust attacks the door bottoms, front wings and rear valance
- Engines are reliable, durable, and easy to work on, but check for low oil pressure and a cracked cylinder head
- Gearboxes are always noisy, but grinding noises mean that bearings are wearing out; worn CV joints will click
- Take extra care when buying a Cooper, because fakes exist; always get expert advice

LEYLAND MINI AND ROVER MINI: FACTS AND FIGURES

Pressed steel monocoque bodyshell with front and rear sub-frames; two doors and four seats. Transversely mounted front engine driving front wheels.

Engine 848cc 4-cylinder with 34bhp at 5,500rpm (to 1984)
998cc 4-cylinder with 38bhp at 5,250rpm (to 1990)
1275cc 4-cylinder petrol with 59bhp at 5,300rpm (1275GT models) 78bhp at 6,000rpm (Cooper S); 63bhp at 5,700rpm (Cooper 1.3i)

Gearbox Four-speed manual; optional four-speed automatic

Dimensions

Length 3,079mm (121.25in) (standard models)
3,165mm (124.625in) (with Clubman-style front)
3,299mm (129.875in) (estates and commercials)
3,404mm (134in) (estates with Clubman-style front)

Wheelbase 2,032mm (80in) (saloon) 2,134mm (84in) (estates and commercials)

Width 1,410mm (55.5in)

Height 1,346mm (53in)

Kerb weight 587–660kg (1,294–1,455lb), depending on model

Leyland Mini and Rover Mini: Statistics

Performance 0–60mph in 20.3sec (848cc, manual)
0–60mph in 18.7sec (998cc, manual)
0–60mph in 14.6sec (1275cc, manual)

Max. speed 72mph (116km/h) (848cc)
75mph (120.6km/h) (998cc)
90mph (145km/h) (998cc Cooper)
90mph (145km/h) (1275cc)
97mph (156km/h) (1275cc Cooper)

Fuel consumption 35–40mpg (8–7ltr/100km)

Production numbers

5, 300,000 (all models, 1959–2000)

the 1275GT ten years earlier, and adding plastic wheel-arch extensions. Only 998cc engines were now available, and a new era began, of boosting Mini sales through special editions that traded on its fashionable appeal.

In this guise, the Mini lived out the British Leyland era. In 1988 it was renamed a Rover Mini. The outrageous Mini ERA Turbo followed in 1989, the Cooper returned in 1990, and from that year all engines were 1275cc types. Fuel injection followed in 1991, and a cabriolet derivative in 1993. By this stage, most sales were in Japan, but they were strong enough (around 40,000 a year) for BMW to invest in upgrading the Mini soon after they acquired the Rover Group in 1994. So 1996 brought a new injection system, a driver's airbag, side impact beams and a front-mounted radiator. The very last of 5.3 million Minis was built at Longbridge in October 2000.

Leyland Princess (1975–81)

The Leyland Princess was the second stage in the life of the ADO71 models, which were introduced in the first half of 1975 with Austin, Morris and Wolseley badges. Just six months later, in September 1975, that whole range was cleared away and was relaunched as the Leyland Princess. The Princess name was one already in the corporate cupboard, as it had been used for many years on the big Austin limousines and also on Vanden Plas models.

The catalyst for change was almost certainly the Ryder Report, which was completed at about the same time as the ADO71 was announced. It recommended that all BLMC's individual marques should be scrapped in favour of a corporate Leyland identity – and the Princess was the first range to fall into line.

In fact, Leyland Cars made some cost savings with the introduction of the Princess range. The seven models of the old 18-22 range were cut back to four, and the humped bonnet

Renamed the Leyland Princess, the 18-22 range had a few cosmetic differences as well. This is a 1978-model 2200 HLS, at the top of the range.

British Leyland designs all seemed to suffer from unappealing plastic dashboards in the 1970s, and the one for the Princess was no exception.

of the Morris and Wolseley versions disappeared in favour of the Austin-style flat bonnet. The new Princess now came as an 1800, 1800HL, 2200HL or 2200HLS; the 1800s had twin headlamps, and the 6-cylinder 2200s had trapezoidal headlamps. All of them had a crown badge on the bonnet and the Princess name on the grille, together with black vinyl covers for the rearmost body pillars.

The Princess showed great promise and was much admired in some quarters. However, build quality was affected by poor quality control and constant industrial disputes, and as a result the cars gained a reputation for unreliability. A particular problem arose in early 1977, by which time driveshaft failure on the 6-cylinder manual cars had reached epidemic proportions. The cars were taken out of production while the problem was fixed (the solution was to change the engine mountings), and in March a special edition of 1200 automatic-gearbox 2200 Special Six models was released to keep sales afloat. These were all black with silver side stripes, and a number of features otherwise reserved for the HLS models.

Princess 2

Major changes came in July 1978, and the revised models were sold as Princess 2 types. The old 1800 B-series engine disappeared, and in its place came two versions of the new O-series engine. There was a 1.7-litre size that in the UK came

The Princess was, of course, gradually developed, and this is the rear view of a Princess 2 1700 HL, with the new 1.7-litre O-series engine and distinctive decal stripe at the rear.

A vinyl roof always helped… this is a late model Princess 2000 HLS, with metallic paint and the 2-litre O-series engine.

below the 1.8-litre tax-break point, and a 2.0-litre size that provided a third engine for the range and was intended to eat into the fleet market then dominated by the Ford Cortina.

The 6-cylinder 2200 models remained available as before, but now with two different levels of trim. The full range of six models was now 1700L, 1700HL, 2000HL, 2000HLS, 2200HL and 2200HLS. From May 1979, a 1700HLS model joined the range, but this was withdrawn after less than a year, in March 1980.

The Princess 2 was replaced by the Austin Ambassador from November 1981, and for that car BL finally provided the hatchback that customers wanted. Demand was enough to persuade two companies – Crayford in Kent and Torcars in Devon – to develop aftermarket hatchback conversions of the Princess. However, the conversion cost was a deterrent, and neither was very numerous.

4-cylinder Princess models were assembled in New Zealand from CKD, beginning with 1800 models in 1977 and changing to 2000 models in early 1979. The last ones were built in June 1982.

IF YOU WANT ONE....

The relatively small number of viable survivors today means that the Leyland Princess does not have a large following in the classic world. However, the cars are distinctive, spacious and comfortable, and in 6-cylinder form, remarkably smooth to drive. For anyone interested in what is commonly described as the Wedge, membership of The Princess and Ambassador Owners' Club (www.princessandambassador.org.uk) is indispensable.

Key purchasing points:

- Bodies last quite well if decently maintained, but if mud build-up is ignored, they will rust in the wings, door bottoms and around suspension mountings
- 6-cylinder engines can overheat, so watch the temperature gauge and check for leaks
- Hydrolastic fluid needs to be changed every five years to avoid pipes corroding and leaking; also check front suspension bushes, because worn ones can stress the Hydrolastic displacers
- Check the front footwells under the carpets for water leaking through a perished windscreen seal
- Seat backrests fade and deteriorate, and driver's seats can sag; headlinings also discolour, sag and tear

LEYLAND PRINCESS: FACTS AND FIGURES

Pressed steel monocoque with four doors and five seats. Transversely mounted front engine driving front wheels.

Engine	1.7: 1695cc O-series in-line 4-cylinder, with 88bhp at 5,200rpm
	1800: 1798cc B-series in-line 4-cylinder, with 82bhp at 5,250rpm
	2.0: 1994cc O-series in-line 4-cylinder, with 92bhp at 4,900rpm
	2200: 2227cc E-series in-line 6-cylinder, with 110bhp at 5,250rpm
Gearbox	Four-speed manual; optional three-speed automatic

Dimensions

Length	4,454mm (175.35in)
	4,456mm (175.4in) (Princess 2)
Wheelbase	2,667mm (105in)
	2,673mm (105.25in) (Princess 2)
Width	1,730mm (68.1in)
Height	1,409mm (55.5in)
Kerb weight	1,085kg (2,390lb) (Princess 2 1700)
	1,090kg (2,400lb) (Princess 2 2000)
	1,160kg (2,557lb) (1800)
	1,197kg (2,638lb) (2200)
	1,215kg (2,677lb) (2200HLS)

Leyland Princess: Statistics

Performance	0–60mph in 13.5sec (2200)
Max. speed	96mph (154km/h) (1800)
	104mph (167km/h) (2200)
	98mph (158km/h) (1700)
	98mph (158km/h) (2000)
Fuel consumption	28mpg (10ltr/100km) (1700)
	23mpg (12.3ltr/100km) (2000)
	27mpg (10.5ltr/100km) (2200)

Production numbers

41,134	(1700)
84,867	(1800)
35,498	(2000)
63,443	(2200)

THE MG-BADGED MODELS

MG fell from favour for a time under British Leyland, probably because top management had an understandable preference for Triumph – which had, of course, belonged to the Leyland group since the early 1960s. The Midget lasted only until 1979, and the MGB just a year longer, and the only new MG sports car was a V8-powered version of the B. Even that was more or less forced on British Leyland by the activities of an after-market conversion specialist, although it must be said that having Rover (who built the engine) in the same group as MG (who built the car) did make its creation easier.

However, the MG name was revived to good effect in the 1980s on some performance versions of the Metro, Maestro and Montego saloons.

MGB GT V8 (1973–76)

The MGB GT V8 was not really British Leyland's own idea. They simply capitalized on a popular conversion available since 1970 from Ken Costello's Costello Motor Engineering Company Ltd in Sidcup, Kent. The MG engineers at Abingdon were given a strictly limited budget, and instructed to deliver their own production version.

The Rover 3.5-litre V8 was a fairly straightforward fit in the MG's engine bay, and as its weight was roughly the same as that of the 1798cc B-series 4-cylinder that normally lived there, the car's existing handling balance was not upset. MG took the low-compression version of the Rover engine, but designed their own special carburettor installation that placed the twin SUs transversely behind the engine, with distinctive 'lobster claw' air intakes. This meant that the standard bonnet could be retained: the Costello conversion had needed a bonnet hump to clear the standard Rover carburettor installation.

The Abingdon-built V8 MG was only ever available as a fixed-roof GT, and not as an open roadster. With 137bhp, the Rover engine delivered a big boost in performance, but MG's timing was unfortunate. They released the car in autumn 1973, just before the first oil crisis caused a huge increase in fuel prices, and buyers began to shun cars with large engines. The high cost of the MGB GT V8 was a further deterrent to sales, and the special wheels and V8 badges were seen as insufficient to distinguish it from its 4-cylinder sibling.

So only just under 2,600 examples were sold before British Leyland decided to end production in 1976. The only significant change during the model's production life was the switch from chrome bumpers to black bumpers in September 1974, a change shared with 4-cylinder MGBs and dictated by legislation in the US market. Ironically, perhaps, the MGB GT V8 was never sold in the USA.

As this picture makes clear, the MGB GT V8 was not all that easy to tell from a standard MGB GT. These are rubber-bumper models; the V8 car is the one on the right with the distinctive wheels.

IF YOU WANT ONE....

The MGB V8 may have a V8 engine, but it is fundamentally an MGB GT. That alone makes it an established classic, welcome at any enthusiast event. Like the 4-cylinder MGBs, it is a fully usable car, and although costs are likely to be slightly higher with the V8 engine, they will not be a serious deterrent for most people. The car is well served by specialists, and is welcome in several clubs, including the MG Car Club (www.mgcc.co.uk) and the MG Owners' Club (www.mgownersclub.co.uk).

Key purchasing points:

- Rust can be a big problem, so check sills, behind the headlights, and all body seams
- The V8 engine needs regular lubrication maintenance, so check how clean the oil is; however, 20psi when hot is normal because this is a low-pressure system
- The high torque of the V8 causes early wear to first and second gears, and also to the overdrive; many cars now have Rover five-speed gearboxes for these reasons
- Steering is unassisted and will feel heavy to many drivers; if there's a knocking against the steering column, the engine mountings are worn
- Beware rusty rims on the composite Dunlop wheels; centres are alloy, but rims are steel and cannot be successfully re-chromed

MGB GT V8: FACTS AND FIGURES

Pressed steel monocoque with two side doors and hatchback tail door; 2+2 seating. Front engine driving rear wheels.

Engine 3528cc Rover V8, with 137bhp at 5,000rpm
Gearbox Four-speed manual with overdrive

Dimensions

Length	3,929mm (154.7in) (chrome bumper models) 4,020mm (158.25in) (black bumper models)
Wheelbase	2,311mm (91in)
Width	1,524mm (60in)
Height	1,270mm (50in)
Kerb weight	1,108kg (2,442lb)

MGB GT V8: Statistics

0–60mph	7.7sec
Max. speed	125mph (201km/h)
Fuel consumption	26mpg (10.9ltr/100km)

Production numbers 2,591

MG Metro (1982–90)

The MG marque was in abeyance at the start of the 1980s, as the MG factory at Abingdon was closed down after assembly of MGBs ended in 1980. But there was a new focus on 'hot hatch' models in the marketplace, and British Leyland determined to get a piece of the action. So from 1982 the MG marque was reinvented as the maker of small sporting saloons, the first model being the MG Metro.

The MG Metro was introduced in June 1982, and was promoted as a sports model. It came with the 1275cc engine in Mini Cooper specification. That meant a modified cylinder head with bigger valves and better porting, different cam profiles, and a bigger carburettor than the standard Metro 1.3 had. A sporty interior with red carpets and red seat belts reinforced the car's image. The MG Metro was interesting, but not yet a contender in the Volkswagen Golf GTi stakes, or even against the recently introduced Ford Fiesta XR2.

Meanwhile, the finishing touches were being put to the real performance Metro with the assistance of Lotus Engineering at Hethel. That car was announced in October 1982 as the MG Metro Turbo, and its launch was timed to coincide with that of the new high-performance Rover Vitesse.

Key to the Metro Turbo was a turbocharged 1275cc engine, boosted by a Garrett T3 turbocharger with a two-stage electronic boost control to regulate torque and protect the standard four-speed gearbox. The engine had been considerably reworked to cope with the extra stresses, and among the changes was a stronger crankshaft. Stiffer suspension and low-profile tyres played their part in making this Metro fun to drive – and a 115mph (185km/h) top speed made clear what

The sporty version of the Metro wore MG badges, and the sportiest of them all was the MG Metro Turbo. The black lower panels and large decals were unmistakable.

IF YOU WANT ONE....

The MG Metro is much rarer today as a classic than its specification might suggest. The main reason is that poor build quality has accounted for many, while low levels of owner maintenance have sent many more to the scrapyard. Nevertheless, a well preserved example provides plenty of MG-style entertainment, and there are plenty of specialists who can help with its upkeep. Among the clubs that welcome MG Metro and Metro Turbo owners are the MG Car Club (www.mgcc.co.uk), the MG Owners' Club (www.mgownersclub.co.uk), and the Metro Owners' Club (http://metroownersclub.boards.net).

Key purchasing points:

- Rust is a big problem, so check the sills, the rear heelboard (where the sub-frame mounts to it), wheel-arches, valances and door bottoms
- Gearboxes were pushed to their limits with the turbocharged engine's torque, and worn synchromesh (when the gearbox jumps out of second) is a warning sign
- Check the Hydragas suspension for leaks from pipes and unions, and that the ride height is even all round
- The turbocharged engine may look similar to a standard A-series, but it has a lot of uprated parts; be careful when buying spares
- The MG Metro is really a Metro 1300 with some performance enhancements and MG badges, so don't expect it to be a high-performance car!

Later Metro Turbos had these rather controversial part-octagon decals, together with cross-spoke alloy wheels.

it was all about. Servo-assisted brakes with ventilated discs and four-piston calipers at the front kept performance under control. The Metro Turbo looked the part, too, with a bodykit of wheel spats and front and rear spoilers, plus special flat-faced cast alloy wheels.

Both models shared the October 1984 facelift applied across the Metro range, but it was about this time that the Metro Turbo encountered its nemesis in the shape of the new Peugeot 205GTi. Nevertheless the car remained a popular purchase for several more years.

Later versions of the Metro Turbo switched to cross-spoke alloy wheels, and even lower-profile tyres. Changes to both models for the 1989 model year proved controversial, in particular the large split octagons and MG logo decals that were applied to their flanks. The basic MG Metro also had a slightly less powerful engine for this final year. From 1990, both would be replaced by versions of the Rover Metro.

MG METRO: FACTS AND FIGURES

Pressed steel monocoque with two side doors and hatchback tail door; five seats. Transversely mounted front engine driving front wheels.

Engine	MG Metro: 1275cc A-Plus in-line 4-cylinder, with 72bhp at 6,000rpm; 69bhp at 5,450rpm (1989 models) MG Metro Turbo: 1275cc A-Plus in-line turbocharged 4-cylinder, with 93bhp at 6,130rpm
Gearbox	Four-speed manual

Dimensions

Length	3,403mm (134.05in)
Wheelbase	2,251mm (88.62in)
Width	1,563mm (61.58in)
Height	1,359mm (53.53in)
Kerb weight	810kg (1,785lb) (Metro) 840kg (1,852lb) (Metro Turbo)

MG Metro: Statistics

0–60mph	10.1sec (MG Metro) 9.9sec (Metro Turbo)
Max. speed	105mph (169km/h) (MG Metro) 112mph (180km/h) (Metro Turbo)
Fuel consumption	40mpg (7ltr/100km) (MG Metro) 35mpg (8ltr/100km) (Metro Turbo)

Production numbers

120,197 (MG Metro 1300)
21,968 (MG Metro Turbo)

MG Maestro (1983–91)

MG Maestro 1600

The MG Maestro got off to a bad start. Keen to follow the sales momentum generated by the MG Metro Turbo in 1982, Austin Rover Group had an MG version of the new Maestro rushed through to production. Launched along with the Austin versions of the Maestro in March 1983, the MG Maestro 1600 was sadly underdeveloped, and made do with a twin-carburettor version of the R-series engine, whose development had also been rushed.

On the cosmetic front, Austin Rover had done a great job. Front and rear spoilers, red inserts for the bumpers and side bump-strips, plus distinctive alloy wheels underlined the car's sporty pretensions. The grey interior trim combined herringbone cloth with velour and red accent piping, while the front seats had rally-style bolsters. An interesting (but ultimately unloved) innovation on the MG Maestro was computer LCD instrumentation.

Even though a close-ratio five-speed gearbox made the most of what the R-series engine had to offer, it soon became apparent that the engine itself had problems (see Appendix I). Dealers were also unfamiliar with the twin Weber carburettors on this version. So from July 1984 the new S-series engine was fitted instead. This cured most of the problems, but sadly the damage had already been done to the MG Maestro's image.

The focus on MG as the sporting brand gave rise to the MG Maestro. Though the 1600 was not a big success, the 2.0 EFi seen here was very much liked.

The digital dashboard of the MG Maestro 1600 was supposed to give the car a modern image, but it did not go down very well with the customers – especially when the accompanying voice command system started playing up.

MG Maestro 2.0 EFi and 2.0i

The MG Maestro 1600 was replaced from October 1984 by the 2.0 EFi model which, as its name suggests, had an injected 2.0-litre engine. Not only more powerful, the O-series engine was also much sweeter than the 1600 had been. It also drove through the Honda PG1 end-on gearbox, which brought five speeds and a slick change action.

The car looked much the same as before, although there was a new style of grille, now painted in the body colour. Suspension and brake changes helped the Maestro 2.0 EFi become Austin Rover's first serious rival for the Volkswagen Golf GTi and the Ford Escort XR3i, which were then dominating the hot hatch market. A PAS option was also listed.

The unfortunate image generated by the earlier MG Maestro 1600 probably did nothing to help sales of this much improved car, and Austin Rover did little to help it by way of production changes. In late 1984 it was renamed a Maestro 2.0i, and the EFi terminology was dropped. New 15in alloy wheels were fitted when the MG Maestro Turbo arrived in 1989. However, the focus was now on the turbocharged car, and the MG Maestro 2.0i faded quietly away, going out of production in 1991.

MG Maestro Turbo

Austin Rover had been planning a turbocharged Maestro by 1984, but the prototypes were said to be too fast (a strange way to describe a performance-oriented car!), and so the

IF YOU WANT ONE....

The MG Maestro and Maestro Turbo are still practical as 'everyday' classics, and are also quick and economical. Arguably, the early digital dashboard has its own appeal now, too. Specialists are not numerous, but there is plenty of support to be had from the clubs: the MG Maestro Turbo Register (www.maestroturbo.org.uk), the Maestro & Montego Owners' Club (www.maestro.org.uk), the MG Car Club (www.mgcc.co.uk), and the MG Owners' Club (www.mgownersclub.co.uk).

Key purchasing points:

- As with all Maestro variants, look for serious rust, especially in the rear suspension turrets, the inner sills, the wheel-arches, door bottoms and tailgate
- R-series engines are chain-driven, but the S-series has a belt, which needs changing at regular intervals; fortunately it is arranged so that a broken belt does not wreck the engine
- Blue smoke from the exhaust of a Maestro Turbo will indicate that the turbocharger is on the way out
- Gearboxes are more prone to wear in the turbocharged models, which may also suffer from whining differential bearings
- All interiors will creak and rattle; although the electronic dashboard on the early 1.6 can be troublesome, it can be repaired by specialists

MG MAESTRO: FACTS AND FIGURES

Pressed steel monocoque with four doors and hatchback tail door; five seats. Transversely mounted front engine driving front wheels.

Engine	1600: 1598cc R-series in-line 4-cylinder (early models); 1598cc S-series in-line 4-cylinder from July 1984; both with 103bhp at 5,600rpm 2.0 EFi: 1994cc O-series in-line 4-cylinder, with 115bhp at 5,500rpm Turbo: 1994cc O-series in-line turbocharged 4-cylinder, with 150bhp at 5,100rpm and 169lb/ft at 3,500rpm
Gearbox	Five-speed manual

Dimensions

Length	4,050mm (159.5in)
Wheelbase	2,507mm (98.7in)
Width	1,687mm (66.4in)
Height	1,429mm (56.3in)
Kerb weight	980kg (2,160lb) (2.0 EFi)

MG Maestro: Statistics

0–60mph	9.6sec (1600) 8.5sec (2.0 EFi) 6.7sec (Turbo)
Max. speed	111mph (178km/h) (1600) 115mph (185km/h) (2.0 EFi) 128mph (206km/h) (Turbo)
Fuel consumption	28–34mpg (10–8.3ltr/100km) (2.0 EFi) 22.2mpg (12.7ltr/100km) (Turbo)

Production numbers

Over 15,000 (Maestro 1600)
32,249 (Maestro 2.0 EFi and 2.0i)
505 (Maestro Turbo)

turbocharged powertrain was made available only for the Montego. A later change of heart brought the MG Maestro Turbo for 1989, but only as a limited-edition model. There were just 500 cars for the public, plus five press demonstrators (or four, depending on your source), and although the car was announced at the Motor Show in October 1988 there were no customer examples until early 1989.

Essentially, the MG Maestro Turbo used the Montego Turbo drivetrain and suspension, suitably adapted. Some of the development work had been done in conjunction with Tickford, and it was Tickford who applied the bodykit and graphics to the cars after they had been built at Cowley. The bodykit incorporated very bold front and rear bumpers, with Lucas driving lamps integrated into the front one. There were then large 'Turbo' graphics on the sides, and, of course, alloy wheels.

The MG Maestro Turbo disappeared when all 500 examples had been sold. It was in many ways an excellent car, but it had arrived too late in the Maestro's production life to make the impact it deserved. Besides, GTi versions of the new Rover 200 and 400 were in preparation, and there was no room for internal competition.

MG Montego (1984–91)

MG Montego 2.0 EFi

The drive to create a credible range of MG performance saloons continued in 1984 with the MG Montego. This had the O-series 2.0-litre engine with a Lucas hot-wire injection, plus a new cylinder head with paired inlet ports. The gearbox was a five-speed Honda PG1, and a maximum speed of 115mph (185km/h) was quite respectable.

On the outside, the car was distinguished by a deeper front spoiler than on other Montegos, a lip spoiler on the boot lid, red highlights running around the bumper tops and bump strips, and low-profile tyres on special alloy wheels with puncture-retaining rims. The interior followed the lead of the MG Maestro, with red highlights on grey upholstery, and the car came with a decent stereo radio-cassette as standard, plus central locking and electric front windows. On the down side, it had a further updated version of the computer Liquid Crystal Display instrumentation pioneered in the Maestro.

RIGHT: Another well regarded car was the MG Montego Turbo, a keenly priced performance package but with some wayward handling characteristics.

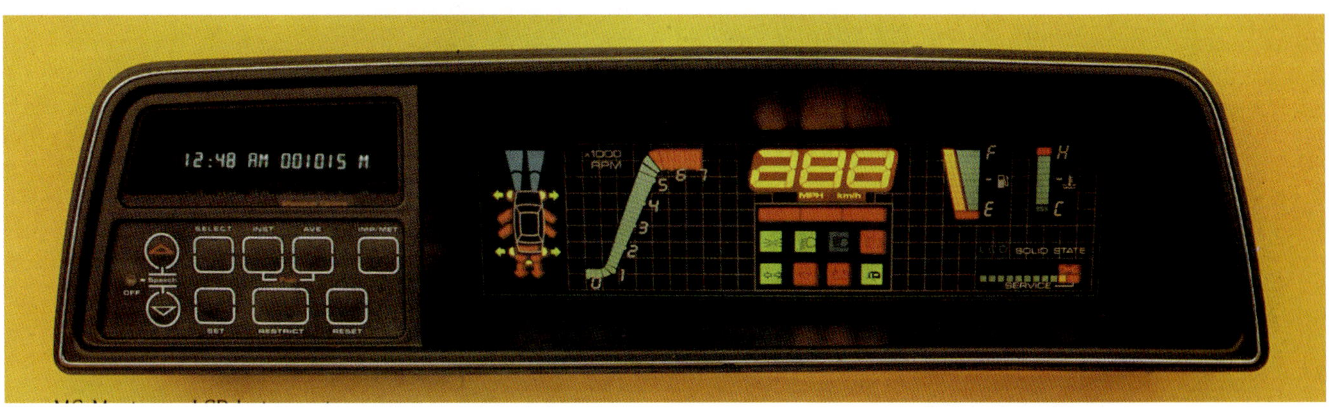

BELOW: The MG Montegos also had a digital dashboard. This demonstration example appears to have a fault already: what exactly is that character in yellow in front of the 88?

Conventional analogue instruments became standard towards the end of 1984, and changes after that broadly followed those on the MG Maestro. The EFi element in the name disappeared, and the car became an MG Montego 2.0i. The alloy wheels changed to a cross-spoke design, and there was a new 2.0i badge on the boot lid, while the MG motif was relocated from grille to bonnet and made smaller. Colour-keyed door mirrors were added, and a tilt-and-slide glass sunroof became standard. Grey carpets replaced the earlier red ones, and plain grey upholstery replaced the earlier herringbone pattern. Dashboard switches were changed, and there was a better quality, four-speaker sound system.

The MG Montego went out of production in 1991, as the focus on MG as a maker of performance saloons changed.

MG Montego Turbo

The next stage, almost inevitably, was a turbocharged model. Developed with some assistance from Tickford, the MG Montego Turbo was introduced at the start of April 1985, and depended on a Garrett T3 turbocharger forcing air through its single SU carburettor. This delivered a 126mph (203km/h) top speed and very rapid acceleration – give or take the sometimes alarming turbo lag that so often compromised the driving experience of turbocharged cars in the 1980s.

To handle the extra performance, Austin Rover had increased spring rates, fitted wider tyres, and added an anti-roll bar at the rear with a fatter anti-roll bar at the front. Power-assisted steering was standard, and the Montego Turbo came with a tilt-and-slide sunroof, central locking, electric-heated door mirrors and a four-speaker radio-cassette system.

Although the car was competitively priced, its handling could be a little wayward, and so could its stability. So for 1986 there were changes to the front suspension with different track control arms, and the steering ratio was changed; the overall gearing was raised, and the front air dam was redesigned to improve stability at high speeds. Thus modified, the MG Montego Turbo carried on until production ended in 1991, but it would always be very much less common than its naturally aspirated sibling.

IF YOU WANT ONE....

The MG Montego and Montego Turbo are the most desirable of the Montego variants, combining practicality with performance; however, good examples of the Montego Turbo are not easy to find, and many have been modified, driven into the ground, or both. There are a few specialists around, and the clubs to investigate are the Maestro & Montego Owners' Club (www.maestro.org.uk), the MG Car Club (www.mgcc.co.uk), and the MG Owners' Club (www.mgownersclub.co.uk).

Key purchasing points:

- Look for rust in the rear suspension towers, sills, door bottoms, rear wheel-arches, and metal around the windscreen; repair costs could well rule out a purchase, even if it is a relatively rare Montego Turbo
- The MG Montego Turbo is not as rare as the MG Maestro Turbo, so don't be fooled into paying over the odds for one
- Blue smoke from the exhaust of a Montego Turbo means there are problems with the turbocharger
- Engines are noisy by modern standards, and also have oil leaks; a favourite is oil leaking from the head gasket close to the distributor
- Wheels on early cars required metric (TD) tyres, which can be hard to find today; many owners change these wheels for imperial sizes

MG MONTEGO: FACTS AND FIGURES

Pressed steel monocoque with four doors; five seats.
Transversely mounted front engine driving front wheels.

Engine	Montego: 1994cc O-series in-line 4-cylinder, with 115bhp at 5,500rpm Montego Turbo: 1994cc O-series in-line turbo-charged 4-cylinder, with 150bhp at 5,100rpm
Gearbox	Five-speed manual

Dimensions

Length	4,468mm (175.9in)
Wheelbase	2,565mm (101in)
Width	1,710mm (67.3in)
Height	1,420mm (55.9in)
Kerb weight	1,043kg (2,300lb) (Montego) 1,079.6kg (2,380lb) (Turbo)

MG Montego: Statistics

0–60mph	8.9sec (Montego) 7.3sec (Turbo)
Max. speed	114mph (183km/h) (Montego) 125mph (201km/h) (Turbo)
Fuel consumption	29.3mpg (9.7ltr/100km) (Montego) 23mpg (12.3ltr/100km) (Turbo)

Production numbers 34,476 (Montego)
7,276 (Montego Turbo)

THE MORRIS-BADGED MODELS

In the beginning, BLMC treated Morris as just another name for volume-produced saloon cars, and indeed the Morris models it inherited were for the most part badge-engineered clones of Austins. However, the distinction between Austin and Morris soon became clearer: Morris was best exemplified by the simple, reliable Minor, while Austin was primarily responsible for the advanced front-wheel-drive cars with transverse engines. So when BLMC came to choose marque badges for new products, the issue was not whether a design originated at the Morris works in Cowley or at the Austin works in Longbridge, but whether its engineering was conventional or advanced. In future, new Morris models would be conventional, uncomplicated designs.

That is why the Marina became a Morris, and why it remained a Morris when it was later revitalized as the Morris Ital. But there were not enough new cars for the policy to become well established. The plan to market the 18-22 range with Morris badges as well as Austin and Wolseley badges was torpedoed after six months, and the Marina was the only model to carry the Morris name forwards into the 1980s.

The Morris name was retained for the Ital that succeeded the Marina, although that model went out of production in 1984. The final gasp for the Morris marque was the van version of the Austin Metro, which initially carried Morris badges. It kept that name until 1985, when the Morris name was finally extinguished.

Not much had changed by 1978, when this Marina 1.8 Super was built. The Sandglow colour was somehow typical of BL cars in the 1970s. MAGIC CAR PICS

There was a two-door coupé version of the Marina as well, seen here in its most powerful TC guise. Despite the warpaint, it was still very much a Marina. MAGIC CAR PICS

Morris Marina (1971–81)

The Marina had two major problems in its life: first, it was designed in too much of a hurry; and it was then kept in production for twice as long as had originally been planned. It was always intended as a 'conventional' car, so should not really be criticised for that (after all, Ford were doing very well with conventional cars in Britain at the time). However, British Leyland's industrial relations problems contributed to poor build quality, while the company's cash crises during the 1970s meant that the Marina could not be updated as time went on. So it became the public image of everything that was wrong with British Leyland – an outdated model that never fulfilled its own limited potential.

For all that, it was remarkably popular during its ten years in production. In the UK, it regularly figured in third or fourth place in the top ten best-selling new cars, and in 1973 actually achieved second place. Its conventional engineering also

The Marina's interior was bland and colourless, unless you liked the multiple shades of brown in this 1.8 Super. Once again, it seemed to typify BL cars of the 1970s. MAGIC CAR PICS

helped to make it quite a good seller in export markets that demanded rugged, simple cars.

The Morris Marina, or ADO28, was a pure British Leyland confection. It started life very soon after the BLMC merger, when the corporation's new head, Lord Stokes, reviewed the former BMC's future model plans. Appalled that there was nothing on the stocks to tackle Ford's domination of the company-car market in Britain, he swiftly made some management changes, moving Alec Issigonis sideways out of the top engineering spot and replacing him with Harry Webster, who had been the chief engineer at Leyland-owned Triumph. His brief to Webster was to initiate a new model programme for the Austin and Morris marques, and to get on with it as quickly as possible.

The plan for ADO28 came together very quickly. Webster knew that he would have to use as much existing hardware as possible to save development time. Stokes wanted the car to be simply and conventionally engineered so that it would appeal to the fleet market and company car buyers, who were a major factor in Ford's success in Britain. That meant it was to be badged as a Morris; the Austin name was to be kept for technically more advanced designs, such as those for which Issigonis had been responsible. Simple and rugged construction was also expected to be an important factor in gaining sales in overseas territories like Australia, New Zealand and South Africa.

Webster did his best, and in double-quick time. By May 1968, detailed plans for ADO28 were in place, and by August that year Roy Haynes had styling mock-ups ready for viewing. Stokes really wanted the car ready for launch in October 1970, as he planned a major barrage of new models from British Leyland for that summer, but there was simply not enough time. Nevertheless, the styling was frozen that month and tooling began for a launch early in the second quarter of 1971.

There was much more to the ADO28 project than the car itself. Among the models it would replace were the ageing Morris Minor and the larger Morris Oxford; both were built at the old Morris plant in Cowley, and so it was logical that the assembly lines for the new car should go into that factory. However, Stokes wanted quality improvements as well, and part of the old factory was gutted and completely rebuilt as the ADO28 assembly hall. This was to be fed by a covered conveyor running across the road from the old Morris plant where the bodyshells would be built, saving time in transportation and also eliminating the risk of shells stored in the open going rusty before they were painted. It was all a massive and costly upheaval.

On the engineering side, Harry Webster chose to use the simple, cheap, but seriously outdated front suspension from the Morris Minor. This used longitudinal torsion bars as the springing medium, with lower arms pivoting on trunnions and hydraulic lever-arm dampers – a truly ancient form of damping that was almost extinct by the late 1960s. At the rear, a 'live' axle on leaf springs was the quick and cost-effective solution, although the conventional telescopic dampers would have their top mounts on the strong transmission tunnel that reinforced the bodyshell – a simple and ingenious design that nevertheless left the dampers too close to the horizontal to be fully effective.

Webster's original thinking focused on the E-series engines as used in the Maxi, but these were giving some problems in service and ADO28 was a car with which no risks could be taken. So the engine choice switched to the 1.3-litre A-series and the 1.8-litre B-series, both proven and reliable engines even though they were elderly designs. Drive would be to the rear wheels, and Webster chose to use the four-speed Triumph manual gearbox, whose design he had recently overseen when the Toledo models had been created from the front-wheel-drive 1300 and 1500. Design complication would be avoided by mounting powertrain and suspension directly to the monocoque bodyshell without the use of sub-frames.

Meanwhile, Roy Haynes was working on the shape of the car. He was an ex-Ford man – designer of the Ford Cortina Mk II, to which ADO28 would have some resemblance – and could see the advantages of spinning two models off a common set of mechanical underpinnings. So he suggested a four-door saloon as the core model, plus a more prestigious and specialist two-door coupé; the strategy was similar to that which Ford would employ from 1969 with the related Cortina and Capri models. However, Haynes left BLMC in 1970, before ADO28 was ready for production and when the Cowley styling studio where he worked was absorbed into the Longbridge studio.

Under his successor, Harris Mann, the design was compromised by cost-saving measures imposed by BLMC management. The coupé was given the same front doors as the saloon, which made it look like a derivative of that car rather than a separate model. This completely changed the plan for ADO28: instead of the two-door being a sporty derivative, it was now redefined as the entry-level car that would compete with the entry-level two-door Ford Escort and Hillman Avenger models. So British Leyland lost a potentially interesting additional model, and the relationship between saloon and coupé versions of ADO28 would forever be a source of confusion.

Meanwhile, the competition for ADO28 was getting stiffer. In 1969 it had been aimed to beat the Cortina Mk II, the Hillman Hunter and the smaller Vauxhall Viva HB. But in 1970 Hillman expanded their range downwards with the Avenger, and Ford switched to the dramatically more modern-looking and larger Cortina Mark III, which now also had engines as large as 2.0 litres. Vauxhall, meanwhile, delivered more space and more attractive styling with their Viva HC. ADO28, conceived before the goalposts had been moved and committed to tooling in late 1970, was left looking outdated before it even reached the showrooms.

BLMC were probably not too concerned at these developments. ADO28 was deliberately intended to be conventional, and in any case had been drawn up as a stop-gap model that would be replaced by something more considered after five years or so. Sadly, that plan never came to fruition.

So ADO28 was introduced as the Morris Marina in late April 1971. That name was not wholly new, as it had been used on Morris 1100 and 1300 models for Denmark since 1962, but it was new for most markets where ADO28 would be sold. There were three engine options, and the cars came badged as Marina 1.3, Marina 1.8, and Marina 1.8TC, the latter with a twin-carburettor engine lifted straight from the MGB sports car and tweaked to give a little extra power.

All three engines were available in both two-door coupé and four-door saloon bodies, making six variants in all, and there was an automatic gearbox alternative to the standard four-speed manual. However, all was not yet well, and the journalists invited to the press launch in Cannes quickly highlighted a couple of oddities about the Marina. One was that RHD cars had windscreen wipers apparently set up for LHD cars, and vice versa. This was actually a last-minute decision taken when test drivers reported airflow causing the driver's side wiper to lift off the screen at speed; a swap to the other 'hand' cured the problem, and Marinas would always have this oddity.

The second oddity was much more serious: the car suffered from bad understeer at speed. This was certainly a result of the unseemly haste with which the Marina had been put into production, and Harry Webster put his engineers to work to sort it out at once, with the aim of having a remedy before cars began to reach the public through dealers.

Their solution was a redesigned lower front suspension arm that reduced camber change in cornering, and this was rushed into production. The higher-powered 1.8-litre models sold to the public theoretically all had it (although a few escaped unmodified), but the 1.3-litre cars had to wait until production of the new components had built up; fortunately, their lighter front ends meant they suffered less from understeer. One estimate is that around 30,000 cars in all reached the public with the unmodified suspension. Many of these were modified by dealers under warranty, and by about September 1971 the modified suspension was being installed on the assembly lines.

This was not a good start, but Cowley ramped up production as planned, adding an extra night shift in May 1971 to meet anticipated demand. And that demand did come, although not in quite the volumes that BLMC had expected. At the car's launch, they bullishly suggested that they might sell 5,000 cars a week, but even in its first few years the Marina sold nowhere near that many. A press announcement in March 1972 trumpeted the production of the 100,000th Marina – which meant that production was being pegged at under 2,000 cars a week. In February 1972 the 250,000th example left the assembly lines, which suggested an increase in production volumes to give a weekly average of about 2,500 cars. Later, production would settle down to around 70,000 a year, or 1,350 a week.

The early increase in production volumes was certainly helped by the arrival of additional models, and also by the start of CKD assembly overseas (discussed in Chapter 4). During 1972, a four-door estate derivative joined the coupés and saloons, and then van and pick-up models broadened the range further. The first facelift came in 1975, and wisely brought anti-roll bars alongside the new radiator grilles, new seats and dashboard, and better soundproofing. Then in May 1977 Marinas took on the rather more comfortable seats designed for the Austin Allegro. That year also brought a further expansion of the model range, but for export markets only. This was a diesel-engined variant, with a 1.5-litre engine developed from the B-series petrol type and available in the old Morris Oxford diesel taxi up to 1971. Only four-door saloon variants were available, and Britain, still very much diesel-shy at this stage, never saw it – not even in the light commercial derivatives.

In an ideal world, the Marina would have been replaced in the mid-1970s, but British Leyland's multiple problems meant that no replacement was ready. So in autumn 1978, the model was given a further lease of life with a new engine and some cosmetic improvements. It was rebranded as a Marina 2. The new engine was the 1.7-litre version of the O-series 4-cylin-

For the US market, the Marina gained impact-absorbing bumpers and wore Austin badges.

IF YOU WANT ONE....

The Morris Marina was deeply unpopular for several years, during which time many quite reasonable examples were scrapped. However, it has now developed a sort of cult appeal as a symbol of the 1970s. Inexpensive to buy and look after, and easy to work on, the Marina is a practical classic despite its lack of glamour. Many mechanical parts are common to other British Leyland cars of the time, and can be found fairly easily from specialists. As for clubs, the Morris Marina Owners' Club can be found on the web at www.morrismarina.org.uk

Key purchasing points:

- Look for rust in the sills and floorpans; rust also attacks the front wings, around the headlamps and front valance, the wheel-arches, and the door bottoms
- Clutch judder was always a problem, and judder as the drive takes up may be caused by worn gearbox mountings, propshaft UJs, or even tired rear dampers
- Vibration through the steering and uneven front-tyre wear suggest worn tie-rod bushes
- Early 1.3 models (to October 1975) had an all-drum braking system, but front discs from later models can be fitted quite easily
- Interior trim is not very robust; vinyl seats often crack and split, and the tops of the rear seat and dashboard are prone to sun damage

MORRIS MARINA: FACTS AND FIGURES

Pressed steel monocoque with four doors (saloon and estate) or two doors (coupé); five seats. Front-mounted engine driving rear wheels.

Engine	1.3: 1275cc A-series 4-cylinder, with 60bhp at 5,250rpm
	1.7: 1695cc O-series 4-cylinder, with 88bhp at 5,200rpm
	1.8: 1798cc B-series 4-cylinder, with 72bhp at 4,750rpm;
	85bhp at 5,500rpm for the 1.8TC model
	1.5 diesel: 1489cc B-series 4-cylinder diesel, with 40bhp at 4,000rpm

Note: Other engines were used in Marinas assembled overseas. See Chapter 4 for details

Gearbox	Four-speed manual; optional three-speed automatic

Dimensions

Length	4,140mm (163in) (two-door)
	4,216mm (166in) (four-door)
	4,254mm (167.5in) (estate)
Wheelbase	2,438mm (96in)
Width	1,626mm (64in)
Height	1,426mm (56.125in)
Kerb weight	965kg (2,127lb) (1.3 saloon)

Morris Marina – Statistics

0–60mph	16.8sec (1.3)
	12.1sec (1.8)
Max. speed	86mph (138km/h) (1.3)
	100mph (161km/h) (1.8)
Fuel consumption	31mpg (9ltr/100km) (1.3)

Production numbers

659,852

der, and it created the Marina 1.7 to replace the earlier Marina 1.8 – although it was never made available with the two-door body. All Marina models gained a new grille with driving lights embedded in it, redesigned bumpers, a front chin spoiler and new tail-lights. The dashboard was redesigned, too. In this guise, the 1.3 and 1.7 Marinas ended production during 1980, still available in two-door, four-door, estate, pick-up and van forms. But the ADO28 was not dead yet, and re-emerged in autumn 1980 as the Morris Ital.

The Morris Marina had sold quite strongly overseas, too. As expected, it had done well in those traditional British markets that tended to fight shy of Issigonis's unconventional Austin designs on the grounds that they were not robust enough – or that they were too difficult to repair when they did go wrong. In particular, the car had done well in Australia, New Zealand and South Africa, and in all these countries it was built from CKD kits shipped out from Cowley and supplemented to a greater or lesser extent by locally designed components. (There is more about these versions of the car in Chapter 4.)

Among the overseas markets it is worth mentioning North America here. BLMC was known in the USA and Canada primarily for its sports cars and Jaguar saloons, and the Morris name simply did not figure in the consciousness of the North American car-buying public. However, the Austin name had a resonance – mainly from the Austin-Healey sports cars – and so the North American Marina was badged as an Austin Marina when it went on sale in 1973.

All the North American cars were 1800s, equipped with a power-sapping air-injection system to meet local emissions regulations, and there were both two-door and four-door models. The 1973 models had standard bumpers, but the 1974–75 models had heavy crash-absorbing bumpers to meet new regulations. Sales in the USA ended in 1975, but Austin Marinas remained available in Canada until 1978, when the last 1800 models were made. However, British Leyland did not consider sales strong enough to support the cost of developing and homologating a special Canadian version of the replacement 1.7-litre model.

Back in Britain, BLMC's Special Tuning Division prepared some excellent performance and handling upgrades for the Marina. However, Special Tuning was poorly marketed (as had been the case under BMC), and the general public remained blissfully unaware of how much the Marina could be improved. Special Tuning products were aimed at the dedicated specialist, who was prepared to take the trouble to seek them out. What such enthusiasts discovered included suspension upgrades – a telescopic damper conversion for the front end, and a rear-end conversion that set the dampers nearly vertically in turrets. There was also a bodykit available for the 1.8TC Marina, consisting of front and rear spoilers, alloy wheels, additional lighting and other items.

The Marina did leave a worthwhile legacy. Ironically, perhaps, the most visible element in that legacy was its exterior door handles. Their design met safety legislation around the world, was ergonomically excellent, and looked neat as well. So they reappeared on the Austin Allegro (1973), the Triumph TR7 (1975), the Range Rover (1981 – although they had been tried on a prototype as early as 1972), and the Land Rover Discovery (1989). Other companies bought them, too, and they appeared on cars such as the Lotus Esprit and Reliant Scimitar.

Arguably, the Marina also helped to kick start one of the success stories of the Korean motor industry. Hyundai wanted to make the transition from licence-build manufacturer to building cars of its own design, and in 1974 hired former Austin-Morris managing director George Turnbull. He took to Korea his deep knowledge of the Marina, a clutch of British engineers, and a determination to succeed. The result was the Hyundai Pony, launched in 1975 and unquestionably owing a great deal to the Marina.

Morris 18-22 series

There had to be a Morris version of the new ADO71 to keep dealers happy, but it didn't last long. Ryder Report rationalization provided an excuse to get rid of it and rebadge the whole range as Leyland Princess.

Morris versions have four round headlamps and a 'lumpy' bonnet like the Wolseley versions. In other respects they are virtually identical to the Austin models.

The Morris version of the 18-22 series had four round headlights and a distinctively humped bonnet.

IF YOU WANT ONE....

The Morris 18-22 cars are essentially the same as their Austin-badged equivalents, and the buying advice provided for those applies equally well to the Morris models. With a production run of just six months, and no strong enthusiast following (at the time of writing), these cars are likely to be hard to come by in any condition, let alone good condition.

Morris 18-22 Series: Facts, Figures and Statistics

See the entry for the Austin 18-22 series models.

Morris Ital (1981–84)

As progress was being made under Michael Edwardes towards a new range of medium-size cars, it became obvious that something had to be done to maintain the sales of existing models until around 1983–84. In the case of the Morris Marina, the solution was a major facelift, and for ideas British Leyland engaged the services of the Italian design consultancy ItalDesign.

ItalDesign was a highly respected company run by Giorgetto Giugiaro, and in recent years had been responsible for the first-generation Volkswagen Golf. However, it was invited only to submit ideas, while final responsibility for the new shape rested with Harris Mann at Longbridge. The style chosen for production incorporated a redesigned nose, a longer and restyled tail, black plastic-faced bumpers and new plastic wheel trims. There were new bodyside bump strips, and even the much-liked Marina door handles were changed to help the transformation, although the overall result was still very clearly a derivative of the Marina.

A front and rear restyle from an Italian design house turned the Marina into the Ital, but its origins were still recognizable.

The new style was applied to both saloon and estate models, but no updated two-door body was prepared. Relevant details were changed on the light commercial derivatives, too. Underneath, not very much changed, and the revised cars were planned to have the same 1.3-litre A-series and 1.7-litre O-series engines as the last Marinas, again with four-speed gearboxes or an extra-cost three-speed automatic. There would also be the same two levels of trim, called L and HL. In fact the original plan was to retain the Marina name as well, and to call the new models by the name of Morris Marina Ital. However, it appears that Michael Edwardes favoured the shorter name of Morris Ital, and so that was what they became for most markets.

IF YOU WANT ONE....

Most people probably see the Morris Ital as a slightly less dull variation on the Marina, and the two cars certainly do have a lot in common. As the final development of the ADO28 range, however, it does benefit from all the advances that were incorporated over the years.

For details of the clubs that cater for the Morris Ital, please see the entry for the Morris Marina (the Morris Marina Owners' Club has an Ital Register). Similarly, for key purchasing points, please see the entry for the Marina.

At the launch of the Morris Ital on 1 July 1980, BL publicity played up the part of ItalDesign in its creation, but the reality was that it was simply a modified Marina. Three months later, though, in October 1980, the range was extended with a new 2.0-litre derivative, using the O-series engine and built only with an automatic gearbox. This was called the Ital 2.0 HLS, but never proved very popular. Very much out of sight, the old 1.5-litre diesel engine remained available, but only for versions of the car built from CKD in Portugal by IMA at Setubal. These were badged as Morris Marina 1.5D models.

Upgraded interior trim for the HL and HLS derivatives followed in November 1981, but in the meantime work had been going ahead on a more heavily revised Ital range. This reached showrooms in September 1982, and its arrival coincided with Ital production being moved from Cowley to Longbridge so that the Cowley factory could be prepared for production of the forthcoming Maestro and Montego ranges.

The key changes to the Ital in 1982 were the introduction (at last) of telescopic front dampers, a change to parabolic leaf springs at the rear to improve ride comfort, improved trim and extra soundproofing. Meanwhile, the entry-level L models and the 2.0-litre cars disappeared (only about 1,000 of the 2.0-litre models had been sold when production ended in May 1982), and new trim levels of SL and SLX were introduced. The full range now consisted of 1.3 SL, 1.3 SLX, 1.7 SL and 1.7

MORRIS ITAL: FACTS AND FIGURES

Pressed steel monocoque with four doors; five seats.
Front-mounted engine driving rear wheels.

Engine	1.3: 1275cc A-series 4-cylinder, with 61bhp at 5,300rpm 1.7: 1695cc O-series 4-cylinder, with 78bhp at 5,150rpm 2.0: 1993cc O-series 4-cylinder, with 90bhp at 4,750rpm
Gearbox	Four-speed manual; optional three-speed automatic (standard on 2.0 models)

Dimensions

Length	4,343mm (171in) (saloon) 4,376mm (172.3in) (estate)
Wheelbase	2,438mm (96in)
Width	1,636mm (64.4in)
Height	1,417mm (55.8in)
Kerb weight	939kg (2,070lb) (1.3)

Morris Ital: Statistics

0–60mph	15.2sec (1.3) 12.5sec (1.7) 11.7sec (2.0)
Max speed	91mph (146km/h) (1.3) 98mph (158km/h) (1.7) 101mph (163km/h) (2.0)
Fuel consumption	32mpg (8.8ltr/100km) (1.3) 30mpg (9.4ltr/100km) (1.7)

Production numbers
175,276

SLX saloons, plus 1.3 SL and 1.7 SL estates. Light commercial derivatives remained available, too.

With this specification, the Morris Ital remained in production until 1984, when it was replaced in the BL range by the new Austin Montego. Saloon production ended first, in February that year, and the estate and van models continued for around another six months before they, too, were taken out of production.

The Marina tooling would later be sold to the Chengdu Auto Works in western China, which would build estate, van and pick-up models derived from the Marina until the late 1990s. Among the names these carried was Huandu CAC6430 – which was a 1998 estate model that added Ital bodywork to a separate chassis with deeper bumpers to disguise the extra height. It had a Chinese-built 2.0-litre O-series engine and an LT77 five-speed gearbox.

IF YOU WANT ONE....

The comments already made about the Austin Metro saloons apply equally well to the Morris Metro van.

MORRIS METRO VAN – FACTS, FIGURES AND STATISTICS

Pressed steel monocoque with two-door, two-seat cab.
Front engine driving front wheels.

For further details, please see the Austin Metro entry.

No separate production figures for the Morris Metro Van are currently available.

Morris Metro Van (1982–85)

Just as the Mini had been developed as a light commercial vehicle, so was the Metro, although that had not been part of British Leyland's original agenda for the model. However, several private conversions in the Metro's first year indicated that there would be a market for such a model, and so in 1982 one appeared. It was based on the cheapest version of the Metro – the City model that was also introduced that year.

However, where the Metro was an Austin or an MG, the light commercial derivative was badged exclusively as a Morris. Perhaps the Morris name seemed better suited to light commercial vehicles now that the Austin name was supposed to be attached to products with advanced engineering. One way or the other, the Morris Metro van was on sale for just three years, and disappeared from the showrooms in 1985. It was the last vehicle of any kind to carry the Morris name.

The van itself nevertheless survived for another five years, initially rebadged as an Austin Metro 310, and later simply as a Metrovan.

THE ROVER-BADGED MODELS

Like several other constituent marques of the British Leyland empire, Rover was left alone for a few years after BLMC had been formed. But this honeymoon period was not to last. In 1969, the British Leyland Board reviewed Rover's plans for an exciting new mid-engined sports car (which would probably have been given Alvis badges) and cancelled the project; legend has it that Jaguar's Sir William Lyons argued forcefully that the car would damage sales of his E-type. Then in 1971, Rover's plans for a new, large luxury saloon to replace the stately P5B models were also cancelled, just a few months before pilot production was due to begin. Again, legend has it that Lyons feared a clash with his XJ models.

Lyons can hardly be blamed for protecting his company's interests. However, these two incidents do illustrate that British Leyland had taken far too long to get to grips with what its various marques were doing; both the Rover projects could have been cancelled earlier if anyone in a sufficiently senior position had spotted the potential clashes with other projects. Instead, large sums of money and a lot of engineering development time were wasted, particularly on the big Rover saloon.

By 1971, British Leyland management had also spotted a potential clash between Rover and Triumph, both of which had plans to replace their 'executive' saloons. The Board reviewed the options, and judged in favour of the Rover proposal, giving Triumph the job of developing engines and gearboxes for it. During 1972, Rover ceased to exist as a separate entity, and was merged into Rover-Triumph. That in turn later became the Specialist Cars Division; later still, it was Jaguar-Rover-Triumph, with distinctly reluctant participation from Jaguar.

Rover then became the favoured name for the Honda-designed replacement for the Triumph Acclaim, which was introduced as the Rover 200 series in 1984. And it would be the Rover name that was the only one to survive the whole British Leyland period, when the Rover Group was formed from the reorganized British Leyland in 1986. That same year, a second Rover with Honda origins arrived, as the Rover 800 series took over from the SD1 range – but that car was a joint project with British Leyland designers and engineers. Some had once worked for Rover or Triumph; others were drawn from the old Austin and Morris divisions.

P8: THE CANCELLED ROVER

Rover's plan in the late 1960s was to replace the P5B models with a technologically advanced new car developed with the internal name of P8. Under Leyland Motors, this had been specifically realigned during 1967 to provide a competitor for BMH's big Jaguar saloons, and its introduction was provisionally scheduled for some time late in 1971. However, the BLMC merger that brought Jaguar and Rover into the same fold completely altered the picture: the two marques were now supposed to co-operate with one another instead of producing rival products. Something had to give.

The British Leyland Board belatedly recognized the danger of a clash with Jaguar's XJ6 saloon, introduced in 1968, and Jaguar's Sir William Lyons argued that the Rover should not be allowed to go ahead. His view prevailed, and the new Rover was cancelled in March 1971. Much of the body tooling had already been ordered, and a new 4.4-litre version of the V8 engine had been designed for early introduction. The cancellation proved to be an expensive one, which highlighted British Leyland's problems of control over its constituent marques. Not long after that, British Leyland took a firmer grip and amalgamated the Rover and Triumph marques.

Rover's planned big saloon was the P8, but Jaguar objected. This picture of a prototype suggests that some cosmetic revisions might have been welcome before production.

Rover 3500 and 3500S

When Rover took on the manufacture of the General Motors V8 engine, the company planned to use it right across the model range. So its initial appearance in the big P5B models in 1967 was swiftly followed by its arrival in the P6 (Rover 2000) body, so creating the Rover 3500 (initially known as a Three Thousand Five). The new model was announced in April 1968, just after the formation of BLMC. However, the launch press material, prepared in advance, carried Leyland identification rather than BLMC identification.

The 3500 was only available with a three-speed Borg Warner automatic gearbox, as Rover had not been able to find a suitable manual alternative in time. It was nevertheless highly regarded as a cross between a sports saloon and a (rather cramped) luxury car.

A special version, badged as 3500S, was prepared for the US market and released in 1969. It anticipated many of the changes that would be made to the Mark II versions in autumn 1970, but sold poorly. There were quality control problems, and Rover's tiny distribution network caused servicing problems for many customers; the model was therefore withdrawn in 1971. As it disappeared, so other markets were given a 3500S that was simply a manual-gearbox version of the 3500, using an uprated version of the 2000's four-speed gearbox. The 3500S was distinguished by a vinyl roof covering and, initially, by special wheel trims. This model attracted enthusiast drivers, and was also much liked as a police motorway patrol car.

The 3500 and 3500S remained in production until 1977, overlapping by a few months with production of the replacement Rover 3500 SD1 model. These cars were always well liked, as they combined excellent performance with compact dimensions and high build quality. So saying, it was a Rover 3500 that won the Automobile Association's Square Wheel Award in 1974 for the most troublesome new car delivered to a UK owner. Even Rover's legendary build quality had suffered from British Leyland disease.

IF YOU WANT ONE....

The Rover 3500 and 3500S are popular classic saloons that are still fully usable as everyday cars, thanks to their dynamic qualities. Drawbacks are poor rear legroom and a boot that is not very capacious – but for the owner who rarely, or never goes out with family in tow, they make a good choice. There are several specialists who provide spares support, and there are three clubs to investigate: the P6 Rover Owners' Club (www.p6roc.co.uk), the Rover P6 Club (www.p6club.com) and the Rover Sports Register (www.thersr.co.uk).

Key purchasing points:

- Sills, lower D-posts, front bulkhead, inner wings and the panel behind the headlamps can all rust out; on late models, paint blistering is also a problem
- Gearboxes can wear on enthusiastically driven 3500S models; some owners have replaced them with the later five-speed from the Rover SD1
- Rear brakes are mounted inboard alongside the differential and are awkward to work on, which means they are often neglected
- Leather upholstery can sometimes shrink, leaving the edge beading looking weirdly wavy; however, the cloth alternative is hard-wearing
- If there are electrical problems, check the fusebox, which can melt or crack on some cars

The Rover 3500 was one of the first new cars to be announced after BLMC was formed. This 1968 car has the bright metal bonnet finisher that distinguished the early models.

The facelifted Rovers had an additional side-trim strip, and in 3500S guise also had a vinyl roof. This is a 1974 model, without the special wheel trims of the first manual gearbox cars.

ROVER 3500 AND 3500S: FACTS AND FIGURES

Pressed-steel base unit with unstressed skin panels; four doors and five seats. Front engine driving rear wheels.

Engine	3528cc Rover V8, with 184bhp at 5,200rpm (1968–73); 143bhp at 5,000rpm (1974–77)*
Gearbox	Three-speed automatic (3500) or four-speed manual (3500S)

Dimensions

Length	4,554mm (179.3in)
Wheelbase	2,626mm (103.4in)
Width	1,676mm (66in)
Height	1,403mm (55.25in)
Kerb weight	1,298kg (2,862lb) (3500) 1,301kg (2,868lb) (3500S)

* Rover quoted power figures to SAE standards in 1968, but to DIN standards in 1974. Despite a lower compression ratio, the 1974 and later engines actually had only 1bhp less than the earlier types by DIN standards.

Rover 3500 and 3500S: Statistics

0–60mph	10.5sec (3500) 9.1sec (3500S)
Max. speed	114mph (183km/h) (3500) 122mph (196km/h) (3500S)
Fuel consumption	19mpg (14.9ltr/100km) (3500) 23mpg (12.3ltr/100km) (3500S)

Production numbers
79,057

Rover 2200 (1973–76)

The only new versions of the Rover P6 range actually developed under British Leyland were the 2200 models, which arrived in autumn 1973 to replace the 2000SC and 2000TC. The major change was an enlarged bore size, which had originally been developed when Rover was planning a 16-valve slant-four derivative of the 2000 engine for use in the forthcoming P10 model. That eventually became the Rover SD1, but the slant-four engine disappeared into oblivion.

Both 2200SC (single-carburettor) and 2200TC (twin-carburettor) came with the same four-speed manual gearbox as before, and the single-carburettor model could also be had with an automatic gearbox. Although these were quite old designs

The orange paint – called Paprika – was very 1970s in intent, but was never very popular. This is a 2200SC model; all of them had vinyl-trimmed rear roof pillars.

ROVER 2200: FACTS AND FIGURES

Pressed-steel base unit with unstressed skin panels; four doors and five seats. Front engine driving rear wheels.

Engine	2205cc Rover 4-cylinder, with 98bhp at 5,000rpm (2200SC); 115bhp at 5,000rpm (2200TC)
Gearbox	Four-speed manual; optional three-speed automatic on 2200SC

Dimensions

Length	4,554mm (179.3in)
Wheelbase	2,626mm (103.4in)
Width	1,676mm (66in)
Height	1,403mm (55.25in)
Kerb weight	1,280kg (2,822lb) (2200SC) 1,295kg (2,855lb) (2200SC Automatic) 1,283kg (2,829lb) (2200TC)

Rover 2200 – Statistics

0–60mph	9.1sec (2200SC manual) 10.4sec (2200SC automatic) 8.0sec (2200TC)
Max. speed	101mph (162.5km/h) (2200SC) 107mph (172km/h) (2200TC)
Fuel consumption	29mpg (9.8ltr/100km) (2200SC manual) 22mpg (12.9ltr/100km) (2200SC automatic) 24mpg (11.8ltr/100km) (2200TC)

Production numbers 31,810

IF YOU WANT ONE....

Everything said above about the Rover 3500 and 3500S also applies to the 2200 models – except that the 4-cylinder cars do not destroy their own gearboxes like the 3500S. It is also worth knowing that, unlike the earlier 2000TC, the 2200TC idles smoothly when properly set up, even though as a big 4-cylinder it is not perfectly smooth.

by 1973, having been introduced ten years earlier, they were still highly regarded, and Rover remained a prestigious make. Their main failing was a lack of legroom for rear-seat passengers.

The last examples were built in 1976, and these Rovers were replaced by the 6-cylinder models of the Rover SD1 that arrived in spring 1977.

Rover SD1 (1976–86)

By the end of the 1960s, Rover had started work on their P10 project, planned as a replacement for the P6 range and for autumn 1974 introduction. Chief stylist David Bache wanted to create a fastback design with a big hatchback, which would be ground-breaking in that class of car. In the meantime, however, Triumph were working on a replacement for their 2000/2500 range, always a direct rival for the Rover P6.

By late 1970, top management at British Leyland had realized what was happening: a classic design competition in February 1971 resulted in the Rover proposal being chosen, and Triumph being given the job of developing new 6-cylinder engines for it. The two engineering teams were instructed to work together on the car, which briefly became RT1 (Rover-Triumph No. 1) before becoming SD1 (Specialist Division No. 1) in April.

During 1972, David Bache realized the styling lacked impact, and he radically altered it by borrowing some ideas from Ital-

RIGHT: The stunning shape of the Rover SD1 is seen against the background of the new assembly plant at Solihull where it was built. This is an early 3500 model, with the optional alloy wheels.

BELOW: The 3500 Vanden Plas EFi model was the flagship of the SD1 range. It combined strong performance with a luxury specification.

ian supercars of the day – notably the Ferrari Daytona, which inspired the overall profile and the distinctive wrapround front sidelights and the scallop in the body side. Several delays later, the car was finally announced in summer 1976, initially only as a 3500 model with the latest version of the Rover V8 engine. Later, the 6-cylinder models would follow as the 2300 and 2600.

In line with 1970s thinking, the interior was very plain, and disappointed established Rover buyers. Build quality was often dreadful, and sales never reached British Leyland's original projections. By the end of the decade, funds were found for more luxurious appointments in top models, and the V8-S (1979) and Rover Vanden Plas (1980) delivered more of what the buyers expected. Unfortunately, build quality was still poor – and that, combined with a thin dealer network, meant that the SD1's foray into North America was ended prematurely in summer 1981 after just 1,254 sales in a year.

British Leyland management finally gripped the problem and pulled the SD1 out of Rover's Solihull factory (where it was being built alongside the Triumph TR7). From the end of the year, production restarted at the former Morris plant in Cowley, and the cars built there quickly demonstrated how good the fundamental SD1 design really was.

There were model changes and specification upgrades to support the change in production standards. A deeper hatchback window, flush headlights, and a chin spoiler on top models were all new. A 2000 model with the O-series 4-cylinder engine joined the range for 1982, together with a 2400SD Turbo, which used a 4-cylinder turbocharged diesel engine bought in from VM in Italy. These helped sales on the European continent, and were followed in autumn 1982 by a new Vitesse model, with an injected version of the V8 engine giving 190bhp and 135mph (217km/h) performance.

This started life as a 'homologation special' to allow Rover to take the injected car racing in the European championships, and at the end of production a number of cars were produced with a special 'twin plenum' specification (it was actually twin throttles) so that this specification could also be used in racing. From 1984 the engine also found its way into a flagship model called the Vanden Plas EFi, which combined performance with the top level of luxury.

These final SD1s showed the car's true potential – but it was all too late. There had been thoughts about reskinning the SD1 for a mid-1980s replacement, but these were cancelled when British Leyland's links with Honda gave birth to Project XX for a new, executive-class saloon. That became the Rover 800, and it replaced the SD1 from 1986. Meanwhile, the SD1 tooling was sold to Standard Motors in India, who briefly produced a version called the Standard 2000 with a locally manufactured engine.

The SD1's hatchback was ground-breaking in a car of this class. Unfortunately, poor build quality destroyed Rover's hopes for the model.

IF YOU WANT ONE....

The Rover SD1 is still a very practical car for everyday use, although its numbers have been hugely diminished by owners who have despaired of examples with multiple problems. The best ones to go for are the V8 and 2600 models, and the full experience comes with the Vanden Plas trim level. There are several specialists who support these cars, and there are also two clubs: the Rover SD1 Club (www.roversd1club.net), and the Rover Sports Register (www.thersr.co.uk).

Key purchasing points:

- Look for rust in wheel-arches, door bottoms and at the bottom of the tailgate; it can be more serious in sills, front inner wings, front chassis legs, and around rear radius arm mountings
- Sunroofs, windscreens and tail-lights all leak – the latter into the boot; check for damage to the plastic bumpers of 'Series II' cars, and to the front spoiler if fitted
- Few diesels survive; check for top-end rattle and overheating in V8s, and remember that sixes have a cambelt to renew and can suffer from top-end oil starvation if poorly maintained
- Early interior trim is fragile, especially the door trims and the quirky choke lever, and headlinings can sag
- Electrics were always a weakness, so check that everything works properly

ROVER SD1: FACTS AND FIGURES

Pressed-steel monocoque with four doors; five seats. Front engine driving rear wheels.

Engine 2000: 1994cc O-series 4-cylinder, with 101bhp at 5,250rpm
2300: 2350cc Rover-Triumph PE146 6-cylinder, with 123bhp at 5,000rpm
2600: 2597cc Rover-Triumph PE166 6-cylinder, with 136bhp at 5,000rpm
3500: 3528cc Rover V8, with 155bhp at 5,250rpm; 133bhp at 5,000rpm (North American models)
Vitesse & Vanden Plas EFi: 3528cc Rover V8, with 190bhp at 5,280rpm
2400 diesel: 2393cc VM HR492 4-cylinder turbo-charged diesel, with 90bhp at 4,000rpm

Gearbox Five-speed manual, except four-speed manual on 2300 before 1982; optional three-speed automatic

Dimensions

Length	4,699mm (185in)
Wheelbase	2,814mm (110.8in)
Width	1,778mm (70in)
Height	1,397mm (55in)
Kerb weight	1,310kg (2,888lb) (2000) 1,264–1,369kg (2,717–3,018lb) (2300) 1,527kg (3,366lb) (2400SD Turbo) 1,300–1,475kg (2,866–3,252lb) (2600) 1,305–1,414kg (2,877–3,117lb) (3500) 1,439kg (3,173lb) (Vitesse)

Rover SD1: Statistics

0–60mph	12.4sec (2000) 11.9sec (2300 manual) 14.2sec (2400SD Turbo) 10.4sec (2600 manual) 8.9sec (3500 manual) 9.8sec (3500 automatic) 7.1sec (Vitesse, manual) 8.9sec (Vanden Plas EFi)
Max. speed	104mph (167km/h) (2000) 109mph (175km/h) (2300 manual) 103.4mph (166km/h) (2400SD Turbo) 116.1mph (187km/h) (2600 manual) 125mph (201km/h) (3500 manual) 119mph (191km/h) (3500 automatic) 135.4mph (218km/h) (Vitesse, manual) 129.5mph (208km/h) (Vanden Plas EFi)
Fuel consumption	22.8mpg (12.4ltr/100km) (2000) 24mpg (11.8ltr/100km) (2300 manual) 29.6mpg (9.6ltr/100km) (2400SD Turbo) 18.9mpg (15ltr/100km) (2600 manual) 22.5mpg (12.6ltr/100km) (3500 manual) 20mpg (14.2ltr/100km) (3500 automatic) 22.3mpg (12.7ltr/100km) (Vitesse, manual) 20.2mpg (14ltr/100km) (Vanden Plas EFi)

Production numbers
303,345

Rover 200 series (1984–89)

The car that became the Rover 200 series in 1984 was planned as early as November 1981, when British Leyland and Honda agreed to work together on a replacement for the Acclaim, which would be ready for launch in 1984. In practice they chose to work on Honda's new Ballade, for which the Japanese company had already done most of the groundwork, and so the BL input to the new car was somewhat limited. It was, though, greater than it had been for the Acclaim itself, while falling well short of the full joint engineering programme that would be put in place for the Rover 800 and its Honda Legend twin.

The new Ballade was to be a compact four-door, three-box saloon with front-wheel drive. Its basic lines had already been settled, and were very much in the Japanese idiom. Nevertheless, BL had plenty to do to adapt the car for UK manufacture and to suit its own customers, and the Ballade became known at Longbridge as the SD3 project, and as the 'new Acclaim' or 'Acclaim facelift'.

However, it would never be given Triumph badges. Production of Triumph sports cars had stopped in the summer of 1981, and by the following summer BL had decided to drop the Triumph marque altogether. So the SD3 came to market as a Rover, the additional prestige of that name allowing BL – Austin Rover from 1982 – to charge higher prices. In practice, SD3 was mid-way

Some buyers found it hard to accept the Acclaim's replacement as a Rover, but that was how it was badged. This is a 216S model, with a British engine in the Japanese-designed bodyshell.

IF YOU WANT ONE....

The Rover 200 series was a competent, small family car without a lot of character, and it was well respected when new. However, such qualities do not make a classic, and few enthusiasts bother with surviving examples today. Although Rover no longer exists as a source of spares, many mechanical items are available from Honda, and specialists can often help with other items. There is no specific club for these cars (even though there is one for their R8 Rover 200 successors), but owners will be welcome in the Rover Sports Register (www.thersr.co.uk).

Key purchasing points:

- Severe rusting in the structure has accounted for many of these cars: check the sills and jacking points, floorpans, suspension mounting points and the boot floor
- Cosmetic rusting can also be severe, as the panels are of quite light-gauge metal: examine wheel-arches, front wings, door bottoms, bonnet leading edge and boot-lid trailing edge; even the windscreen pillars can rot
- The 1.3-litre Honda engine is generally very reliable and long-lasting, but it needs regular cambelt changes and the right anti-freeze to prevent aluminium corrosion
- The 1.6-litre S-series engine is prone to top-end oil leaks, noisy tappets, and head gasket problems, as well as ECU and electronic sensor faults; misbehaving EFi engines will need specialist attention
- Interior trim generally wears well, but replacement will involve finding a donor car, or major expense with a specialist

between the Maestro and Montego models in size, but it would cost more than either of them. Although many traditional Rover buyers considered this was moving the brand down-market, there were more than enough buyers who welcomed the availability of the aspirational brand at a more affordable price.

The SD3 project focused on designing new front and rear panelwork, modifying the interior, retuning the suspension, and engineering the car to accept BL engines. It was ready for launch in June 1984, by which time Austin Rover had developed a new model naming strategy, and the SD3 became a Rover 200.

Only the 213 models were launched initially, with Honda's 70bhp EV2 1.3-litre engine and three levels of trim: base, S and SE. There was a 213 Vanden Plas briefly, too. The 216 models followed in March 1985, with British Leyland's own 1.6-litre S-series engine in either 85bhp carburettor tune, or with fuel injection and 102bhp. These had four levels of trim: 216S and 216SE models had the carburettor engine, but the 216 Vanden Plas EFi and the 216 Vitesse came with the injected engine. The Vitesse also had a deeper front spoiler, stylish alloy wheels, and Vitesse decals on its rear doors. All models came with five-speed Honda manual gearboxes as standard; automatic 213s had a Honda three-speed gearbox, and automatic 216 derivatives used a German-built ZF automatic.

The 200-series cars went through minimal production changes over the next five years. In October 1986 the boot lid was altered to give a lower sill height, a glass sunroof became available, and the interior was restyled. Then in May 1988 there was a Sprint special edition of the 216. Beyond that, no changes were really needed. They attracted the nickname of Rondas (Rover-Hondas) in some quarters.

The 200s sold very well, and at times there were waiting lists of up to three months. They were regularly among the top ten best-selling cars in Britain, and did a lot to improve the public perception of Rover quality. In fact, the Rover 200 played an important part in the longer-term survival of what had once been British Leyland.

ROVER 200: FACTS AND FIGURES

Pressed-steel monocoque with four doors; five seats. Transversely mounted front engine driving front wheels.

Engine	(213) 1342cc Honda EV2 4-cylinder, with 70bhp at 6,000rpm (216) 1598cc S-series 4-cylinder, with 85bhp at 5,600rpm (216 EFi) 1598cc S-series 4-cylinder, with 102bhp at 5,600rpm
Gearbox	Honda five-speed manual; optional three-speed Honda automatic (213), or four-speed ZF automatic (216 and 216 EFi)

Dimensions

Length	4,156mm (163.6in)
Wheelbase	2,450mm (96.5in)
Width	1,623mm (63.9in)
Height	1,378mm (54.3in)
Kerb weight	860–884kg (1,896–1,950lb), dependent on the model (213) 941kg (2,075lb) (216S) 946kg (2,086lb) (Vitesse)

Rover 200: Statistics

0–60mph	11.7sec (213) 10.1sec (216) 9.2sec (216 Vitesse)
Max. speed	96mph (155km/h) (213) 102mph (164km/h) (216) 112mph (180km/h) (216 Vitesse)
Fuel consumption	41mpg (6.9ltr/100km) (213) 35mpg (8.1ltr/100km) (216)

Production numbers 418,000

THE TRIUMPH-BADGED MODELS

British Leyland saw Triumph as their manufacturer of affordable sports cars, fitting in below Jaguar in the sports-car hierarchy. MG, as explained in the section on that marque, was to some extent suppressed. Rover was chosen as the marque for executive and large saloons (as long as they did not rival Jaguars), but Triumph was allowed to continue as a maker of what would now be called 'premium' medium-sized saloons.

Even so, the Triumph sports range was eventually severely rationalized. At the start of the British Leyland era, Triumph had large (TR) and small (Spitfire) roadsters; it had the GT6 coupé, and swiftly followed up with the Stag grand tourer. But that was far too many, and the 1975 TR7 replaced all except the Stag, which lingered on for only two years more.

On the medium saloon front, the front-wheel-drive 1500 was simplified into a successful rear-wheel-drive range that was broadened to provide Triumph models with both larger and smaller engines. The large saloon range of 2000 and 2500 types remained available until 1977, when it gave way to the 6-cylinder (Triumph-engined) versions of the Rover SD1. And then Triumph badges were applied to the first car to be built under the alliance with Honda, which was the 1981 Acclaim.

As for Triumph itself, the company had been merged with Rover in 1971, and although it survived as a marque into the 1980s, it was simply another name in the British Leyland catalogue. The old Triumph factory at Canley was closed in 1980 (although the site was retained as an administrative centre), and when Acclaim production ended in summer 1984, the Triumph name disappeared with it.

Triumph TR6 (1969–76)

The Triumph TR6 just about qualifies as a British Leyland car, although it was developed during the days when Triumph belonged to the earlier Leyland Motor Company. Available from early 1969, it used the same chassis frame as its TR5 and TR250 predecessors, plus the same body centre-section. However, the front and rear ends had been restyled by Karmann in Germany to look more modern and more aggressive.

The TR6 came with Triumph's 2.5-litre 6-cylinder engine, initially for most countries in the same 150bhp form as in the TR5, with Lucas fuel injection. However, the injected engine could not be made to meet US emissions regulations, and so TR6s shipped to the USA and Canada had a tamer carburettor version, with just 104bhp.

A few changes were made during production. Changed gearbox ratios arrived in autumn 1971, but the biggest changes came a year later, when the injection engine was detuned to 125bhp to improve drivability, and a new type of overdrive became available. A chin spoiler was added, along with a new type of overdrive and a revised facia, but wire wheels disappeared from the options list. The last major change affected North American models, which were saddled with big black bumpers for 1975 and later model years.

The TR6 sold very well indeed, partly perhaps because there was almost nothing else like it on the market; it has often been described as the last of the hairy-chested British sports cars. It became the best selling of all the TR models,

Triumph's TR6 continued the great traditions of the TR range, despite its sometimes troublesome fuel injection system.
MAGIC CAR PICS

A removable hardtop was optional for the TR6 models, and is seen here in a publicity shot from the early 1970s.

although its sales total was then surpassed by that of the TR7 that replaced it. The TR7 – quite a different proposition – actually arrived in late 1975, and the TR6 was discontinued for the UK at that stage. However, the North American cars remained in production until mid-1976 to provide a smooth transition to the new model in the showrooms.

IF YOU WANT ONE....

The Triumph TR6 is a classic favourite, and although it is not fast by modern standards, it can be exhilarating to drive. Plenty of spares and specialist support are available; the clubs are the TR Drivers' Club (www.trdrivers.com), the TR Register (www.tr-register.co.uk), Club Triumph (www.clubtriumph.org.uk) and the Triumph Sports Six Club (www.tssc.org.uk) – although the cars are welcome in any club for the Triumph marque.

Key purchasing points:

- Look for rust in the joints between the rear wings and rear deck, or for signs of filler; body side curvature should be the same on each side!
- Check the chassis frame for signs of accident damage, often betrayed by ripples in the side members or by misalignment around the T-shaped pressing in front of the differential
- Check the chassis for rust, too, especially where the trailing arms are attached to the chassis
- Driveline clunks may be caused by torn differential mounts or by failing UJs in the propshaft or driveshafts; rear hub bearings often fail
- If the clutch will not disengage properly, check for a worn thrust washer by levering the front pulley with the engine off; the main source of fuel injection problems is the injection pump, and many owners fit a modern Bosch replacement

TRIUMPH TR6: FACTS AND FIGURES

Separate chassis with two-door roadster body; two seats. Front engine driving rear wheels.

Engine	2498cc 6-cylinder, with 150bhp at 5,500rpm (early models) or 125bhp at 5,000rpm (from mid-1972); North American engines with 104bhp at 4,500rpm (106bhp at 4,900rpm from mid-1972) and carburettors instead of fuel injection
Gearbox	Four-speed manual, with optional overdrive

Dimensions

Length	3,950mm (155.5in)
Wheelbase	2,235mm (88in)
Width	1,550mm (61in)
Height	1,270mm (50in)
Kerb weight	1,122kg (2,473lb) 1,084kg (2,390lb) (North American cars, 1969–74) 1,106kg (2,438lb) (North American cars, 1975–76)

Triumph TR6: Statistics

Performance	
0–60mph	8.2sec
Max. speed	119mph (191.5km/h)
Fuel consumption	20mpg (14ltr/100km)

Production numbers 94,619

Triumph 2000, 2500 and 2.5PI (1969–77)

Restyled front and rear ends distinguished the Mark 2 versions of the big Triumph saloons. This is a 2500S model from the mid-1970s.

As before, there were capacious estate versions of the Mark 2 Triumph range, converted for them by Carbodies.

New versions of the Triumph 2000 saloon family were introduced under British Leyland in October 1969. Although their engines were carried over from the earlier models, the Mark 2 Triumph saloons had an extensively revised bodyshell, with new front and rear ends by its original designer, Michelotti. The front and rear ends were deliberately designed to resemble those of the Stag, which would be introduced a year later.

These revised models were known as the Innsbruck types, after the code name used during their development. As before, there were both saloon and estate types, a minor detail being that the estates retained their original rear panels and so were now slightly shorter than the Mark 2 saloons with their lengthened tails. There were also now four models rather than the two of the final Mark I range. The 1998cc 2000 remained the core of the range, but above it were three models with the 2498cc engine: the 2500, 2500TC and 2.5 PI. Confusingly, both 2500 and 2500TC had twin carburettors, and the TC letters simply indicated higher levels of equipment.

The 2.5 PI remained the quickest of the new models, but its Lucas fuel-injection system was notoriously unreliable – just as it was in the contemporary TR6 sports cars which had the same engine. Nevertheless, when it was functioning as intended, it was an excellent engine, and in 1970 a pair of 'works' 2.5 PI saloons claimed second and fourth places in the London to Mexico World Cup Rally.

Only detail production changes were made to the range before June 1975, when a new model called the 2500S replaced both the 2500TC and the 2.5 PI, whose petrol-injection equipment had always been a source of problems. Triumph had for some time been planning to re-engine these cars with variants of a new ohc 6-cylinder they had been developing, but British Leyland earmarked that for the Rover SD1, and so the 2000 and 2500S remained unchanged until their production ended in 1977. The 6-cylinder Rovers were their replacements in the British Leyland corporate product plan.

Even though production at Canley ended in 1977, overseas assembly of Mark 2 Triumphs from CKD carried on for another couple of years. In New Zealand, the New Zealand Motor Corporation at Nelson assembled 7,977 Mark 2 2000s between January 1970 and December 1973, plus 10,776 2500TC models from April 1973 to April 1978, and 576 2500S models from April 1978 to March 1979. In South Africa, 5,723 Mark 2 2000s were assembled between 1970 and 1975, plus 922 2.5 PI Mark 2 models between 1971 and 1975. Between 1973 and 1976, locally assembled 2500TC models were sold with the name of Triumph Chicane, and the Triumph Chicane Mark 2 of 1976–78 was a locally assembled 2500S. These two models accounted for a further 5,733 cars built in South Africa.

IF YOU WANT ONE....

Like its contemporaries and rivals of the Rover P6 range, the Triumph 2000 family is still viable for everyday use, although of course its dynamics are nothing like those of a modern car. The 6-cylinder engines are smooth and torquey, although the injected ones (shared with the TR6) can be troublesome. There are plenty of spares and specialist support available, and the cars are welcome in several Triumph clubs, but also have their own, the Triumph 2000 2500 2.5 Register (http://triumph2000register.co.uk).

Key purchasing points:

- Rust attacks the rear of the sills, the front floor pans, and the boot floor; also check the mountings for the IRS, the top mountings for the MacPherson struts, and the inner wings ahead of the front wheels
- Neglected oil changes cause rocker shaft wear; timing chains clatter when old, and a worn crankshaft washer (see TR6) needs urgent attention
- Sliding splines on the rear axle shafts can seize, which will produce a lurch when cornering
- Back-axle whine results from loss of lubricant when an oil seal fails
- Erratic overdrive operation is caused by a failed solenoid (difficult to get at) or by oil that needs changing

TRIUMPH 2000 MARK 2 FAMILY: FACTS AND FIGURES

Pressed-steel monocoque with four doors; five seats. Front engine driving rear wheels.

Engine	2000: 1998cc 6-cylinder, with 84bhp at 5,000rpm 2000TC: 1998cc 6-cylinder, with 91bhp at 4,750rpm 2500: 2498cc Triumph 6-cylinder, with 99bhp at 4,700rpm 2.5PI: 2498cc Triumph 6-cylinder, with 132bhp at 5,500rpm
Gearbox	Four-speed manual with optional overdrive; optional three-speed automatic

Length	4,630mm (182.3in) (Saloon) 4,502mm (177.25in) (Estate)
Wheelbase	2,692mm (106in)
Width	1,664mm (65.5in)
Height	1,422mm (56in)
Kerb weight	1188kg (2,620lb) (2000 Saloon) 1,247kg (2,750lb) (2000 Estate) 1,252kg (2,760lb) (2.5PI Saloon) 1,303kg (2,873lb) (2.5PI Estate) 1,216kg (2,681lb) (2500TC Saloon) 1,270kg (2,801lb) (2500TC Estate)

Triumph 2000 Mark 2 Family: Statistics

0–60mph	15.8sec (2000 Estate) 11.0sec (2.5PI Saloon) 13.8sec (2500TC Saloon)
Max. speed	93mph (150km/h) (2000 Estate) 110mph (177km/h) (2.5PI Saloon) 104mph (167km/h) (2500TC Saloon)
Fuel consumption	23mpg (12.3ltr/100km) (2000 Estate) 18–25mpg (15.7–11ltr/100km) (2.5PI Saloon) 23mpg (12.3ltr/100km) (2500TC Saloon)

Production numbers

194,978 overall, broken down as follows:

2000 (1969–1977)	104,580
2.5 PI (1969–1975)	49,742
2500TC (1974–1977)	32,492
2500S (1975–1977)	8,164

Triumph 1500 (1970–1973)

As early as 1967, Triumph began work on a bigger-engined version of their front-wheel-drive 1300 model, whose sales had been disappointing. Their thinking was that this bigger engine would help to justify the higher price of the front-wheel-drive design, and in the meantime they would develop a cheaper rear-wheel-drive car to take over from the 1300.

The new front-wheel drive car was to use a long-stroke version of the existing 4-cylinder engine, but would not have the independent rear suspension of the 1300. To distinguish the new model visually from the old, Michelotti came up with a restyled front end that incorporated a vertically divided grille and twin headlights. He also lengthened the tail to give a larger boot, and provided this with horizontally mounted rear light units. An interior redesign brought a different dashboard and door cards, although the upmarket touch of wooden door cappings was retained.

The Triumph 1500 was introduced in 1970, at the same time as the first of the rear-wheel-drive models. From 1972, power went up from the original 61bhp to 65bhp, thanks to a different carburettor on a new inlet manifold. The nose badge of these cars also switched to silver from

The front-wheel-drive Triumph 1500 was probably one of the most attractive versions of the Michelotti-designed medium saloon.

the black type on the original cars. However, Triumph's commitment to its rear-wheel-drive range was now total, and the 1500 was withdrawn in 1973 to be replaced by the rear-wheel-drive 1500TC.

IF YOU WANT ONE....

The Triumph 1500 always presented itself as a cut above rivals such as the BMC 1100s and 1300s, and it was certainly better equipped. Inexplicably perhaps, the cars have never attracted a very strong enthusiast following. Spares back-up is far better on the mechanical side than for body and trim elements, and an indispensable aid to ownership is membership of the Triumph Dolomite Club (www.triumphdolomite.co.uk), although owners are also welcome in several other Triumph clubs.

Key purchasing points:

- Check for rust in the sills, which have three-piece construction and have often been patched up with oversills
- Rust also attacks the bottoms of the front wings, and the wing strengthener behind the road wheel; check around the fuel tank, too
- Engines are fairly robust, and a certain amount of timing-chain rattle was always normal
- Synchromesh baulk rings wear, particularly on first gear
- Hard-used cars will have knocked out their CV joints

TRIUMPH 1500: FACTS AND FIGURES

Pressed-steel monocoque with four doors; five seats.
Front engine driving front wheels.

Engine	1493cc 4-cylinder, with 61bhp at 5,000rpm; 65bhp at 5,000rpm from October 1971
Gearbox	Four-speed manual

Length	4,115mm (162in)
Wheelbase	2,454mm (96.6in)
Width	1,567mm (61.7in)
Height	1,372mm (54in)
Kerb weight	965kg (2,128lb)

Triumph 1500: Statistics

0–60mph	16.5sec
Max. speed	85mph (137km/h)
Fuel consumption	28mpg (10ltr/100km)

Production numbers

66,353

Triumph Toledo (1970–76)

As explained above in the entry for the Triumph 1500, the front-wheel-drive 1300 on which it was based was replaced by a rear-wheel-drive 1300 that used a comprehensively re-engineered version of the same bodyshell. The floorpan was changed to accept a conventional propshaft and a live rear axle with coil springs instead of independent suspension. The shell was also converted from four doors to just two, and for good measure the front-end styling was altered to take rectangular headlamps. The cost cutting that was essential to the exercise was clear from the all-drum braking system and the loss of wood trim from the doors, and of course only a manual gearbox was available.

The new mid-size Triumph was introduced in September 1970 with the name of Toledo, and reverted to the short boot of the old 1300 (the new 1500 had a longer tail). However, while UK buyers were still only able to have two doors and the 1296cc engine, in March 1971 a four-door Toledo was announced for export with a 1500 engine in 61bhp single-carburettor or 64bhp twin-carburettor forms. The four-door body became available for UK Toledos that autumn, but the larger engine did not. Four-door models gained radial tyres, but the two-doors retained their original cross-ply types, and the four-doors also gained wraparound bumpers, while the two-doors again did not – at least, not yet.

The Triumph Toledo had rear-wheel drive, but had a short-tail bodyshell instead of the long-tail type seen on the Dolomites. It also had single rather than twin headlights. This is a 1975 car. MAGIC CAR PICS

Toledos were built at Triumph's Liverpool no. 2 (Speke) factory in the beginning, but in late 1974 their place on the assembly lines was taken by the new TR7 sports car, and the Toledos moved to Canley. The two-door body ended production at the same time, so all later Toledos had four doors. The

IF YOU WANT ONE....

The Toledo was designed as an entry-level mid-size saloon for the Triumph range, and as such it was never intended to set any pulses racing. It still does not, although it is uncommon enough now for good ones to attract some attention from classic car enthusiasts. Many of its mechanical elements and some of its body panels are shared with other Triumph models, which eases the problem of parts availability, but some parts unique to the Toledo will be hard to find. Membership of the Triumph Dolomite Club (www.triumphdolomite.co.uk) is recommended, although owners are also welcome in several other Triumph clubs.

Key purchasing points:

- Severe rust makes a Toledo beyond economic repair, and the most expensive areas to repair are the sills (especially at their front ends), the rear of the front inner wings (which intrude on the footwells), and the nose panel that carries the hinges for the bonnet
- On four-door cars, check for rust in the D posts, and make sure that the bases of the B/C posts are solid where they meet the sills
- Other rust areas are the wheel-arches and door bottoms, and the folded-over seams of the bonnet and boot lid; some cars rust in the lower windscreen pillars, too
- The 1296cc engines suffer from worn crankshaft thrust washers, which must be attended to as soon as possible; rock the front pulley to test for movement
- Seat coverings are brushed nylon, which will suffer with sunlight and age, and may tear as well

TRIUMPH TOLEDO: FACTS AND FIGURES

Pressed-steel monocoque with four doors; five seats.
Front engine driving rear wheels.

Engine	1296cc 4-cylinder, with 58bhp at 5,300rpm 1493cc 4-cylinder, with 61bhp at 5,000rpm; 65bhp at 5,000rpm from October 1971
Gearbox	Four-speed manual

Dimensions

Length	3,962mm (156in)
Wheelbase	2,464mm (97in)
Width	1,575mm (62in)
Height	1,372mm (54in)
Kerb weight	890kg (1,960lb)

Triumph Toledo: Statistics

0–60mph	17.1sec
Max. speed	83mph (133.5km/h)
Fuel consumption	34mpg (8.3ltr/100km)

Production numbers

Around 96,000 (exact figures not available)

1975-model Toledos took on the single-rail gearbox from the Spitfire 1500, and were facelifted with a black grille and body trims plus higher levels of equipment.

This remained the case until March 1976, when the 'short nose, short tail' Toledo body went out of production altogether, and Triumph based its new Dolomite range on a long nose, long tail shell. The new range would include direct replacements for the Toledo models called the Dolomite 1300 and Dolomite 1500.

Nevertheless, production of the Toledo continued until 1977 in New Zealand, where CKD bodyshells were still being built up into complete cars until stocks were exhausted.

Triumph Dolomite and 1500TC (1971–80)

One of the last major decisions that Harry Webster took at Triumph before moving to Austin-Morris was the one to focus on rear-wheel drive for the mid-size Triumph saloons. When the existing Michelotti-designed front-wheel-drive bodyshell was re-engineered for rear-wheel drive, the first of the new range was the Toledo, discussed above. Then in 1971 came the first of Triumph's planned Dolomite range of rear-wheel drive cars.

Dolomite

The first Dolomite was announced at the October 1971 Motor Show, but industrial unrest delayed its availability for a year. Confusingly, the car combined the four-lamp, long-tail bodystyle of the front-wheel-drive 1500 with a rear-wheel-drive floorpan. Its task was to replace the Vitesse, and its name was taken from a legendary Triumph model of the 1930s.

Re-engineered for rear-wheel drive, this was Michelotti's medium saloon as a Dolomite 1850 HL in 1980.

It came with a high level of standard equipment, and was distinguished by black vinyl D-pillars and a black tail panel. There were new wheel trims as well. The engine in this car was Triumph's new ohc 1.8-litre slant four, the engine that the company was already supplying to Saab for that company's 99 model. As an alternative to the standard four-speed gearbox, buyers could order a three-speed automatic.

From March 1973, overdrive was made available as an option, and soon after that, more members of the rear-wheel-drive family were introduced. In 1975, a front spoiler was added. From autumn 1975, when the whole Dolomite range was overhauled and given new names, the car was renamed a Dolomite 1850HL; at this change it gained another design of wheel trim. It remained available until 1980.

1500TC

Introduced in 1973, the 1500TC had the Dolomite body and rear-wheel-drive floorpan, with a twin-carburettor version of Triumph's 1.5-litre engine. The name was designed to show that this was related to, but more powerful than, the old front-wheel-drive 1500 that it replaced – but really it just caused confusion. Or perhaps that was the idea…

It even looked like the old 1500, retaining that car's wheel trims, and would do so until autumn 1975, when it was replaced in the big range reshuffle that year. From that point, it picked up the more luxurious specification of the Dolomite 1850 and, logically at last, was renamed a Dolomite 1500HL.

Dolomite Sprint

The original Dolomite was not quite fast enough to compete with the BMW 2002 that was its main rival, although it was certainly more keenly priced. So a more powerful version was planned, with a new 2-litre version of the slant-four engine featuring an advanced 16-valve cylinder head that was drawn up under Spen King's leadership of the company. A 1972 introduction was envisaged, but in practice the car arrived in June 1973.

Dressed up with alloy wheels and a vinyl roof, the Triumph Dolomite Sprint delivered what it promised, thanks to a clever 16-valve cylinder-head design.

Smaller-engined Dolomites followed, replacing the front-wheel-drive cars. This is a Dolomite 1500 from the mid-1970s.

On test, the new engine gave upwards of 135bhp, but production examples could not all meet this figure. So the plan to call the car a Dolomite 135 was dropped at the last minute, and the car was renamed a Dolomite Sprint. Trim was similar to the standard 8-valve Dolomite of the time, but there were special features. These included a front spoiler, alloy wheels (the first on a British production car), lowered suspension, and twin exhausts. Bodyside coachlines added distinction, and the vinyl quarter pillars were matched by a full vinyl roof covering. Seats were upholstered in the same cloth that was now used on the 8-valve Dolomite.

On the mechanical side, there were bigger rear brakes and harder brake pads, plus a load-sensing valve. Gearbox and differential were those of the Triumph 2000 and TR ranges, but with close-ratio gears. A limited-slip differential was optional, and so were overdrive and an automatic gearbox.

The first examples were available only in Mimosa Yellow, which certainly got them noticed; other colours joined the range in 1974. The first round of revisions came in May 1975, when overdrive and tinted window glass were standardized. So were body side trims and some cabin upgrades. Headrests, a radio, and a laminated windscreen became standard in March 1976, and the final changes came just before production ended in 1980, when twin rear fog lamps were added to meet new UK legislation.

Customers rapidly recognized that the Sprint was a quite sensational car; it was also developed as a race-winning Group I saloon. To homologate the high performance parts that the works-supported cars needed, BL's Special Tuning division made them available as extras. They included bigger carburettors, a less restrictive exhaust system, and competition camshafts.

Dolomite 1300 and 1500

The 1300 and 1500 were added to the range in 1976, and replaced the Toledo models. So from that point on the Dolomite range consisted of five models: from the bottom, the hierarchy was now Dolomite 1300, Dolomite 1500 (single carburettor), Dolomite 1500HL (twin carburettor), Dolomite 1850HL, and Dolomite Sprint. The HL models and the Sprint had higher levels of equipment than the two entry-level models.

The 1300 was essentially the old Toledo (see separate entry), but now with the long-tail bodyshell of the other Dolomites, and only available with four doors. The 1500 was a new model with the single-carburettor 1493cc engine, but the same low level of trim and equipment as the 1300. Both were distinguished by the rectangular headlamp nose of the old Toledo. Overdrive and an automatic gearbox were options for the 1500, but not for the 1300.

In 1979, a special edition Dolomite 1500SE was introduced, with the basic 1500 single-headlamp bodyshell finished in black with silver side stripes and SE decals. There were 2,163 of these cars, which had Spitfire road wheels and a front spoiler, the SE designation being justified by their more luxurious interior trim that incorporated burr walnut and grey velour upholstery.

The End

Dolomite production ended in August 1980, when BL closed the old Triumph factory at Canley. Just over a year later, the whole Dolomite range was replaced by the single model Triumph Acclaim, which was a very different kind of car.

There had been thoughts of replacing the Dolomite much earlier, notably with a new hatchback saloon that was devel-

TRIUMPH DOLOMITE AND 1500TC: FACTS AND FIGURES

Pressed-steel monocoque with four doors; five seats.
Front engine driving rear wheels.

Engine 1300: 1296cc 4-cylinder, with 58bhp at 5,300rpm
1500: 1493cc 4-cylinder, with 65bhp at 5,000rpm
1500TC: 64bhp at 5,000rpm
1500HL: 1493cc 4-cylinder, with 71bhp at 5,500rpm
1850: 1854cc 4-cylinder, with 91bhp at 5,200rpm
Sprint: 1998cc 4-cylinder, with 127bhp at 5,700rpm

Gearbox Four-speed manual; overdrive optional from March 1973 on all models except the Dolomite 1300; overdrive standard on the Sprint from May 1975 Optional three-speed automatic on all models except the Dolomite 1300

Dimensions

Length 4,115mm (162in)
Width 1,568mm (61.75in)
Height 1,372mm (54in)
Wheelbase 2,454mm (96.6in)
Kerb weight 864kg (1,905lb) (Dolomite 1300)
935kg (2,061lb) (1500TC)
951kg (2,097lb) (Dolomite 1500)
956kg (2,108lb) (Dolomite 1500HL)
965kg (2,127lb) (Dolomite and Dolomite 1850HL)
1004kg (2,214lb) (Dolomite Sprint)
1,941kg (2,295lb) (Dolomite Sprint with overdrive)

Triumph Dolomite and 1500TC: Statistics

0–60mph 20.1sec (1300)
14.2sec (1500)
11.1sec (Dolomite and Dolomite 1850HL)
8.4sec (Dolomite Sprint)
Max. speed 83mph (133.5km/h) (1300)
91mph (146km/h) (1500)
100mph (161km/h) (Dolomite and Dolomite 1850HL)
119mph (191km/h) (Dolomite Sprint)
Fuel consumption 28mpg (10ltr/100km) (1850)
23mpg (12.3ltr/100km) (Sprint)

Production numbers

25,549 (1500TC)
32,031 (Dolomite 1300)
43,235 (Dolomite 1500)
79,010 (Dolomite 1850)
22,941 (Dolomite Sprint)

IF YOU WANT ONE....

The star of the Triumph Dolomite range was undoubtedly the Dolomite Sprint, the smaller-engined models really being little more than upmarket mid-size saloons. As with all Triumphs, there are plenty of spares and maintenance support available, and the Dolomites are welcome in most Triumph clubs, the dedicated one being the Triumph Dolomite Club (www.triumphdolomite.co.uk).

Key purchasing points:

- For structural problems, see the entry for the Triumph Toledo
- The condition of the Sprint's engine valve gear is important; blue smoke warns of worn guides, and clearances must be set laboriously with shims
- The Sprint's aluminium head suffers if incorrect or too little coolant is used; look for leaks between head and block
- The Sprint's chain tensioner needs to be renewed every 65,000km (40,000 miles)
- Wayward cornering behaviour, where the whole rear axle seems to move sideways, is caused by worn mounting bushes in the upper rear suspension arms

oped under the code name of SD2. This was during Triumph's days as part of the Specialist Division, and the name followed on from that of the big Rover SD1 hatchback introduced in 1976. However, SD2 was cancelled in 1975. Triumph then looked at facelifting the Dolomite range, and asked Michelotti to update his body design for the car. A single prototype was built, based on Dolomite Sprint mechanical elements, but the idea went no further, as British Leyland's parlous financial state in the late 1970s ruled it out of the equation.

Triumph Stag (1970–77)

'Alfa and Merc look out! Triumph leap in with the Stag!' That was the confident strap-line of the first press advertisements for the Triumph Stag grand tourer in 1970. 'This summer,' the copy continued, 'with the hood down, roll-over bar exposed, and twin exhausts ebulliently burbling, you can overtake the Continentals in style.'

The Stag seemed to have everything going for it when it was announced in June 1970. The attractive styling was by Triumph's regular consultant Michelotti, the handling was as sporty as Triumph buyers expected, and the brand-new 3-li-

The Triumph Stag was one of British Leyland's major disappointments... and it could have been such a good car if only they had built it properly. This is an early model, wearing the optional removable hardtop.

The Stag went through a mid-life facelift and emerged looking all the better for it. Note in particular the stylish alloy wheels and twin coachlines.

tre V8 engine made glorious noises. This looked like a truly great car from British Leyland, and the company's Chairman Sir Donald Stokes had thought so, too. He had asked for its launch to be brought forward to give BL a strong portfolio of new products that summer, when the Range Rover was also launched.

Both the Stag and the Range Rover would go on to become acknowledged classics, but the Stag never fulfilled its promise. That lovely V8 engine quickly developed a reputation for overheating and other problems, and the Stag never recovered from this setback. Sales stalled in the USA, and were not helped by the general turn away from large-engined cars after the 1973 oil crisis. So the Stag was taken out of production in June 1977 after just under 26,000 had been made.

The origins of the Stag predated British Leyland. The car grew out of Michelotti's wish to build a show special to advertise his talents, and for which Triumph provided him an old 2000 saloon. The company's Harry Webster liked the design so much that he agreed to take it as the basis of a new Triumph model, and the V8 engine that had been under development since 1963 was a natural choice to provide the performance for what was clearly going to be a glamorous new addition to the Triumph range.

The first prototypes had Triumph's 6-cylinder engine because no V8s were available. In a moment of clear thinking, somebody within BL suggested that it would make better sense to use the existing Rover V8 engine instead of spending money on putting a second large-capacity V8 into production. However, the Triumph engineers seem to have found ways of proving that the Rover engine would not fit, and in any case every engine that Rover could make was already spoken for. So Triumph got their V8. Ironically, the Rover V8 became a popular aftermarket conversion for Stags that had suffered terminal engine problems.

Stags were 2+2 models, the rear bench really only being suitable for children. They could be had with manual, overdrive, or automatic gearboxes, and with either a foldaway soft-top or a rather heavy demountable hardtop. Few production changes were made over the car's seven-year life, the major ones creating a Mark II specification in 1973. These included stylish alloy wheels and a coachline down each side.

IF YOU WANT ONE....

The Stag is greatly appreciated as a usable classic today, and aftermarket specialists have developed reliable cures for the engine's well-known weaknesses. There is also an excellent Stag Owners' Club (www.stag.org.uk).

Key purchasing points:

- Overheating or water in the coolant are both signs of major and expensive engine problems
- Timing chains stretch and should be changed every 25,000 miles (40,000km)
- Structural problems result from rust in the joins between sills and floor pan. More obviously, the wheel-arches rust
- Rust can also form around the top mountings of the rear springs
- Replacement soft-tops are available but are expensive; hardtops are prone to rust

TRIUMPH STAG: FACTS AND FIGURES

Pressed-steel monocoque with structural rollover bar, foldaway convertible top and/or demountable hardtop; 2+2 seating. Front engine driving rear wheels.

Engine	2997cc V8, with 145bhp at 5,500rpm; 146bhp at 5,700rpm (from 1973); 127bhp at 6,000rpm (US engines); 127bhp at 5,500rpm (US engines from 1973)
Gearbox	Four-speed manual; overdrive initially optional, then standard for most markets from October 1972 Optional three-speed Borg Warner automatic; initially Type 35, then Type 65 from October 1976

Dimensions

Length	4,420mm (173.75in)
Wheelbase	2,540mm (100in)
Width	1,612mm (63.5in)
Height	1,258mm (49.5in) with soft-top erected
Kerb weight	1,355kg (2981lb) with hardtop

Triumph Stag: Statistics

0–60mph	9.3sec (manual) 10.4sec (automatic)
Max. speed	116mph (187km/h) (manual with overdrive) 112mph (180km/h) (automatic)
Fuel consumption	22mpg (12.9ltr/100km) (manual with overdrive) 20mpg (14ltr/100km) (automatic)

Production numbers 25,939

Triumph TR7 (1975–81) and TR8 (1980–81)

By the early 1970s, British Leyland was in need of a modern sports car to sell alongside its old-school MGs and Triumph TRs. Triumph suggested creating one by using existing or planned production components in a deliberately modern-looking bodyshell, and their proposal was approved. It was developed under the code name of Bullet.

Stylist Harris Mann, who had already designed the new 18-22 saloon range, came up with another dramatic wedge shape for what would become the TR7. As there were fears that open cars might become unsalable in the USA, it was drawn up as a fixed-head coupé, which of course incurred the wrath of traditional TR buyers. The sharp nose demanded electrically operated pop-up headlamps.

The engine was a 2-valve version of the Dolomite Sprint's 2-litre slant-four, and both the four-speed gearbox and rear

From this angle, the Triumph TR7 looked sleek and exciting, but unfortunately in straight side view it tended to look rather dumpy. This is an early hardtop model.

All could be forgiven when the TR7 drophead appeared, but sales never matched expectations, and the model lasted only three years in production.

Almost as rare as the car itself, this is the US-market sales catalogue for the Triumph TR8. The model name was displayed prominently across the nose of the V8-engined car. MAGIC CAR PICS

axle came from the Marina. All might eventually have been well, but British Leyland chose to build the car at the Triumph plant in Speke. Industrial relations were at an all-time low here in the middle 1970s, and the constant stoppages and other disruptions led to abysmal build quality for the TR7.

The cars were launched in the USA, expected to be their most important market, in January 1975, but did not reach UK buyers until May 1976. Rover's new five-speed gearbox entered production (for the SD1) a few months later, and was matched to the Rover axle as a 1977-season option. However, supply shortages soon saw the option withdrawn. A three-speed automatic option also became available for the 1977 season.

However, an all-out strike at Speke in October 1977 tried the patience of BL's new Chairman, Sir Michael Edwardes. He closed down the TR7 lines, and no more examples would be built until a year later, by which time production had been transferred to the Triumph plant at Canley. Plans for a TR7 Sprint, using the Dolomite Sprint's 16-valve engine, were unfortunately scrapped at the same time.

There was much better quality control at Canley, and it showed on the TR7s built there. Meanwhile, the threat of legislation against open cars in the USA had receded, and by mid-1977 a TR7 drophead was ready for launch, designed for Triumph by Michelotti. Its introduction was delayed by the Speke strike, but the model was introduced in early 1979 and broadened interest in the TR7; the USA got it first, UK sales being delayed until early 1980.

The next development was the TR8, created primarily for the power-hungry US market by putting the Rover V8 into the TR7 shell. This was a development that had been planned

IF YOU WANT ONE....

The TR7 and TR8 are both popular classic sports cars today, the TR8 being highly prized in the UK, where it is very rare; there have been many aftermarket conversions of TR7s to V8 power. Spares and expertise are readily available, and the cars find a ready home with the TR Drivers' Club (www.trdrivers.com), the TR Register (www.tr-register.co.uk), Club Triumph (www.clubtriumph.org.uk), and the Triumph Wedge Owners' Association (www.triumphwedgeowners.org). They are, of course, welcome in any club for post-1945 Triumph models.

Key purchasing points:

- Structural rust affects the inner and outer sills, the floorpans, the boot floor, the inner wings and the MacPherson strut top mountings
- Cosmetic rust affects the headlamp pods (which can also jam), the panel between them and the bumper, the insides of the front and rear wheel-arches, the rear of the front wings, and the door bottoms
- The TR7 engine is sensitive to use of the correct anti-freeze mixture, and will suffer from waterway corrosion and overheating if mistreated
- The TR8 engine also requires the correct anti-freeze; listen for top-end noise indicating a worn camshaft, often caused by neglected lubrication services
- The four-speed gearbox has weak synchromesh and may jump out of gear on the over-run; the five-speed can baulk when changing into second gear unless filled with automatic transmission fluid

TRIUMPH TR7 AND TR8: FACTS AND FIGURES

Pressed-steel monocoque with two doors and two seats; coupé and convertible bodies available. Front engine driving rear wheels.

Engine	TR7: 1998cc 4-cylinder, with 105bhp at 5,500rpm TR8: 3528cc Rover V8, with 137bhp (49-State) or 133bhp (California) at 5,000rpm
Gearbox	Four-speed manual, 1975–78 Five-speed manual, 1978–81 (and on some early 1977 cars) Optional three-speed Borg Warner automatic, 1976–81.

Dimensions

Length	4,066mm (160.1in)
Wheelbase	2,159mm (85in)
Width	1,681mm (66.2in)
Height	1,258mm (49.9in) (coupé)
Kerb weight	1,016kg (2,241lb) (four-speed TR7 coupé) 1,068kg (2,355lb) (five-speed TR7 coupé) 1,163kg (2,565lb) (TR8)

Triumph TR7 and TR8: Statistics

0–60mph	11sec (TR7) 8.4sec (TR8)
Max. speed	114mph (183km/h) (TR7) 130mph (209km/h) (TR8)
Fuel consumption	28–30mpg (10–9.4ltr/100km) (TR7)

Production numbers

112,368 (TR7)
2722 (TR8)

from the beginning, but the later stages of the project became entangled with Rover's plan to develop a US-market version of their SD1 saloon. TR8 and SD1 were to share powertrain components, with engines in both '49-State' and Californian specifications to suit different emissions control requirements.

Both projects failed miserably, in the case of the TR8 mainly because of build quality issues. During 1980, production of both TR7 and TR8 models was moved again, this time to occupy empty space in the big assembly hall at Solihull built to assemble far more Rovers than were ever ordered. There were more detail changes, the most recognizable being a switch to a chrome bonnet badge instead of the earlier wreath decal. However, sales still did not meet expectations, especially in overseas markets, and in late 1981 TR7 and TR8 production was brought to an end for good. A very small number of right-hand-drive TR8s, intended as pre-production samples for an eventual UK launch, escaped on to the market.

The Triumph Acclaim was desperately ordinary, but it offered reliability that British buyers welcomed after many years of poor build standards from British Leyland.

Triumph Acclaim (1981–84)

The Triumph Acclaim was a quite unremarkable family car, except for the fact that it was better built and more reliable than any other car that British Leyland had produced. In fact, it was neither more nor less than a mildly modified Honda Ballade that was built under licence in Britain, and was the first (major) fruit of the BL-Honda collaboration. BL learned a lot from building it – not least about how to design a car for straightforward manufacture.

The Acclaim's role in life was to give BL a decent middle-sized saloon to hold the fort until the new family of the Maestro and Montego was ready, in 1983 and 1984 respectively. It replaced the whole Dolomite range in the Triumph hierarchy, and although there was never a variant with any sporting qualities or to match the performance of the Dolomite Sprint, its high-revving, 1.3-litre engine turned in a performance equal to that of many 1.6-litre types of the time. The Acclaim replaced the Austin Maxi on the assembly lines at Cowley. Inevitably, it took some sales from the Allegro and the Ital.

IF YOU WANT ONE....

Triumph fans were not impressed when this wholly Japanese saloon was launched with Triumph badges, but it did go on to become the second best-selling Triumph of all time. That said, the Acclaim has a very small fan base today, and is probably appreciated as much for nostalgic reasons as for its almost bullet-proof reliability.

Spares can be a problem, and even Honda garages have difficulty because their parts system works on Honda VINs, not British Leyland ones. An attempt to establish an Acclaim club in 2004 foundered, but the cars are welcomed by the Acclaim Registers of Club Triumph (www.clubtriumph.org.uk), and the Triumph Sports Six Club (www.tssc.org.uk).

Key purchasing points:

- Eradicating rust around the rear suspension mountings can be costly, and rusted sills are part of the monoside and not separate items, so have to be treated accordingly
- Cosmetic rust will be found around the wheel-arches and often under the trim strips on bonnet and boot
- The cambelt must be changed every 72,400km (45,000 miles); the advance-and-retard mechanism on the distributor can fail, and carburettor jets can block, leading to rough idling
- Wiper shafts can seize and move off-centre, damaging the surrounding metalwork
- The boot floor's hardboard panels are not very robust and can split

TRIUMPH ACCLAIM: FACTS AND FIGURES

Pressed-steel monocoque with four doors; five seats. Transversely mounted front engine driving front wheels.

Engine	1335cc Honda EJ1 4-cylinder, with 69bhp at 5,500rpm
Gearbox	Five-speed Honda manual optional Honda Trio-Matic three-speed automatic

Dimensions

Length	4,089mm (161in)
Wheelbase	2,311mm (91in)
Width	1,600mm (63in)
Height	1,346mm (53in)
Kerb weight	809kg (1,784lb)

Triumph Acclaim: Statistics

0–60mph	11.7sec
Max. speed	97mph (156km/h)
Fuel consumption	35mpg (8ltr/100km)

Production numbers

133,626

The truth was that the Acclaim was rather dumpy-looking, with less interior room than was ideal. That did not hurt its appeal to the British public – in particular to retired couples. Triumph die-hards winced, especially at the marketing slogan 'Totally equipped to Triumph' – but the name did make sense, as Triumph had been known for its range of quality, medium-sized family saloons. If the car was unashamedly a Japanese design, the high percentage of local content in its manufacture made it a British car in the eyes of the European Economic Union. That mattered at the time, because the Japanese car makers were restricted by a 'voluntary' limit to 11 per cent of total car sales in the EEC. The Acclaim was the first Japanese car to be built in Europe, and it got around that restriction. In practice, the vast majority were sold in the UK.

The main differences between the Acclaim and its Honda parent were a more powerful engine (with twin carburettors instead of the unusual triple-choke original), revised suspension settings, and better seats. Generally, the Acclaim had better equipment levels than its Japanese counterpart, which was not sold in the UK. Four trim levels were available, ranging from L through HL and HLS up to CD. The end-on gearboxes were both Honda designs, either a five-speed manual or a three-speed Trio-Matic automatic, which gave a degree of manual control and was much liked by elderly buyers.

The Acclaim was introduced in October 1981, and remained much the same for all its production life. Revised versions arrived in 1983, with better equipment for the mid-range HL and HLS models, some minor interior revisions, and new exterior door handles. BL dealers also sold a small number of rather smart Avon Acclaims, converted by Ladbroke Avon, who were then building estate-car conversions of the Jaguar XJ6. These had two-tone paint, a vinyl roof covering, and leather upholstery with wood trim. Avon also built a few 105bhp turbocharged Acclaims (using a Turbo Technics kit), distinguished by special wheels, a deep front spoiler and 'Turbo' side graphics.

Acclaim production was brought to an end in summer 1984, and with it the Triumph marque passed into history. The car was replaced by the Rover 200-series, which was another British derivative of a Honda design.

THE VANDEN PLAS-BADGED MODELS

Under British Leyland, the Vanden Plas name continued to denote more expensively trimmed versions of what were essentially Austin designs, although the Vanden Plas coachworks was also responsible for building and trimming the bodies for the big Daimler DS420 limousine models until it closed in 1979.

Just two models built under the British Leyland regime were actually badged as Vanden Plas types. These were a continuation of the Vanden Plas 1300 range, and its replacement, which was based on the Austin Allegro.

From 1980, Vanden Plas as a separate marque disappeared. Nevertheless, the name was retained for luxury versions of other models, such as Daimlers, Jaguars and Rovers, and Austin's Ambassador, Maestro, Metro and Montego.

Vanden Plas 1500, 1.5 and 1.7 (1974–80)

Sales of the Vanden Plas derivatives of the ADO16 range were strong enough for British Leyland to commission a direct replacement when the cars were replaced by the Austin Allegro in 1973, and unsurprisingly that new replacement was also based on the Allegro. However, it never carried the Allegro name. Introduced in September 1974, a year or so after the mainstream Allegros, the new model was simply called a Vanden Plas 1500. Unlike its Vanden Plas predecessors, the car was never given the Princess name either (which would re-emerge in autumn 1975 as the new brand name for the car, introduced as the Austin-Morris 18-22 series).

The formula for the Vanden Plas 1500 was the same as before: this was a luxuriously equipped small car designed for retirees who wanted a quality driving environment with affordable running costs. It had a wood and leather interior, complete with traditional picnic tables on the back of the front seats, all designed and built by Vanden Plas at Kingsbury.

It also had a distinctive front end, which many people thought was simply ugly. The big Vanden Plas grille gave the car an unmistakable 'snout', which seemed to overwhelm the rest of the Allegro shape. The design was by Vanden Plas' Managing Director, Roland Fox, who claimed the Daimler Double Six as his inspiration and insisted that the 'snout' gave the type of view over the bonnet that Vanden Plas buyers liked. Perhaps he was right, because the Vanden Plas 1500 sold quite well despite its high price – £1,951 at launch, when the entry-level Austin Allegro cost just £1,159.

The major changes to these cars came in autumn 1979, after they had been on sale for five years. British Leyland closed

The bright yellow was very 1970s, but it is unlikely that many Vanden Plas Allegro models were this colour. Most were painted in much more conservative hues, as befitted their image of small, discreet luxury saloons for the elderly. This is a 1978 1500 model.

Figured wood trim, leather upholstery, and picnic tables for the rear-seat passengers said everything there was to say about the Vanden Plas versions of the Allegro.

the Vanden Plas factory at Kingsbury, and so production was transferred to the MG plant at Abingdon. At the same time, automatic models took on the 84bhp 1748cc engine seen in mainstream Allegro 1750 models, while cars with manual gearboxes changed to a 77bhp twin-carburettor version of the 1485cc '1500' type. The models were renamed Vanden Plas 1.5 and Vanden Plas 1.7 types.

Rationalization finally killed off these Vanden Plas models because BL closed the Abingdon factory in 1980. Sales volumes did not justify a further transfer of assembly, and so the Vanden Plas models were withdrawn; mainstream Allegros would remain in production for another two years.

IF YOU WANT ONE....

Even though the mainstream Allegro remains a minority taste in the classic car world, the Vanden Plas models have developed something of a cult appeal. They are welcomed by two clubs: the Allegro Club International (www.allegroclubint.org.uk), and the Vanden Plas Owners' Club (www.vpoc/info).

Key purchasing points for the Vanden Plas Allegro are the same as those for the Austin Allegro to which it is related, and are discussed under the heading for that model. The Vanden Plas models of course have leather trim, which normally lasts well but is inevitably expensive to replace.

VANDEN PLAS 1500, 1.5 AND 1.7: FACTS AND FIGURES

Pressed-steel monocoque with four doors; five seats.
Transversely mounted front engine driving front wheels.

Engine	1500: 1485cc E-series in-line 4-cylinder, with 69bhp at 5,600rpm 1.5: 1485cc E-series in-line 4-cylinder, with 77bhp at 5,000rpm 1.7: 1748cc E-series in-line 4-cylinder, with 84bhp at 5,000rpm
Gearbox	Five-speed manual (1500 and 1.5) Four-speed automatic (1.7)

Dimensions

Length	3,861mm (152in)
Wheelbase	2,438mm (96in)
Width	1,600mm (63in)
Height	1,397mm (55in)
Kerb weight	907kg (2,000lb) approx.

Vanden Plas 1500, 1.5 and 1.7: Statistics

0–60mph	16.7sec (1500)
Max. speed	90mph (145km/h) (1500)
Fuel consumption	27mpg (10.5ltr/100km) (1500)

Production numbers

11,840

THE WOLSELEY-BADGED MODELS

It would probably be fair to say that the Wolseley brand was largely an encumbrance to British Leyland, although they did keep it going for the top models of the ADO17 'Land Crab' range. When these went out of production in 1974, it might have been time to say goodbye to Wolseley – but no, the name was revived for the top models of the 18-22 'wedge' saloons that replaced them. At least, it was revived briefly: the top models were subsumed into the renamed and remarketed Leyland Princess range after six months on sale.

IF YOU WANT ONE....

The Wolseley is mechanically and structurally the same as 6-cylinder Austin and Morris versions of the 18-22 range. Buying advice given under the entry for the Austin versions applies just as well to the Wolseleys. However, it is important to note that the short production run, and the relative exclusivity of the Wolseley variant, means that examples will now be very hard to find.

Wolseley (1975)

As befitted the top model of the range, the Wolseley version of Harris Mann's wedge-shaped saloon came only with the 2.2-litre 6-cylinder engine. It had a unique grille design, recognizable as belonging to a Wolseley by the illuminated marque badge, rather than by its shape. It also shared its four round headlights and bonnet bulge with Morris versions of the range.

There were several items of equipment not seen on other models in the 18-22 range, and the Wolseley had nylon velour upholstery and circular instruments in a wood veneer instrument panel. Both manual and automatic gearboxes were available. The Wolseley – it was simply known as the new Wolseley saloon – lasted in production from March to August 1975 only.

WOLSELEY: FACTS AND FIGURES

Please see the details for 6-cylinder models in the entry for the Austin 18-22 range.

Wolseley: Statistics
For performance and fuel consumption figures, see the details for 6-cylinder models in the entry for the Austin 18-22 range.

Production numbers
3,800

Wolseley versions of the 18-22 model had the same humped bonnet and four-headlamp arrangement as Morris types – but of course they were far better equipped and had their own grille design.

4 OVERSEAS ODDITIES

THIS CHAPTER IS NOT ABOUT the multiple minor variations of British Leyland models that were built for export territories – nor is it about the British Leyland cars that were manufactured overseas from CKD kits that were shipped out from the UK. Rather, it is about the major variations that were produced overseas under the British Leyland umbrella. Some had different engines from their UK equivalents; some had different bodies from their UK equivalents; one (in Australia) was actually a completely home-grown design.

Four countries in particular stand out in this story: Australia, Italy, South Africa and Spain. All four countries started out assembling British cars from CKD in the era before British Leyland came into being, and all four had progressed to full local manufacture, backed up by sophisticated design and engineering operations. Chile could perhaps be added to this list as a fifth country, although the engineering and assembly operations there were far less sophisticated than in the four other countries listed.

These countries, then, were the home of British Leyland's Overseas Oddities – although the cars were not at all odd as far as those who bought them were concerned. Their story was, of course, very much affected by what was happening to and within the parent company in the UK. So although many overseas assembly operations continued into the 1980s, there were also some that were torpedoed in 1974–75. They were torpedoed because the British Leyland Board decided in February 1974 to close its manufacturing plants outside the UK and realize the assets to help offset the parent company's parlous cash position. Australia was by far the largest of the overseas operations that were summarily closed down, but the plants in Italy, South Africa and Spain were also affected.

The material that follows is organized by car type, and within the car type it is organized in alphabetical order of country. It does not pretend to be exhaustive, but the author would be delighted to hear of additions or corrections necessary to the material here; information should be sent to the publishers in the first instance.

Austin/Morris 1100 and 1300 (ADO16 and Derivatives)

The best-selling ADO16 range was assembled from KD kits in a number of overseas territories, but the Australian and South African operations progressed to developing ADO16 derivatives of their own. The South African derivative also entered production, with modifications, in Spain. In addition, special ADO16 derivatives were assembled in Chile and in Italy.

Australia

When BLMC was formed in 1968, its Australian arm was assembling two versions of the ADO16 series, both with Morris badges. These were the 1098cc 1100 and the 1275cc automatic 1100S, and both had several variations from the UK norm, such as different interior trim and a bench front seat, an outboard handbrake, and a cranked gear lever.

Both of these models went out of production in June 1969, and their replacements were new Morris-badged models that

Australia's YDO9 Nomad was a hatchback derivative of the ADO16 range.

The YDO9 was slightly ungainly in appearance but immensely practical.

had been re-engineered in Australia. The new models also took on their own engineering code names, with a YDO prefix, and although they were clearly based on the ADO16, they were equally clearly special designs.

There were two body designs now, instead of just one. The basic four-door saloon remained available, but in its re-engineered form as a YDO15 model it came as a 1300 Automatic or a 1500 ohc, the latter with the 1485cc E-series engine from the Austin Maxi and that car's five-speed gearbox. The same two powertrains were available for the new YDO9, which was badged as a Morris Nomad and had an extensively reworked bodyshell that now incorporated a hatchback. When the taller 1500 engine was fitted, both models had a bonnet bulge to clear it, and both 1300 and 1500 models had much stronger sub-frames than the UK-designed ADO16s.

The Morris Nomad's new hatchback body had been developed with UK assistance and was certainly no thing of beauty. It was, however, practical and rugged, and these characteristics were expected to suit Australian buyers. Sadly, sales failed to match those of the earlier ADO16s, and gearing changes to improve acceleration during 1971 made little difference. However, YDO9 and YDO15 had been intended only as place-holders until the new Leyland Marina arrived in Australia, and they were taken out of production in 1972.

The Australian operation exported a number of 1500 ohc models to New Zealand, where they were rebadged as Austins.

Chile

The Chilean assembly plant was less than ideally situated at Arica, which was more than 2,500km (1,600 miles) from the centre of the Chilean metal industry. As a result, the Chilean operation worked with UK engineers to develop a two-door body to the ADO16 style for local manufacture in GRP. The result entered production in 1971 with MG 1300 badges, and remained available until 1974.

ABOVE: Innocenti continued to develop its own versions of the ADO16, and by 1972 this was how the company's IM5 model looked.

LEFT: Innocenti's IM4 was the Italian company's take on the ADO16 range. WIKIMEDIA COMMONS/LUC106

Italy

Innocenti had been assembling cars for BMC since 1959, but the company had gradually progressed to full local manufacture. The versions of the ADO16 design in production by the start of 1968 were the IM3S, IM4 and IM4S. IM stood for Innocenti-Morris; all three models were rebadged as Leyland Innocenti models during 1968 and remained in production until 1970.

The IM3S had several cosmetic differences from the UK-built cars, including a better appointed cabin and a steering wheel located at a more orthodox angle. It had the twin-carburettor 1100 engine, with locally sourced Dell'Orto carburettors. The IM4 was a single-carburettor model that was essentially the same as the UK-built 1100, and the IM4S was a twin-carburettor version of it. All these cars had the 'Mark I' body style with its longer rear wings.

A new model developed in the British Leyland era was the IM5, which replaced the earlier models for 1971. This had the Mark I body style again, a twin-carburettor 1100 engine and Rostyle wheels. British Leyland assumed full ownership of Innocenti in 1972, but when the British company ran into financial trouble at the end of 1974 it was no longer able to support its Italian subsidiary. Production of the IM5 ended in September 1975 (by which time it had been joined by Innocenti's version of the Allegro), and that year the Innocenti company was sold to De Tomaso.

South Africa

BLMC's birth in January 1968 coincided with a model change for the South African-assembled versions of the ADO16 range. The cars had been assembled at the Blackheath plant in the Cape since 1963, and at the time consisted of Austin and MG 1100s, a Wolseley 1100, an Austin 1100 Countryman and a Morris 1100 Traveller. All had slightly stronger bodyshells than their UK equivalents, to cope with poor South African roads.

From 1968, the Austin and Wolseley models were both uprated with a larger carburettor and other modifications to produce 55bhp. These revised models were called 11/55 types and remained in production until 1971. In the meantime, the South African subsidiary of BLMC had been renamed Leykor.

When Michelotti's front and rear styling for Triumph was grafted on to a booted ASDO16, the result was the Austin Apache.

This was the Apache with warpaint on: the TC version.

Their replacement was a further derivative of the ADO16 range, but this time quite radically different in appearance. Designed jointly by Leykor and BLMC, the new Austin Apache combined the existing saloon centre section with new front and rear ends by Michelotti – who re-employed several elements of his contemporary designs for Triumph.

The Austin Apache had a 1275cc A-series engine and could be bought with either a manual or an automatic gearbox. It was improved in 1973 with a new rod-operated gearchange and cosmetic alterations. At the same time, a sporty twin-carburettor Apache TC became available, with a vinyl roof covering, Rostyle-pattern wheel trims, a rev counter and other changes. From May 1976 it was joined by a more luxurious special edition Apache 35. By the time Apache production ended in 1978, more than 21,600 had been built – and the basic design had also been picked up by Authi in Spain.

Spain

Authi was established in 1965 as a joint venture company with BMC, and among the cars turned out by its factory near Pamplona at the time of the BLMC merger were MG 1100s. Next came Austin 1300s, which wore special BL-Authi badges on their front wings.

From 1972, Authi built a version of the Austin Apache (see South Africa above), with increased local content, as the Authi Victoria. This was available with either one or two carburettors, and had some cosmetic differences from its South African counterpart. A Mark II version was planned, but was cancelled after a major fire at the factory in October 1974. Meanwhile, 1974 brought an Austin De Luxe model, in effect a standard ADO16 Mark III saloon, but equipped as an economy model with the 55bhp 998cc A-series engine from the Mini.

After BL had to withdraw its financial support at the end of 1974, Authi struggled on for a time but eventually closed down. Austin De Luxe production ended in 1975, and the factory was sold to SEAT in 1976.

Austin Allegro

By the time of the Allegro, British Leyland was already reducing its output, and the car was assembled at far fewer overseas plants than the ADO16 models that it replaced. Locations included Belgium, Italy and New Zealand.

Innocenti in Italy sold their own interpretation of the Allegro as an Innocenti Regent. Recognizable as an Allegro derivative, it had special badges, special wheel trims, a full vinyl roof and the infamous quartic steering wheel. Introduced in 1974, the Regent was not a hit with the buying public and its production was halted in 1975, when Innocenti ceased making British Leyland cars.

Austin/Morris 1800 and 2200 (ADO17 and Derivatives)

Once again, it was British Leyland's Australian arm that developed the ADO17 range, to produce something quite different from the models available elsewhere. The Australian derivatives began with a 'ute' ('truck cab') or pick-up version of the

Uniquely Australian, this very practical pick-up (or 'ute') was a derivative of the Austin 1800 saloon range. To Australians, it was a YDO10 model.

1800, and progressed to a range of 6-cylinder models known as the X6 types.

Austin 1800 (ADO17) models had been built at the Victoria Park plant since 1966, and in 1968 were replaced by Austin 1800 Mark II models. Both types were available with either manual or automatic gearbox. Unique to Australia was a pick-up derivative with the YDO10 designation. This had the 1798cc engine and was built between 1967 and 1969, again with a choice of manual or automatic gearbox, and from 1968 a chassis-cab version became available as well.

Meanwhile, Leyland Australia was working on its own version of the ADO17 design, and central to it was the new 2227cc 6-cylinder E-series engine. The aim was to create a model to compete with the large 6-cylinder family saloons from Ford, GM and Holden, and the result was coded YDO13 and marketed as the Austin X6. It retained the basic body shape of the ADO17 but with new front and rear details, plus recessed exterior handles to meet local safety regulations. YDO13 also retained Hydrolastic suspension and offered the usual choice between manual and automatic gearboxes.

The X6 went on sale in November 1970 in two guises. The entry-level model was the 102bhp single-carburettor Austin X6 Tasman, with single headlights and two bench seats with vinyl upholstery. The more expensive variant was the Austin X6 Kimberley, with paired headlights, a more up-market interior with individual front seats, and a 115bhp twin-carburettor engine. A Tasman utility (YDO14) was also prototyped in 1971 but did not reach production.

Early models developed a questionable quality reputation, and so Leyland Australia addressed this with a redesign that took the YDO19 code. Different wheel trims and front-end details distinguished the Austin Tasman Mark II and Austin Kimberley Mark II models, which were introduced during 1971. However, the damage already done to the car's reputation had been too great and sales were slow. The Mark IIs were built only until December 1972, and the last examples were still being sold when their replacement – the Leyland P76 – was announced in 1973.

The squared-up front end of this Austin X6 Tasman belies its origins in the BMC 1800 range. WIKIMEDIA COMMONS/SIC-NAG

The more up-market Austin Kimberley had a four-lamp front end. WIKIMEDIA COMMONS/SIC-NAG

The interior space of the X6 cars was, of course, just as great as in their UK parents. This is a Kimberley model.

A grand total of 12,194 Tasmans and Kimberleys of all types were sold in Australia. The exact build total (including CKD assembly in New Zealand) was around 15,000. It appears that there were discussions about building a variant of the Kimberley in the UK, and a single Vanden Plas-badged prototype was built as part of the associated investigation.

From 1971 the Australian-designed X6 models were also assembled in New Zealand at the NZMC Petone plant; they were sold as the Morris Tasman and Morris Kimberley.

Land Rover

Land Rover models were assembled at multiple locations around the world during the British Leyland era, and in most cases conformed very closely to the UK build specification, give or take locally sourced items such as glass, tyres, electrical components and paint.

Although the Range Rovers assembled overseas from CKD had only minor variations from the UK specification, there were some significant local variations of the Land Rover utilities in Australia, South Africa and Spain.

Australia

Land Rovers were assembled from CKD kits in Australia by the Pressed Metal Corporation at its plant in Enfield, near Sydney. The Australian line-up included 'tray' (flatbed truck) bodywork in addition to the standard 'ute' (truck cab) and Station Wagons. The Australian colour range was also different from the UK range. Land Rover assembly was not affected when British Leyland closed down the Zetland plant in 1974.

Special Australian models included the Land Rover Game, a 1976 Series III 88 Station Wagon which was decked out as a sporty recreational model – possibly the first of its kind. However, it failed in its objective of creating a new market for the 2235mm (88in) models, and Australian sales remained predominantly of 2769mm (109in) types. Much more special was the Australian adoption of a 3.9-litre 4-cylinder Isuzu diesel engine in 1981 to combat sales of diesel-engined Toyota Land Cruisers. Land Rovers with this were known as 3.9D models, and had the front-end panels otherwise associated with the Stage I V8. Coil-sprung Land Rovers assembled in Australia would also have this engine as an option, and some military variants would have a turbocharged derivative.

Australians preferred long-wheelbase Land Rovers, but in 1976 the local importers created a special colourful short-wheelbase Station Wagon called the Game.

Australia built its own 120in (3048mm) Land Rover, which is seen here with a typically Australian 'tray' body made of aluminium.

Again unique to Australia, this was the six-wheel Land Rover in its civilian guise. Other markets also had six-wheelers, but not to this design.

Using the 3.9-litre Isuzu diesel engine and Stage I V8 front-end panels, these are 3.9D models at a motor show in Australia.

Stage I front-end panels were also used on the South African Series IIIS, seen here in Station Wagon guise. The South African seats had a unique design, with built-in head restraints.

South Africa

British Leyland's South African operation inherited a well established Land Rover assembly plant at Blackheath, in the Cape. It was business as usual throughout the 1970s, as CKD kits continued to be supplied from the UK. However, from 1982 Leyland South Africa introduced new engines in a long-wheelbase (109in) model called the Series IIIS. The new engines made the Land Rover more competitive with local versions of the Toyota Land Cruiser, and also increased the local content in line with South African regulations.

Both petrol and diesel versions of the Series IIIS were distinguished by Stage I front panels. The petrol engine, always known as the R6, was a 110bhp 6-cylinder originally designed in Australia and derived from the British Leyland E-series 6-cylinder. The diesel engine was a locally manufactured Perkins 4.236 (3867cc) 4-cylinder, and took its name of ADE4 from the licence builders, Atlantis Diesel Engines. Both drove through gearboxes sourced from Santana in Spain, and about 5,000 were built before they were replaced in 1986 by new coil-sprung Land Rovers. A best estimate is that around 800 of the Series IIIS models had diesel engines.

Spain

Metalurgica de Santa Ana SA had been licence-building Land Rovers under the Land Rover Santana brand name since 1958. Although the operation was initially one of assembly from CKD, the Spaniards had achieved full local content by the time British Leyland came into being. They continued to use what were essentially Land Rover designs, but gradually modified them to suit requirements on the Spanish domestic market and in the export territories they served.

The first major deviation from the UK Land Rover specification was already in place by 1968, and was the Land Rover Santana 1300, a lighter duty version of the UK-built Forward Control model. Next came special military derivatives of the 88in and 109in models.

When Santana introduced Series III models in 1974, they had multiple detail differences from the UK equivalents, and further deviation came in 1977 when Santana announced two new 6-cylinder engines for their long-wheelbase models. Designed in conjunction with Land Rover in the UK, these were 6-cylinder versions of the existing 4-cylinder ohv types, each with a 3.5-litre swept volume. They were never built anywhere other than in Spain.

A much more major deviation came in 1983, when Santana decided not to follow the UK lead in changing to coil springs, but to continue with further developed leaf-sprung models, which they called Series IIIA types. Not long after that, Santana formed an alliance with the Japanese maker Suzuki to build its small 4x4s for European markets. The 1987 Series IV Santana models looked much like the UK coil-sprung types but were again leaf-sprung.

These moves clearly began to drive a wedge between Santana and British Leyland, and in 1990 Land Rover formally ended its relationship with the Spanish company and began to export UK-built Defender models to Spain. Nevertheless, Santana continued to build ever-more developed versions of

Santana's Series III models looked very similar to the UK type, but the company developed its own models, including this 'window hardtop' rural ambulance.

The Cazorla was perhaps the ultimate development of the long-wheelbase Land Rover by Santana. It was a luxury station wagon, and is seen here as a Series IIIA type.

its leaf-sprung models (now badged purely as Santana types) for several more years.

Leyland P76

By the time BLMC was formed in 1968, it was becoming increasingly clear that the Australian market needed something more than locally modified British car designs. In order to compete effectively with the large, locally made saloons from Ford, Holden and General Motors, British Leyland's Australian operation needed to develop its own special model. So the replacement for the Austin Tasman and Kimberley models was engineered, developed and built in Australia.

The P76 was designed as a big saloon, with the dimensions of its intended rivals. Body styling was by Michelotti in Italy, the long-time Triumph consultant, and among the car's features was a huge luggage boot – big enough, it was claimed publicity, to carry a 2,000ltr (44gal) oil drum. Assembly was undertaken at Leyland's Zetland plant, and the new model was deliberately branded as a Leyland product. There were press leaks about it which had included its development code name

The Leyland P76 saloon was a big car designed specifically for Australian conditions.

Lower-specification models of the Leyland P76 had a bench front seat – odd to UK eyes, but much liked in the car's native Australia.

of P76, and long before it was actually released in autumn 1973 the name of P76 was firmly established in the public mind. So the company decided to go with the welcome advance publicity and use that name on production cars.

The lower-specification models in the P76 range had versions of the 6-cylinder engine designed in Australia on the basis of the E-series engine. These had a 2.6-litre capacity. At the top of the range was a 192bhp 4.4-litre V8 derived from the Rover 3.5-litre V8 then in production in the UK; it had originally been designed for the aborted Rover P8 saloon, and was modified to suit Australian requirements with the aid of Rover's own design staff.

However, as parent company British Leyland slipped deeper and deeper into crisis, the decision was taken in early 1974 to close its overseas manufacturing plants, and among them was the Zetland plant in Sydney where the P76 was being built. This was why P76 assembly in Australia was terminated during 1975, although some commentators have wrongly suggested that the car was a failure in the market and its production was stopped for that reason.

A planned estate derivative was cancelled, and most of the Force 7V Coupé two-door fastback derivatives built for the planned launch were crushed before the model went on sale. The tooling for the 2.6-litre engines was shipped to South Africa, and manufacture of the 4.4-litre V8 was outsourced to an Australian specialist company, which continued to build it for use in locally built Leyland Terrier trucks.

New Zealand initially took the Leyland P76 as a fully built import from Australia, and 100 had been shipped by August 1974. At that point, plans were announced for CKD assembly at the Petone plant in New Zealand, using kits shipped from Australia. Even though the P76 went out of production in Australia at the end of that year, the Petone plant continued to assemble examples for the New Zealand market, and had built around 650 cars by the time the last one was assembled in 1976.

Morris Marina

Not every version of the Marina was sold as a Morris. The USA knew the car as an Austin Marina, and in Australia and South Africa it was sold as a Leyland Marina. Most Marinas assembled outside the UK from CKD were broadly similar to their UK counterparts, but in Australia and South Africa there were unique 6-cylinder versions.

Australia

Marinas were introduced to Australia in 1972, initially with Morris badges but always with high levels of local content added to the CKD sets shipped out from the UK. A notable difference from the UK models was that they were re-engineered to take the 4-cylinder E-series engines, in 1500, 1750 or twin-carburettor 1750 form. They came as coupés and saloons, with four-speed manual or three-speed automatic options, and were different enough from the UK-built models to gain an Australian YDO24 identification code.

All that changed in November 1973, when the cars were relaunched in Australia as Leyland Marinas. A heavily redesigned grille was a distinguishing feature, but most important

The first Australian Marinas were 4-cylinder types with Morris badges. Note the Leyland logo on the grille of this 1972 example. WIKIMEDIA COMMONS/SICNAG

With the 6-cylinder E-series engine, the Australian-built Leyland Marina became a YDO24 model. Badges described it as a '262-Six' (see below left). WIKIMEDIA COMMONS/JEREMY

was that the range now included a 6-cylinder engine that was much more to contemporary Australian tastes. This 121bhp 2622cc engine had been developed in Australia from the earlier 2.2-litre E-series 6-cylinder to suit both the Marina and the Leyland P76, and it powered a new model called the Leyland Marina Six.

The Marina Six had been re-engineered in other areas, too. For a start, its engine was carried on a sub-frame that was not present in the UK-specification cars. The suspension was also modified, with different torsion bars and twin radius arms at the rear. Again meeting contemporary Australian expectations, the car had a three-speed manual gearbox as standard, but the more popular choice was actually a three-speed Borg Warner automatic. Both saloon and coupé models of what were known as the YDO25 types were available.

More than 30,000 Marinas were built in Australia before assembly stopped when British Leyland closed the Zetland assembly plant in 1975. The Australian-built cars were also sold in New Zealand.

South Africa

In South Africa, the Marina came as a 1.8-litre with Austin badges, and its role was to replace the Austin Apache saloons. However, that changed when the Australian assembly operation closed down in 1974. Tooling for both the Marina and its 6-cylinder engine was transferred to the South African plant at Blackheath in the Cape. So from 1975, the Austin Marina sold in South Africa was therefore not only locally assembled, but also used only E-series engines.

The South African-built cars had Rostyle steel wheels as standard, and were available as either 74bhp 1750/4 or 110bhp 2600/6 types. The 2.6-litre 6-cylinder models could be had with a Borg Warner automatic gearbox. Both gained the new padded dashboard at the same time as this appeared on British-built cars in 1975.

There was a range realignment in June 1976, when the cars became known as Marina Series III models. Visually, they were recognizable by a new grille with integrated spot lamps. An automatic gearbox became optional on the 4-cylinder cars, and the manual gearbox was dropped from the 6-cylinder options.

Mini (Austin, Morris and Leyland Versions)

There were multiple CKD assembly operations for the Mini around the world, and as usual most of the cars closely resembled those built in the UK, although varying degrees of local content were incorporated. However, there were significant variations on the UK designs in Australia, Chile and South Africa.

Australia

CKD assembly of Minis began in Australia during 1961, and the cars were always badged as Morris types. However, the sophisticated Australian operation progressed rapidly towards versions of its own design and had these in production by 1965. So in 1968, Leyland Australia inherited four different models, all of which had the YDO codes that indicated an Australian-designed car.

The entry-level model was the Morris Mini Minor (YDO4), available as a saloon or a van-with-windows with rubber cone suspension and a choice between 848cc and 998cc engines. Above that came the Morris Mini Deluxe, with Hydrolastic suspension and the 998cc engine (YDO5). The Morris Cooper S had the 1275cc engine and Hydrolastic suspension, and was a YDO6 model. Then there was also the Morris Mini Moke or YDO7, with 998cc engine, assembled in Australia using UK-sourced body panels. During 1968, Leyland Australia announced the Morris Mini-Matic which, as its name suggested, had the AP four-speed automatic gearbox. This was a 998cc YDO5 model with Hydrolastic suspension, but it did not prove popular and did not last into 1969.

The next group of Australian Minis arrived in 1969, and saloon versions were characterized by the 1098cc engine (except in the Cooper S model) and by wind-up door windows and swivelling front quarter-lights. These were known as Mini K types, the K standing for Kangaroo and tying in with the advertising slogan that these Minis represented a great leap forwards. They were the Morris Mini 1100 (YDO4 with rubber suspension), the Morris Mini 1100 Deluxe (YDO5 with Hydrolastic suspension) and the Morris Cooper S Mark II (YDO6 with Hydrolastic suspension and 1275cc engine). These all lasted until 1971 except for the Cooper S, which ended production in 1970. Their Moke contemporaries were the Morris Mini Moke (YDO8, 1969 only, with Australian body panels) and the Morris Moke (YDO18), introduced with larger 13in wheels and available until 1972. Although theoretically a Morris product, these were always badged simply as 'Moke'.

Then there was a final group of Australian-built Morris Minis in 1971–72, although these were certainly not the last Australian-built Minis of all. They were characterized by the Clubman-style front end. There were both saloon and van-with-windows versions of the Morris Mini Clubman (YDO21 with rubber cone suspension). The Morris Mini Clubman with Hydrolastic suspension was a YDO22 type, and the 'perfor-

The Leyland Moke was far better suited to Australian conditions than to European ones, and found a ready market. This is a 1977 example exported to New Zealand... WIKIMEDIA COMMONS/RILEY

... and this side view shows a 1979 example in Australia. WIKIMEDIA COMMONS/JEREMY

mance' model was now a Morris Mini Clubman GT, a YDO23 with Hydrolastic suspension and the 1275cc engine. The Morris Moke was now for export only, still a YDO18 with 13in wheels and 1098cc engine, but now with the option of four seats instead of the previously standard two.

From 1972, all Australian Minis were rebadged as Leyland Minis or Leyland Mokes. The basic 1098cc model (Leyland Mini) had rubber cone suspension and the YDO21 specification; it came as either a saloon or a van, and remained in production until 1974. The Leyland Mini Super with 1098cc engine was a YDO22 model, and there was also a Leyland Mini GT with the 1275cc engine and Hydrolastic suspension to YDO23 specification. Both of these lasted only until 1973, and at that point the last new Australian Mini model was introduced as the Leyland Mini S with 1098cc engine and the YDO22 specification, but now with rubber cone suspension. This lasted until the end of Australian production in 1974.

The Mokes were available in two guises from 1972 to 1974. The basic Leyland Moke was for export only, with the 1098cc engine. This was a YDO18 model. Above it came the Leyland Moke Californian, a YDO30 type with 1275cc engine. Both models had 13in wheels, and both could be had with either two or four seats.

Chile

For exactly the same reasons as Chilean ADO16s had GRP bodywork, so Mini saloons built in Chile from 1969 had locally made GRP bodies that had been developed in tandem with UK engineers.

Much later, in 1990 and after the British Leyland period, production of a GRP-bodied Mini (called the Mini Cord) began in Venezuela, but the two projects were not related.

Only a close look reveals that this is a GRP-bodied Mini of the Chilean type. SIMON CLAY

The Wolseley 1000 was a uniquely South African version of the Mini. SIMON CLAY

South Africa

Most of the Minis assembled from CKD in South Africa during the British Leyland period were more or less to standard UK specification. However, there were also some interesting local variants.

When BLMC was formed in 1968, production had already begun of a Wolseley 1000 variant that combined Wolseley front-end panels with an otherwise standard Mini saloon body; this also had opening quarter-lights and winding door windows, thanks to engineering input from Australia. Around 450 are thought to have been built between 1967 and 1969.

They were then replaced by a version of the Mark III Mini, which had the booted Riley/Wolseley type shell but with standard Mini or Clubman front panels. Among these were a Mini GTS, which was essentially a 1275GT with Clubman front panels and sporty decals.

Rover SD1

There were just two overseas assembly operations for the Rover SD1. The cars assembled in New Zealand had only minor differences from the UK models, but the ones assembled in South Africa had some major differences.

The SD1 tooling was sold to Standard Motor Products of Madras in India when UK production ended, and that company created from it a model called the Standard 2000 that used a locally made engine. The very first cars, built during 1985 and 1986, had panels shipped out from the UK, but full local manufacture began once the tooling was operational in India. The cars went out of production in 1988.

The Rover SD1 was built briefly as a Standard 2000 in India.

South Africa

The Rover SD1's role in British Leyland's South African line-up was to replace the Triumph Chicane saloon, which was a locally assembled version of the Triumph 2500. The Rover was introduced during 1978, but depended for only about 40 per cent of its content on parts shipped out from the UK. The remaining 60 per cent – a high figure for local content – was achieved partly by local assembly of the bodyshell, partly by local manufacture of interior trim (which was very different from the UK type), and partly by local manufacture of the 6-cylinder engine in the 2600 models.

This 6-cylinder was not the engine used in UK-built cars, but the 2.6-litre 6-cylinder that had originated with Leyland Australia. The tooling had been shipped to South Africa after Leyland's Australian assembly operation closed in 1974. The South Africans called the engine an R6, and used it in Rover SD 2600 and better equipped Rover SDX 2600 models. Both types were available with a choice of manual or automatic transmission.

The Blackheath plant also assembled SD1 3500 models, in this case using V8 engines shipped from the UK. They came as a manual gearbox SDS 3500 or an automatic SDE 3500; the 'S' was probably intended to stand for Sport, and the 'E' for Executive. About 14,400 SD1 models of all types are thought to have been assembled before 1983, when car manufacture at the Blackheath plant ended altogether.

The South African-built Rover SD1s looked much like their UK counterparts, but the seats were quite different.

Rover Quintet

In the early 1980s, British Leyland needed a medium-sized hatchback to strengthen its market presence in Australia. The new collaborative deal with Honda provided an opportunity.

However, the Australians avoided the Honda Ballade, the car that British Leyland built in the UK from 1981 with Triumph Acclaim badges. Instead, Jaguar Rover Australia (as the company was then known) took a car that was built wholly in Japan. This was based on the five-door version of the Honda Quint – a car sold in the UK as a Honda Quintet. Honda was already selling the three-door version in Australia with its own badges, so JRA imported the five-door model from mid-1983 and re-badged it as a Rover Quintet.

There were very few changes to the basic Japanese specification. The cars wore Rover badges and had an improved interior with special velour upholstery and a wood-grain dashboard, but that was all. They had the same Honda EP 1602cc transverse 4-cylinder engine as the Japanese Quint, with the option of five-speed manual or three-speed automatic gearboxes. Production ended in 1985 when the Quint went out of production in Japan. The Rover Quintet was replaced by the Rover 416i, another rebadged Honda, by which time British Leyland had been renamed the Rover Group.

For Australia only there was a Rover Quintet, simply a rebadged Honda model. A swathe of wood on the dash helped to give some of the expected Rover feel to it.

Triumph Herald

Over the years, the Triumph Herald range was assembled from CKD in several different countries. However, the most interesting variants were those built in India by Standard Motor Products of Madras. These initially had the 948cc engine and were sold as Standard Heralds. Production gradually evolved to incorporate a larger proportion of local content, and later, SMP developed four-door saloon and estate models as well, for sale only in India.

In 1971, they introduced a restyled four-door saloon derived from the Herald and called the Standard Gazel. This still had the 948cc engine, but now had the simpler axle design of the Triumph Toledo, introduced because it was better able to withstand the poor road surfaces in India. This remained available until 1977.

The Standard Gazel was not hard to recognize as a Triumph Herald derivative – but no British-built car had four doors like this. WIKIMEDIA COMMONS

Triumph Pony

Triumph began developing a lightweight 4x4 off-road vehicle in 1963, and at the core of its design were engine and drive-train elements from the front-wheel-drive 1300 saloons. They called it the Pony, but decided against putting it into production. Instead, they sold the manufacturing rights to Autocars in Israel, who were already assembling Heralds and 1300s from CKD kits.

Autocars put it into production as the Dragoon in 1967, selling it not only on their home market but also exporting it to Greece and Switzerland, and supposedly also agreeing an assembly arrangement with a company in Persia (now Iran). Two different versions were available, a simple pick-up and a four-door passenger-carrying model with a canvas roof, but there were also adaptations such as tankers.

The Autocars Dragoon was built in Israel, but had started life as a Triumph Pony. This is a tanker-bodied version.

APPENDICES

APPENDIX 1: THE ENGINES

Note that power was expressed according to different standards over the years, so it can be misleading to compare figures.

When British Leyland was formed in 1968, most figures were quoted to SAE (Society of Automotive Engineers) standards, which were American in origin and, roughly speaking, were bench-test figures for the engine with no power-sapping ancillaries and a straight-through exhaust. From 1972, figures were usually quoted according to DIN (Deutsche Industrie Normen, or German Industry Standards) guidelines. These gave a much more accurate impression of the power available once the engine was installed in the car.

In more recent times, power figures have been quoted to German PS (*Pferdestärke*, or horsepower) standards, which in turn are different: 10PS equates to about 9.88bhp.

A-series and A-Plus

The legendary A-series ohv 4-cylinder engine had already been in production for nearly seventeen years at the time of the BLMC merger, but its life was not even close to ending. It remained a staple of the British Leyland range right through that company's existence, and in further revised form it continued until 2000, so achieving an astonishing production life of forty-nine years.

When BLMC was formed in 1968, the A-series engine was in production in three different sizes. These were 998cc, 1098cc, and 1275cc. The 998cc engine was being built as a transverse type only for the Mini range. The 1098cc size came as a north-south engine for the Morris Minor, and in transverse form for the ADO16 '1100' cars. The 1275cc also came in both transverse and north-south forms – transverse for the Mini and ADO16 '1300', and north-south for the Austin-Healey Sprite and MG Midget sports-car twins.

The engine would remain a core feature of the smaller models and of the smaller-engined medium-sized cars under British Leyland. It remained in the Mini range throughout the British Leyland period, and was used in the new Morris Marina from 1971 and Austin Allegro from 1973. Nevertheless, British Leyland was under no illusions about the age of the basic A-series design, and in the first half of the 1970s its engine designers did look hard at replacing what was already an elderly engine.

On the one hand, they tried to convert it to a more modern ohc layout, and on the other they began work on a completely new, small capacity 4-cylinder – but nothing came of

By the time of this 1.3-litre engine for an Austin Montego, the A-series had become an A-Plus and was, of course, a transverse engine with an end-on gearbox.

The additional trunking is not easy to see here, but this is the turbocharged A-Plus engine in an MG Metro Turbo.

their exertions. Then the all-pervasive preoccupation with fuel economy that followed the oil crisis of 1973–74 persuaded the engine designers to take a fresh look at the existing engine, and they realized that it already delivered the good fuel economy and high torque at low speeds that customers were now demanding.

So the A-series was put through a major re-engineering programme that focused on the existing 998cc and 1275cc sizes, and emerged at the other end as the A-Plus engine – the name emblazoned on its rocker cover. The re-engineering programme delivered a stronger block and crankshaft, lighter pistons with improved rings, revised manifolding with more modern carburettors, and longer service intervals from detail changes such as a new timing chain tensioner.

The first car to benefit from the A-Plus engines was the Austin Metro in 1980, but these engines would also go into the Austin Maestro (1983) and Austin Montego (1984). The final development under British Leyland was a special turbocharged derivative of the 1275cc engine for the 1982 MG Metro Turbo, developed with the assistance of Lotus Engineering.

The twin-carburettor version of the 1.3-litre A-series engine, in a Mark II MG 1300 saloon.

B-Series

The B-series engine design could be traced right back to the early 1950s, when the newly formed BMC needed a single 4-cylinder engine of between 1.2 and 1.5 litres to replace a variety of older engines in the models it inherited from Morris and from the Nuffield Organization. So this ohv 4-cylinder engine was introduced in 1953. The original capacities were 1200cc and 1489cc, however the smaller size was discontinued in 1957, and the engine was then further developed to 1588cc (for the 1959 MGA 1600), 1622cc (1959 for Australia but 1961 elsewhere) and 1798cc (for the 1962 MGB).

There were several variations, including a dohc type for the 1958 MGA Twin Cam and a 2.4-litre 6-cylinder built in Australia during the early 1960s, but the versions still in production at the time of the BLMC merger were the 1622cc and 1798cc 4-cylinders. The 1.6-litre engine was in the BMC Farina saloons – Austin A60, Morris Oxford, Riley 4/72 and Wolseley 16/60 – and would go out of production in 1971. The 1.8-litre engine was used in north-south form in the MGB, and in transverse form in the Austin 1800, Morris 1800 and Wolseley 18/85 versions of the ADO17 'Land Crab'.

British Leyland then re-employed it as a north-south engine in the Morris Marina (1971–78), and as a transverse engine in the Leyland Princess and its short-lived 18-22 predecessor (1975–78). In the MGB it soldiered on until 1980, when production finally ended.

The ubiquitous B-series engine is seen here in twin-carburettor 1798cc form, in an MGB.

There were even diesel versions of the B-series, although they were made in far smaller numbers. The first was introduced in 1961 and shared its 1489cc swept volume with the contemporary petrol engine. This was still in production for taxi models of the Morris Oxford when the BLMC merger occurred, and remained so until 1971. It then reappeared a little later in small volume, export versions of the Morris Marina and its Morris Ital successor; it finally went out of production in the early 1980s.

The other diesel B-series engine shared the 1798cc size of the MGB version, and was developed by British Leyland for the Leyland Sherpa van introduced in 1974. It remained available in that application – and that application only – until 1989, when it was replaced by the Perkins Prima diesel developed from the British Leyland O-series engine.

A real rarity: this is the B-series diesel in a 1971 Morris Oxford VI.

C-Series

The C-series ohv 6-cylinder engine that BLMC inherited in 1968 was a very recent redesign of the original C-series type, introduced by BMC in 1954. That original engine had a 2.6-litre capacity and was designed by Morris Engines to replace both the older 2.2-litre ohc '6' that BMC had inherited from the Nuffield Organization, and the 2.5-litre 4-cylinder Riley engine. It had a small number of parts in common with the 4-cylinder B-series (which was drawn up in the Austin offices), but was in no sense designed as a 6-cylinder version of it.

In 1959, the C-series was bored out from 77mm to 83.6mm to give 2912cc, and subsequently appeared in big saloons wearing Austin, Vanden Plas and Wolseley badges. It also became the power unit of the Austin-Healey 3000 sports car. However, these engines all had just four main bearings, which limited further development. So in the mid-1960s BMC thoroughly redesigned the C-series around the same bore and stroke dimensions but with seven main bearings, smaller and slightly lighter block and head castings, and improved breathing to gain extra power.

The revised C-series engine went into the MGC sports car in 1967 – BMC's replacement for the Healey 3000 – and into the big Austin 3-litre that was introduced the same year. However, neither application exploited its extra power potential, which was realized in only six special racing MGCs built for the 12 Hours of Sebring races in 1968 and 1969. Production of the MGC ended in 1970, and that of the Austin 3-litre in 1971. The engine was not directly replaced, although the 2.2-litre 6-cylinder E-series filled a similar place in British Leyland's engines' line-up from 1972.

As re-engineered in the mid-1960s, this is the C-series 6-cylinder engine in an MGC.

E-Series

The E-series was designed in the last days of BMC to be a family of 4-cylinder and 6-cylinder engines that could be built on common tooling. Their purpose was to replace B-series and C-series engines, the 4-cylinders being intended for transverse installation, but the 6-cylinders being designed to suit both transverse and north-south installations. None of these engines entered production until after the BLMC merger.

The original plan was to develop the 4-cylinder engine with 1.3-litre and 1.5-litre sizes, and to create a 2-litre 6-cylinder by adding 2 cylinders to the 1.3-litre size. However, that plan changed when the 1.3-litre size looked like offering no real benefits over the 1275cc A-series engine then being developed. This meant that in effect the engine moved up a size, starting at 1.5 litres.

Meanwhile, the requirement for a transverse version of the 6-cylinder put constraints on the length of the block. The designers got round this by using narrow bores (siamesed to save further space) with a long stroke. This made for a tall engine, whose height was increased by an ohc layout.

The E-series engine entered production as a 1.5-litre 4-cylinder for the Austin Maxi in 1969. From 1973 it was also used in the Austin Allegro. The designers then had some trouble creating a larger capacity derivative because the siamese bore design of the block meant that larger bores were not feasible, while the gearbox-in-sump design limited what could be done to lengthen the stroke. However, a 1748cc 4-cylinder E-series with lengthened stroke was ready for the Maxi 1750 in 1971. This subsequently appeared in the Allegro and the Marina. Unfortunately, the siamese bore design was already earning the E-series a reputation for overheating, oil burning, and head gasket failures.

The engine was meanwhile enthusiastically adopted by Leyland Australia, who saw the advantage of making 4-cylinder and 6-cylinder versions on the same production tooling. The 1.5-litre 4-cylinder went into the Morris 1500 and Morris

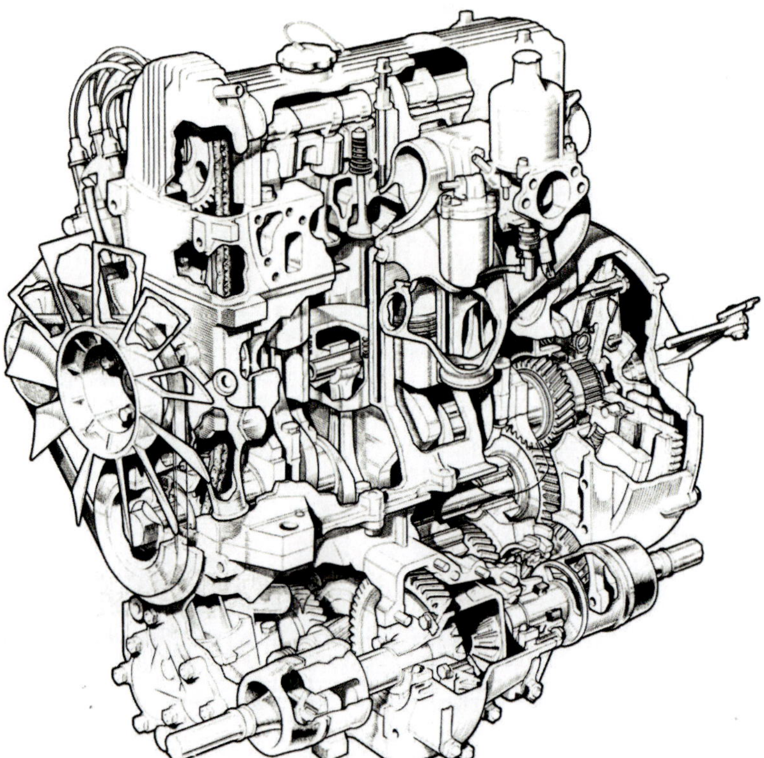

The 4-cylinder E-series was designed for a gearbox-in-sump installation. This cutaway shows the original 1485cc version for the Austin Maxi…

… and this is the 1748cc version in a Maxi 1750.

The E-series was designed to be built as a 6-cylinder as well; this is the 'E6' 2.2-litre in an ADO17 'Land Crab'.

Another view of the E-series 'E6' 2.2-litre engine.

Nomad models released in 1969, both based on the old BMC 1100/1300 range. A year later, the first 6-cylinder E-series engines entered production in Australia for the Austin Tasman and Austin Kimberley derivatives of the ADO17 range. (*See* Section 4 'Overseas Oddities' for further details of all these Australian models.) These had a 2.2-litre capacity, created by using the bore and stroke dimensions of the 1.5-litre 4-cylinder. No 6-cylinder E-series engines would be built in the UK until 1972, when the 2.2-litre was introduced for the ADO17 'Land Crab' saloons.

Cars built in Britain only ever used the 2.2-litre version of the 6-cylinder E-series, but a larger 2.6-litre version was created by using the longer stroke of the 1.7-litre 4-cylinder, and this entered production in Australia and South Africa. Its first use was in the Australian Leyland Marina Six, and in 1973 it appeared in the Australia-only Leyland P76. When the Australian operation closed down in 1975, the engine tooling was passed to Leyland South Africa, and the engine then appeared in that country's Austin Marina, Rover SD1 and Land Rover Series IIIS.

Production of both the 4-cylinder and 6-cylinder E-series engines ended in 1982. New engines were on the stocks for 1983, notably the 4-cylinder R-series that arrived with the Maestro. However, the 6-cylinder E-series was not directly replaced.

The 4-cylinder E-series engine was also used in a pair of interesting 'might-have-beens'. The 1.5-litre size was used in mid-mounted, transverse form in the 1969 MGE concept, which would have replaced the MGB but was cancelled. Issigonis also had one in the gearless Mini that he developed during his retirement.

O-Series

The O-series engine was developed in the mid-1970s from the old BMC B-series, and was intended to replace it. It was intended to suit both north-south and transverse (gearbox-in-sump) installations, and its key advances over the B-series were an aluminium cylinder head and a belt-driven overhead camshaft. Two different sizes were planned, a 1.7-litre with 1695cc and a 2.0-litre with 1994cc. Both had iron blocks and alloy cylinder heads.

The first production installation was in transverse form in the Leyland Princess during 1978. This was swiftly followed by a north-south installation in the Morris Marina. Next came another north-south version in the Leyland Sherpa van. The engine also appeared in the Morris Ital from 1980 and the Austin Ambassador from 1982. At one point around 1980, the engine was even considered for use in Land Rovers, mainly to overcome a supply shortage of that vehicle's standard petrol engine.

Meanwhile, a twin-carburettor version of the 2.0-litre O-series was being developed for use in British Leyland's sports cars. The plan was to use it in both the MGB (for which a production-ready specification was worked up) and the Triumph TR7, but both models were taken out of production before this plan came to fruition. The twin-carburettor engine nevertheless did enter production for the Rover 2000 version of the SD1 in 1982. A multi-point fuel injection specification was also prepared for the MGB version of the engine but did not enter production.

The O-series 4-cylinder is seen here in transverse form with end-on gearbox for an Austin Montego.

The O-series engine was later further developed to provide high-performance derivatives of the Maestro and Montego ranges, and there were both EFi and turbo-charged versions. These later versions were also adapted to take an end-on gearbox, and in practice were used with the Honda PG1 type.

Derivatives of the O-series continued long after the end of the British Leyland era. From 1987, work with Perkins delivered a diesel version that was known to the Rover Group as the MDi engine, and to Perkins as the Prima. It went into some versions of the Maestro and Montego. The petrol engine was further developed with twin overhead camshafts and a 16-valve cylinder head for the Rover 800, and in this guise it was known as an M-series or M16 engine. The Rover 800 also briefly used a modified version of the original 8-valve O-series engine.

The final development of the engine was the T-series, introduced in 1992 and in production until 1999 for versions of the Rover 200, 400, 600 and 800, plus the Land Rover Discovery and special versions of the Defender. Land Rover engineers even developed a turbocharged version of the T-series, but did not put it into production.

R-Series

British Leyland intended that the 1.6-litre engine in its 1983 Austin Maestro should be a derivative of the 1748cc E-series engine with a smaller bore. But the decision to use bought-in Volkswagen gearboxes demanded an additional redesign, as the E-series had been designed to take the gearbox in its sump, while the VW gearboxes were end-on types. However, the redesigned engine was not going to be ready in time for the Maestro's launch, and so the engine designers switched to a stop-gap design that could be got ready quickly. This became the R-series.

It was essentially a small-bore E-series engine rotated through 180 degrees to allow the Volkswagen gearbox to be mounted end-on. However, the speed with which it was developed meant that some problems remained. One was that the carburettors were now at the front of the engine, which led to icing and starting problems in cold weather. Another was that the E-series relied on the heavy gearbox-in-sump assembly for some of its bottom-end strength; a special cast alloy sump was fitted in its place but it did not provide enough strength. As a result, the crankcase could flex, and this would lead to crankshaft failure. Like the E-series, the R-series was

The R-series engine proved troublesome and had a short production life. This one is hiding under the twin carburettors and branded air filter of an MG Maestro.

prone to head gasket failure, and suffered from timing chain noise – both problems that there had been no time to develop out.

R-series engines went into the first 1.6-litre Austin Maestro models in 81bhp single-carburettor form, and into the MG Maestro with twin Weber carburettors and 103bhp. Electronic carburettor control provided an automatic choke and regulated the idling speed, and an over-run fuel cut-off contributed to fuel economy. However, these engines were in production for less than two years, and were replaced during 1984 by the S-series engine – the more fully developed engine that had been planned for the Maestro in the beginning.

The S-series replaced the R-series as soon as it was ready. This is a carburettor version in an Austin Maestro.

S-Series

The S-series engine was intended to create a 1.6-litre powerplant for the Austin Maestro, and was a further development of the E-series types. Work started on it sometime around 1981, but it soon became clear that it would not be ready in time for the Maestro's launch in 1983. So some of the features planned for the S-series were incorporated into a stop-gap engine called the R-series (see above), and the Maestro was introduced with that. By 1985 the S-series was ready, and replaced the R-series altogether.

It is probably easiest to see the S-series engine as an improved R-series, and in many ways it was exactly that. It took the development programme to its intended conclusion, providing more bottom-end strength (to prevent crankcase flexing), turning the top end configuration around so that the carburettor was behind the engine, and removing the problem of timing chain noise by changing to a toothed rubber timing belt.

There were versions of the S-series with an end flange to suit the Volkswagen gearbox used in the Maestro, and others with a flange to suit the Honda PG1 gearbox used in the Rover 216. The S-series engines remained in production until 1993, and their demise was brought about by that of the Maestro and Montego models.

In the mid-1980s, some work was done on a 4-valve version of the S-series engine, and the engine that would have resulted was known as the L16 type (not to be confused with the later L-series diesel engine). The aim was to produce a larger-capacity engine for cars such as the R8 (the 1989 second-generation Rover 200 series), but a redesign of the new

The S-series is seen here in cutaway form for a 1.6-litre Montego.

This was the most powerful S-series engine, a 2.0-litre EFi type in an MG Maestro.

K-series engine that was being developed at the same time enabled larger-capacity versions of that to fill the gap. So the 4-valve S-series did not progress beyond the design stage.

The smaller Daimler V8 engine was the 2.5-litre size, as seen here.

Daimler 2.5 V8

Daimler's 2.5-litre V8 engine only just survived into the BLMC era, as Sir Donald Stokes had its production ended in 1969 on the grounds that it was too expensive. Production volumes had always been small, because Daimler had only been able to afford a limited investment in tooling up for the engine when they introduced it in 1959.

Design began in 1956, when former motorcycle designer Edward Turner became managing director of the BSA automotive division which then owned Daimler. Asked to draw up a V8-engined saloon, he and design engineer Jack Wickes examined Cadillac V8 practice. From it they took the basic pushrod ohv design, which allowed Turner to use the cylinder-head design he had drawn up earlier for the Triumph Thunderbird motor-cycle engine. The new engine emerged as a 90-degree V8 (with two different swept volumes) with hemispherical combustion chambers, a cast-iron block and light alloy heads. Carburation was by twin Sus, and in 2.5-litre form the engine delivered 140bhp at 5,800rpm.

The engine was introduced in the Daimler SP250 sports car of 1959, and there was even a marine version offered from 1961. Daimler had been in trouble in the late 1950s and sold out to Jaguar in 1960, and the engine was used in the Jaguar Mark 2 compact saloons to create a Daimler-badged derivative. It remained in production for the 2.5-litre V8 and later V8-250 saloons until 1969, and was always regarded as a compact jewel of an engine.

The outside dimensions of the 4.5-litre Daimler V8 were not much greater than those of the 2.5-litre type. The four-trumpet air cleaner was characteristic of the engine.
MAGIC CAR PICS

Daimler 4.5 V8

Edward Turner also designed a larger V8 for Daimler, this one of 4.5 litres capacity. Despite its much larger swept volume, the 4.5-litre V8 had a very similar design to the 2.5-litre, and even shared its bore spacings. Its external appearance was also very similar, and it was actually hardly larger physically than the 2.5-litre engine, the major difference being 10cm (4in) of height.

With twin SU carburettors, the 4.5-litre V8 delivered 220bhp at 5,500rpm and 283lb/ft of torque at 3,200rpm. Jaguar supposedly once tried it in their Mark X saloon, where it outperformed the standard XK 6-cylinder and delivered a 135mph (217km/h) lap at the MIRA test ground.

However, the 4.5-litre V8 was always a low-volume engine, and only just over 2,000 were built in just over nine years.

It saw service in the Daimler Majestic Major DQ450 and its DR450 limousine derivative, where it always came with an automatic gearbox. That small-volume production counted against it when British Leyland started to call the shots, and like its 2.5-litre sibling, it was declared redundant during 1968 on the grounds of costs. It was not replaced: the Jaguar XK engine would do the job in later large limousines.

Honda EN4

Honda's family of E-series engines were all in-line 4-cylinders of fairly small capacity, the first one being the EA type of 1971. They are also known as the CVCC engines because they employ compound vortex controlled combustion technology, a type of stratified charge system which enabled Honda to meet US emissions regulations in the 1970s without the need for a catalytic converter.

The EN4 was an all-aluminium 1335cc member of the E-series family that was introduced in 1980 for the Honda Civic. For the 1981 Civic S and the Triumph Acclaim it was fitted with twin Keihin carburettors and delivered 70bhp at 5,500rpm with 74lb/ft of torque at 3,500rpm. These engines had a single overhead camshaft operating 2 valves per cylinder.

The 1335cc Honda EN4 4-cylinder in the Triumph Acclaim always had twin carburettors. MAGIC CAR PICS

The Honda EP 4-cylinder was used in the Rover Quintet designated for the Australian market. A large air cleaner dominated the under-bonnet view.

Honda EP

The EP was a further evolution of the Honda E-series family that was introduced in 1980 and was used in the Rover Quintet for Australia – actually a rebadged Honda Quint. It was a 1602cc ohc type with 2 valves per cylinder and a twin-choke carburettor. Power was 79bhp at 5,500rpm, and torque was 95lb/ft at 3,500rpm.

Honda EV2

The EV2 engine built by Honda was used in the 1984 Rover 213 models. It was yet another derivative of the company's E-series family, an all-aluminium design for transverse installation, with 3 valves per cylinder and a belt-driven overhead camshaft. Initially introduced as the 60bhp EV in the 1983 Honda Civic and CRX models, it was further developed as the more powerful (70bhp) EV2.

RIGHT: **Honda's EV2 4-cylinder was the power unit of the Rover 213 models. Like all Honda engines, it rotated in the opposite direction to British-designed types, which meant that gearboxes could not be shared with other engines.**

Isuzu 4BD1

The Isuzu 4BD1 diesel engine was bought in from its Japanese makers to provide a big diesel engine for the Australian Army's military contract, which Land Rover won in the mid-1980s. Before that, however, it became available in civilian market models built in Australia.

This was a big, tough, rugged 4-cylinder engine originally developed for eight-tonne trucks. It had a swept volume of 3856cc, overhead valves and direct injection, and delivered 97bhp at 3,200rpm and 188lb/ft at 1,900rpm. Later, and after the end of the British Leyland period, a turbocharged version (called 4BD1T) was used in some Australian-built military Land Rovers.

Jaguar XK

Jaguar's long-lived XK 6-cylinder engine was designed by the company's engineers while on fire-watching duties during World War II. It was deliberately advanced in design because Jaguar (then SS Cars) was a small company and needed to offset tooling costs over a long manufacturing run. In fact the engine entered production in 1948 and was last manufactured in 1992 – not a bad production run at all.

The XK was an iron-block engine with an alloy cylinder head, and among its advanced features in 1948 was a twin overhead-camshaft layout. It had also been designed to suit a variety of bore and stroke dimensions, and by the time British Leyland was formed in 1968 it was available in four different

The Isuzu diesel engine used in Australian Land Rovers was really a truck engine. This is the later turbocharged type in a military model.

The legendary XK 6-cylinder is seen here in late 2.4-litre form.

sizes – 2.4, 3.4, 3.8 and 4.2 litres – and a fifth of 2.8 litres would follow later in the year. There were also special 3.0-litre engines for racing after 1959.

There were actually two different blocks, a 'short' block for the 2.4 and 2.8-litre sizes, and a 'full-size' block for the others. There were also two different 3.4-litre engines, the 1975 version introduced after a gap of several years being based on the then-current 4.2-litre rather than the older engine. Either two or three carburettors were used, depending on the model, although fuel injection gradually took over from 1978. Over the years, Jaguar quoted power and torque figures to several different standards, so it is impossible to give a concise picture of how the engine's outputs changed. However, by way of example, the final injected 4.2-litre engine gave 205bhp to DIN standards, and this was a far more powerful engine than the 3.8-litre in the 1961 E-type, which was claimed to deliver 265bhp to SAE standards.

XK engines of one size or another were used in every Jaguar model of the British Leyland era except for the XJ-S (which had the V12, see below). They were also used in Daimler-badged models, and in tracked military vehicles of the CVR(T) family, and were sold to Panther for use in their J72 and De Ville models.

Jaguar V12

There had been discussions about a V12 engine at Jaguar as early as 1954, but when the company withdrew from racing in 1956 the idea was shelved. It was resurrected after Wally Hassan rejoined the company when Jaguar took over Coventry Climax in 1963. This first design was loosely based on an earlier one for a planned Le Mans car, the XJ13. In the later 1960s, the design was simplified with a view to using it in a planned limousine model, but that was cancelled. It was then resurrected for the 1971 Series E-type, and later the XJ12 models as well.

The production engine was an all-alloy design with removable wet liners, over-square dimensions and a single overhead camshaft on each cylinder bank operating a single inlet and single exhaust valve for each cylinder. A planned Brico injection system was cancelled, and all versions up to April 1975 had four Zenith-Stromberg carburettors with a Lucas Opus electronic ignition system. The Opus system remained after April 1975 when a Lucas injection system (based on the Bosch D-Jetronic type) became standard. Then in 1982 a new Lucas CEI system with its own ignition arrangements took over.

Meanwhile, an HE (high efficiency) version of the engine had been announced in 1981, using 'Fireball' high-swirl combustion chambers designed by Swiss engineer Michael May. From 1992, the V12 engine was stroked to 6.0 litres for the

The V12 was massively complicated to work on – and looks it in this picture of one in a 1979 Jaguar XJ-S.

XJ-S, XJ12 and Daimler Double-Six models, and in that form it ended production during 1997 after a long production run of twenty-six years.

The Jaguar V12 was also supplied to Panther for their J72 and De Ville models, and from 1985 there were racing versions developed for the 'works' Jaguars by TWR.

Jaguar AJ6

Jaguar replaced the long-serving XK 6-cylinder with a newly developed straight-6 type in 1983. This was called the AJ6 (Advanced Jaguar Six) and had an aluminium cylinder block to save weight, inclined at 22 degrees from the vertical to allow lower bonnet lines. The engine was developed with both sohc and dohc cylinder heads.

The engine first appeared in 3.6-litre form in the Jaguar XJS as a dohc type, and this was the only version produced in the British Leyland era. From 1986, a 2.9-litre sohc engine was introduced for the new XJ40 saloon models, and later on there would be 3.2-litre and 4.0-litre sizes. The AJ6 was further developed into the AJ16 for 1995's XJ300 models, and this was replaced in 1997 by the new AJ-V8 engine.

Land Rover ohv Petrol and Diesel

The Land Rover 4-cylinder petrol and diesel engines were derivatives of a common ohv design that had been introduced in 1956 with a 2.0-litre swept volume. They were the work of

The AJ6 engine certainly looked neat under the bonnet. This is a 4.0-litre type, in a LHD Daimler from 1990.

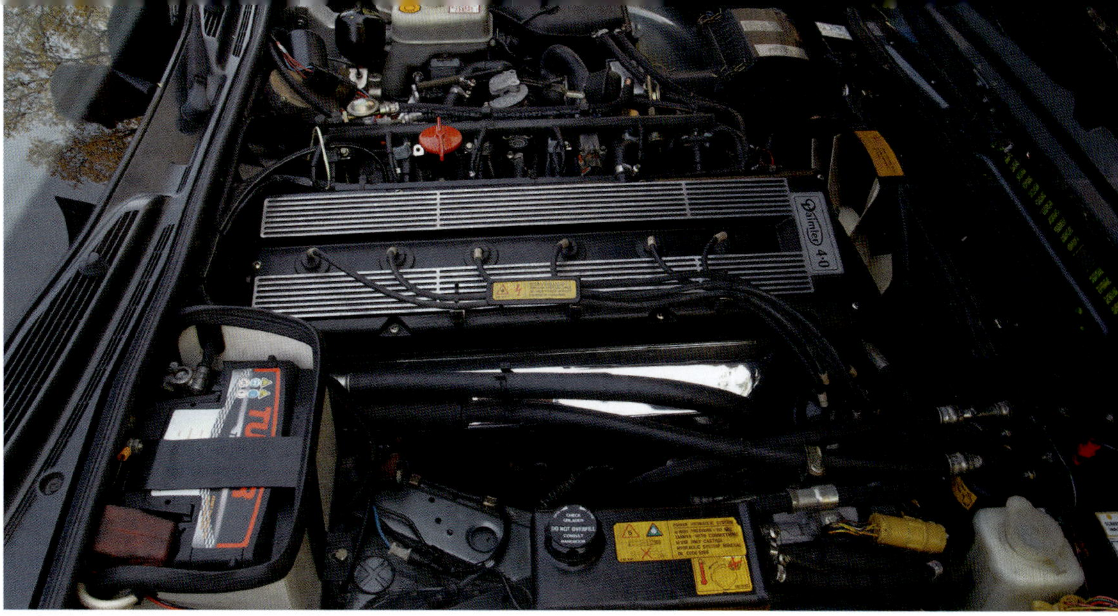

The 4-cylinder Land Rover engines shared a common ohv design. This is the 2.25-litre petrol version...

...and this is the diesel version under the bonnet of a Series III model.

Rover's chief engine designer, Jack Swaine. From 1958, larger-bore derivatives were created with a 2.25-litre (2286cc) swept volume, and the petrol engine was also used in the Rover 80 saloon.

The two engines were changed in only minor respects before 1980. That year, they were re-engineered with five main bearings in place of the original three, and were renamed 2.3-litre types, although the swept volume remained unchanged. In 1984 a long-stroke 2.5-litre (2495cc) diesel engine with belt-driven camshaft was introduced, and the following year the petrol engine was enlarged to the same size but retained its chain-driven camshaft.

In 2.25-litre and 2.3-litre forms the petrol engine had around 75bhp at 4,000rpm (the figures varied over the years) with 120lb/ft of torque, and the diesel had 60–65bhp with between 101lb/ft and 130lb/ft of torque. Low compression petrol engines with less power were available for export to countries where only poor quality fuel could be had. The 2.5-litre diesel had 67bhp, and the 2.5 petrol had 83bhp. Versions of the 2.25-litre engines were made available for marine and some specialist uses during the 1960s.

The 6-cylinder Land Rover petrol engine is seen here in early form with an SU carburettor; later engines had a Zenith type.

Land Rover 6-Cylinder

The 6-cylinder engine available in long-wheelbase Land Rovers was the final descendant of a design drawn up in the late 1940s for Rover cars, and had overhead inlet and side exhaust valves. The block was cast iron, and the head was aluminium alloy. The engine had been re-engineered in the 1950s to allow for a capacity increase to 3 litres for the 1958 Rover P5 saloon, and gained seven main bearings at the same time. A short-stroke version of the engine was then created for the Rover 100 saloon of 1959, and it was a low compression version of this engine that was available in Land Rovers. It had 83bhp at 4,500rpm and 128lb/ft of torque at 1,500rpm.

Rolls-Royce FB60

The Rolls-Royce FB60 just qualifies as an engine used by British Leyland because it was available in the Vanden Plas 4-litre R models during the corporation's first year of existence in 1968.

In the late 1940s, Rolls-Royce started production of their B-series engine range, which provided several different sizes based on an essentially modular design. Most were used for military vehicles, the B40 having 4 cylinders, the B60 6, and the B80 8. The two larger sizes also powered many Dennis fire engines.

British Leyland's only production use of the 4-litre Rolls-Royce FB60 engine was in the Vanden Plas 4-litre R, although there were plans to put it into a re-engineered Austin-Healey as well. MAGIC CAR PICS

The 4-cylinder Rover ohc engine in an early Rover 2000. A 2.2-litre size was developed later.

The Rover V8 was another legendary engine, although it was actually designed by General Motors' Buick division. This is an early 3.5-litre type, with automatic gearbox attached.

The FB60 was a special development of the 6-cylinder design, with an aluminium alloy block and unique bore and stroke dimensions. Like its B-range parents, it had an inlet-over-exhaust valve arrangement. The engine developed 175bhp from 3909cc, and just before BLMC was formed had been earmarked for a new 4-litre version of the Austin-Healey sports car as well; however, this did not pass the pre-production stage.

Rover ohc

The original 4-cylinder ohc Rover engine was designed around 1958 by Rover's Jack Swaine, with a 2-litre (1978cc) capacity and 'square' bore and stroke dimensions. It was introduced in 90bhp (gross) single-SU form in 1963, and was developed with twin SU carburettors for the Rover 2000TC of 1966.

The engine was further developed in the early 1970s. Rover designed a new slant-four 16-valve engine using the existing block with an enlarged bore size. That engine was cancelled in 1971, but the enlarged bores were carried over when a more powerful version of the existing 4-cylinder engine was required. The big-bore versions of the engine were used in the Rover 2200SC (single-carburettor) and Rover 2200TC (twin-carburettor) between 1973 and 1976, when the engine went out of production.

This Rover engine was never used in any other car, although Rover examined the possibility of using both 2000 and 2200 versions in Land Rovers. The company also looked at making 3-litre 6-cylinder, 2.5-litre 5-cylinder and 1.5-litre 3-cylinder versions for various applications, but none of these entered production.

Rover V8

The Rover V8 began life in 1960 as a General Motors (Buick) engine for that company's compact saloons. It was declared redundant in 1963, and Rover bought the manufacturing rights in 1965, adapting it for UK manufacture and conditions and beginning production in 1967. The 3.5-litre (3528cc) V8 was used in the P5B 3.5-litre, P6B 3500 and SD1 3500 models, as well as in the Range Rover, the military-only Land Rover 101 Forward Control and, from 1979, the Land Rover Stage 1 models. It powered the MGB GT V8, and was also planned for Triumph sports cars; the TR8 did enter production but had a short life, and the Lynx coupé was cancelled.

The engine is an all-aluminium V8 with a single central camshaft operating overhead valves. In the British Leyland era, most versions had twin carburettors, but from 1980 fuel in-

Triumph's ohv 4-cylinder engine was produced in many variants. This is the twin-carburettor 1493cc version in a Spitfire.

The slant-four engine also came in several sizes. This is a 1.5-litre twin-carburettor type in a Dolomite.

jection became available to meet emissions control requirements in some overseas markets. The engine was always well liked for its combination of compact dimensions, light weight, simple design, robustness, high torque and tunability. Even fuel economy was acceptable for its day.

Power varied over the years from 91bhp (in Land Rover form) to 190bhp (in injected Rover Vitesse form), with torque from 166lb/ft at 2,000rpm, up to 212lb/ft at 3,000rpm. The engine was later enlarged to 3.9, 4.2 and finally 4.6 litres, and went out of production in 2004. A turbocharged diesel version, codenamed Iceberg, was developed jointly with Perkins in the early 1980s, but was cancelled before production began. Many engines were supplied to other makers, such as Marcos, Morgan and TVR, for use in small-volume sports cars.

Triumph ohv 4-Cylinder

The ohv Triumph 4-cylinder engine, in production when BLMC was formed, had started life as a 803cc size for the Standard Eight in 1953. By 1968 it was available as a 1296cc size with 61bhp. That autumn, a twin-carburettor 1296cc raised power to 75bhp, and from 1970 a long-stroke 1493cc size gave 61bhp, later increased to 65bhp.

Final versions of the 1493cc engine gave 71bhp, and this engine remained in production until 1981. The ohv 4-cylinder in its various guises had powered the Herald, the Spitfire, the front-wheel-drive 1300 and 1500 saloons, the Toledo, and several of the Dolomite range.

Triumph Slant-Four

Triumph had begun work on a new family of engines in 1963. The plan was to save both tooling and development costs by making an ohc slant-four and a V8 which would be in effect two slant-fours on a common crankshaft. One or the other would suit all Triumph's models, because the capacities envisaged ranged from 1.5 litres of the smallest four-cylinder to four litres in the largest feasible V8.

The slant-four was ready first, and was supplied to Saab in 1.7-litre form from 1965 for their 99 model. That company would later develop it further for its own cars. Triumph announced it for their own cars in 1971, when it had an 1854cc swept volume for the Dolomite 1850 and 91bhp. Bored out to 2.0 litres to give 105bhp, it would also power the TR7 sports car from 1974, although emissions control gear reduced that output to 92bhp on North American cars.

Under Spen King, Triumph developed this engine further with an ingenious 16-valve cylinder head in which all the valves were

Triumph designed a 16-valve head for the 1854cc version of their slant-four to get maximum performance in the Dolomite Sprint

The Triumph 3-litre V8 proved an embarrassment for its makers, but subsequent development by specialists has made it into a reliable engine. This is a late example, with thermostatically controlled air intake.

operated by a single camshaft acting directly on the inlet valves and through rocker arms on the exhaust valves. This became the highly acclaimed 2.0-litre Dolomite Sprint engine with 127bhp, and its cylinder-head design won a Design Council award in 1974. The last of the Triumph slant-fours was built in 1981.

Triumph V8

Although Triumph had their slant-four engine ready by 1965, there was less immediate demand for the related V8, and the first prototypes were not ready until late spring or early summer 1968. These were drawn up with a 2.5-litre size with the development code of PE158, and were immediately tried out in the prototypes of the Triumph Stag; the plan was to use the same engine later in the Triumph 2000 saloons.

These engines lacked low-speed torque in carburettor form, and when fitted with fuel injection could not be made to meet US emissions regulations. When Spen King arrived from Rover as Triumph's new chief engineer, he suggested trying a larger bore size to give a 3-litre engine, and this was under development as the PE188 type by July 1968.

The 3-litre engine was carried through to production, but BLMC insisted that its castings were made within the group, rather than at the foundry that had made the prototypes. 'Their quality standards were just awful,' remembered King many years later, 'but nobody would listen to me. BL said manufacture had to be kept within the company, and that was that.' His misgivings were well founded: an alarmingly high percentage of production cylinder blocks had to be rejected, and quality control was so bad that some completed engines were found still to contain casting sand. In tandem with design shortcomings such as a high-mounted water pump that was intolerant of drops in coolant level, these problems led to a series of failures in service.

The 3-litre V8 was never developed any further and was never used in any other car, and British Leyland probably breathed a collective sigh of relief when it was taken out of production in 1977.

Triumph Six

The Triumph 6-cylinder engine that British Leyland inherited had first appeared in 1960 in 1998cc form in the Standard Vanguard. From 1963, with twin carburettors and 90bhp, it powered the Triumph 2000, and would continue to do so until

The Triumph 6-cylinder was another engine with its origins in a Standard. This is the 1998cc size in a GT6 Mark 3.

The largest of the Triumph sixes was the 2498cc size, here in twin-carburettor 2500TC form.

that car's production ended in 1977. Throughout its production life, it remained a highly respected engine, and from 1966 was also used in the Vitesse and the GT6 coupé.

From 1967, a long-stroke 2498cc version was made available in the TR5 sports car, with Lucas fuel injection for most models, but twin carburettors for the USA. The injected engine powered the 2.5PI saloon from 1968, and power rose to 132bhp and later to 150bhp in the TR6. However, the Lucas system became notorious for reliability problems. From 1975, all engines were carburettor types.

Triumph 'SD1' Six

Triumph began work in 1970 on a new 6-cylinder engine, which they intended to use in a new big saloon and also in an eventual replacement for the Dolomite. It was also earmarked as an upgrade for the last few years of Triumph 2000 and 2500 production.

Spen King, then Technical Director, proposed to create this by adding Dolomite Sprint-type valve gear to the existing

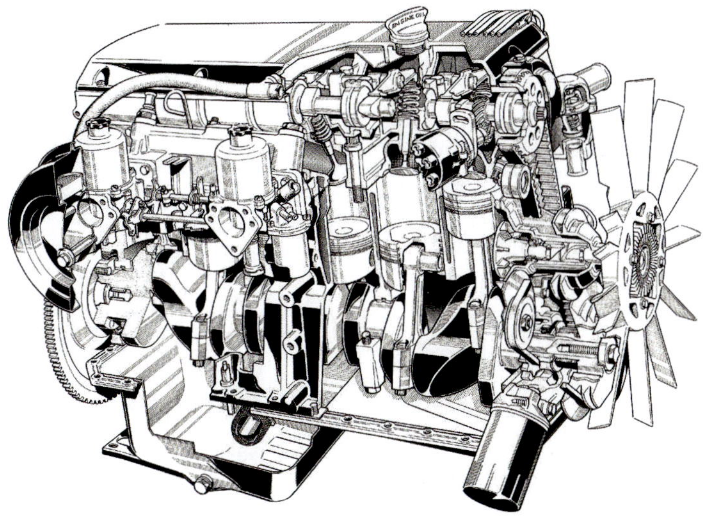

ABOVE: Although it was always associated with the Rover SD1, this ohc 6-cylinder engine originated with Triumph.

BELOW: In this overhead view of the ohc 'six', the Rover labelling on the rocker box is very clear.

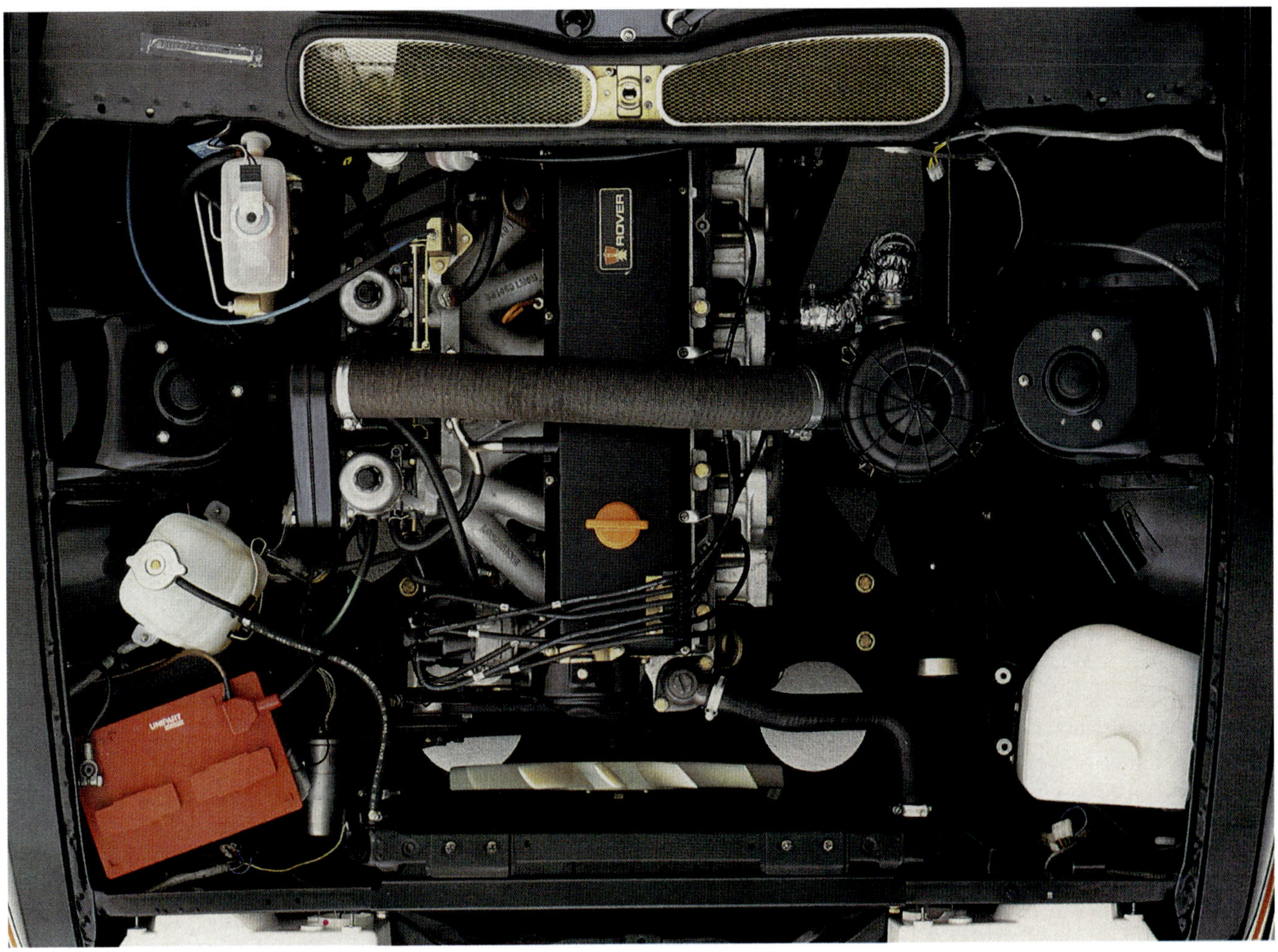

The ADE4 diesel engine is seen here in a South African Series IIIS Land Rover, carrying labels that brand it as an ADE 236 – 236 being its size in cubic inches....

... and this is what it really looked like, although this is actually the UK-built Perkins 4.236 parent engine.

6-cylinder block to create a new ohc engine. However, his idea seems not to have gone beyond the design stage before Triumph increased the budget for the new engine in early 1972. This allowed a redesign of the cylinder block around repositioned bores. By this time both projected Triumph models had been cancelled, and the engine was intended for the new Rover SD1.

Two versions were drawn up, beginning with the PE146 (petrol engine, 140cu in or roughly 2.3 litres, 6 cylinders), which was followed by the PE166 with a swept volume of approximately 160cu in (2.6 litres). A further redesign in 1973 gave the theoretical possibility of making a 3-litre version (actually 2928cc), but this was never built. All versions would have twin SU carburettors and a toothed rubber belt camshaft drive – the first time this had ever been used in an engine from the Leyland group.

Delays in bringing these engines into production were caused to some extent by friction between the Triumph engineers and those from Rover. They were finally ready by early 1977, and powered the Rover 2300 and 2600 models. They would go on to become highly regarded, especially the 2.6-litre size, despite occasional problems with a blocked oilway in the cylinder head that caused expensive failure. Neither was ever used in any car except the SD1, and both went out of production with that car in 1986.

South African ADE4

The ADE4 diesel engine took its name from the fact that it had 4 cylinders and was manufactured by Atlantis Diesel Engines in South Africa. It was in fact a licence-built version of the British-designed Perkins 4.236 – 4 for 4 cylinders, and 236 for the swept volume in cubic inches, which translates as 3860cc. This indirect-injection engine was used only in the South African-built Series IIIS Land Rover, in 74bhp form, between 1981 and 1985. A best guess is that no more than 800 of the Series IIIS models had it.

South African R6

When British Leyland's Australian manufacturing operation was cut back in 1974, the tooling for the company's 2.6-litre engine was shipped to South Africa. In Australia, the engine had been called the E6 and was used in the Leyland P76. In South Africa, it was modified to suit local conditions and was renamed an R6 (Rover 6-cylinder) for use in locally assembled Rover SD1 saloons from 1978.

The South African changes brought a new camshaft and an uprated cooling system. Power and torque were both reduced from the Australian version, and lower noise levels were a claimed side benefit. The South African R6 had 110bhp at 4,750rpm and 148lb/ft of torque at 2,500rpm, with two SU HIF6 carburettors and an 8.75:1 compression ratio.

As assembly of the SD1 wound down in the mid-1980s, the engine was introduced in the Series IIIS Land Rover, which was a uniquely South African long-wheelbase model designed to offer a more powerful engine to counter local sales of the Toyota Land Cruiser.

The enlarged E6 engine developed in Australia became an R6 when manufacture began in South Africa – here in a South African Rover SD1…

… and here in a South African Series IIIS Land Rover.

One of the few bought-in engines during the British Leyland era was this 2.4-litre VM diesel, displaying its four separate cylinder heads under the bonnet of a Rover 2400SD Turbo.

VM Turbodiesel

When Rover needed a diesel engine for its SD1 models in the early 1980s, there was no suitable in-house engine available. However, Italian diesel engine specialist VM Motori had been trying to interest British Leyland in its engines since the mid-1970s, and now became the favoured supplier.

The VM diesel engine chosen for the Rover was a turbo-charged 2.4-litre (2393cc) 4-cylinder, with indirect injection. It had oversquare cylinder dimensions, overhead valves and a chain-driven camshaft. A key characteristic resulting from its modular design was that each cylinder had a separate cylinder-head casting. It was known as the HR492HT type, and delivered 90bhp at 4,000rpm with 142lb/ft of torque at 2,350rpm. The exhaust-driven turbocharger was made by KKK, and had a maximum boost pressure of 10psi, which was controlled by a wastegate.

A version of this engine would be introduced as the diesel option in the Range Rover in 1986, supplemented by an inter-cooler to boost its output up to 112bhp.

APPENDIX II: CODE NAMES

Despite the attractive names dreamed up by marketing departments to help sell cars to the public, those cars are often known by much more prosaic names during the design and development stages. This is a list of such names associated with the cars discussed in this book. It is unlikely to be exhaustive!

ADO6	Austin Hire Car and Taxi (FL2, FL2D, FX4, FX4D), 1958–71
ADO14	Austin Maxi, 1969–81
ADO15	Austin, Morris (and other marques) Mini, 1959 on
ADO16	Austin, Morris, Riley, Vanden Plas and Wolseley 1100 and 1300, 1963–74
ADO17	Austin, Morris and Wolseley 1800 and 2200 range, 1964–75
ADO19	Austin Ant, 1967–68; cancelled by Leyland
ADO20	Mini Mark III
ADO21	Proposed MGB replacement, in design 1969–70
ADO22	Proposed redesign of ADO16, 1967–68; cancelled in favour of ADO67
ADO23	MGB, 1962–74
ADO24	Austin-Healey 4000, cancelled by BL
ADO25	The E6 engine
ADO26	Initially major facelift of ADO17, but soon cancelled; then became X6 project (Australian YDO19)
ADO28	Morris Marina, 1971–80
ADO32	E4 engine
ADO38	Revised Farina 'B' models, 1961–71
ADO39	FX4 taxi replacement, cancelled by BL; 1967
ADO41	Austin-Healey Sprite Mark II and Mark III
ADO46	Diesel A60 Cambridge (1962–68) and Morris Oxford (1962–71)
ADO47	MG Midget
ADO50	Cooper versions of Mini; Cooper S was ADO50S
ADO52	MGC, 1967–69
ADO59	Morris Minor 1000, 1962–71
ADO61	Austin 3-litre, 1967–71
ADO67	Austin Allegro, 1973–82
ADO68	Also called Condor; proposals for a two-door Marina, 1969–70
ADO69	Second planned replacement for FX4, 1970; cancelled
ADO70	Proposed targa-roof Mini coupé by Michelotti, 1970
ADO71	Austin-Morris and Wolseley 18-22 series, 1975
ADO73	Morris Ital; started as a front-end facelift proposal
ADO74	Ant/Dragonfly/Ladybird; supermini project of 1972–73, shelved by John Barber
ADO75	MGB GT V8, 1972–74
ADO76	Revised MGB, 1974–80
ADO77	Proposed Marina replacement, to rival Cortina; merged with SD2, then became TM1, 1972–75
ADO88	Metro predecessor, cancelled after negative clinic reactions; re-engineered to become LC8 (Austin Metro)
ADO99	Proposed Allegro replacement, instigated by Spen King; followed TM1 and became LC10/LM10 (Maestro)
Ajax	Triumph 1300
AM2	Proposed booted Metro, under development in the late 1970s
AR5	Proposed Rover 200 replacement; cancelled in favour of AR8/R8, which replaced 200 and Maestro together
AR6	Proposed new supermini, under development in 1984–86 and intended to replace the Metro; cancelled for lack of funding
AR7	Proposed Maestro replacement, under development in 1984–85; gave way to AR8
AR8	Started out as YY; became R8 in 1988
AR9	Unconfirmed; possibly rebodied Montego
AR16	Proposed four-door saloon on shortened XX platform, under development in 1984–85
AR17	Proposed five-door hatch, companion to AR16
Bravo	Proposed SD1 rebody with both four-door and five-door variants, 1979–80; abandoned in favour of XX
Bullet	Triumph TR7, from 1975
Condor	Various proposals for a two-door coupé Marina
HD9	Proposed five-door Acclaim; possibly also associated with the Rover Quintet in Australia

HD14	Proposed small hatchback, below Metro, possibly based on Honda City/Jazz, under development in 1980–81
HD17	Early name for XX
HX	Honda Legend (joint with XX)
HY	Honda version of YY
Innsbruck	Triumph 2000/2500 Mark 2 range, 1969–77
LC8	Austin Metro
LC9	Triumph Acclaim, also called Project Bounty, 1981–84
LC10	Austin Maestro, renamed from ADO99; initial stages of LM11 Montego also had this code
LC12	Possibly a coupé version of LC10, 1978–80
LC40	Jaguar XJ40, renamed to fall in line with corporate naming in 1977; reverted to XJ40 in 1978
LM10	Austin Maestro, code used from 1980
LM11	Austin Montego
LM12	Proposed two-door coupé on LM11 floorpan, to be an MG and replace all MGs and TRs; considered in 1980–81
LM14	Proposed hatchback Montego, 1980–81
LM15	Proposed re-skin of SD1, 1980–81
LM19	Austin Ambassador, 1981–84
Lynx	Proposed Triumph coupé, 1970s
P5B	Rover 3.5-litre Saloon and Coupé, 1967–73
P6	Rover 2000, 2200 and variants, 1963–77
P6B	Rover 3500 and 3500S, 1968–76
P8	Proposed Rover replacement for P5B saloons, cancelled in 1971
P9	Proposed mid-engined Rover sports car; could have become an Alvis
P10	First thoughts on Rover replacement for P6 and P6B; later became RT1 and then SD1
P76	Development code for Australian Leyland P76 saloon; the name was retained for the production car
Puma	Proposed Triumph replacement for 2000 and 2500 saloon range
R6	South African-built 6-cylinder engine based on Australian 2.6-litre E6 type
RT1	Joint Rover-Triumph project to replace Rover P6 and Triumph 2000/2500 saloon ranges; later became Rover SD1
SD1	Rover 3500, 2000, 2300, 2400 and 2600 range, 1976–86
SD2	Proposed Dolomite replacement, under development in 1972–75; merged with ADO77 in 1975
Stag	Triumph Stag, 1970–77; the development code name was retained for the production car
TM1	Proposed Triumph-Morris family saloon, under development in 1975
XX	Rover 800
YDO4	Australian basic Mini, with rubber cone suspension
YDO5	Australian Deluxe Mini, with Hydrolastic suspension
YDO6	Australian Morris Cooper S
YDO7	Australian Morris Mini Moke
YDO8	Australian Morris Mini Moke, 1969
YDO9	Australian Morris Nomad; hatchback relative of ADO16
YDO10	Australian Austin 1800 'ute' and chassis-cab
YDO13	Australian Austin X6 (Tasman and Kimberley), Mark I
YDO14	Planned Australian 'ute' derivative of YDO13
YDO15	Australian-engineered and assembled ADO16
YDO18	Australian Morris Moke (with 13in wheels)
YDO19	Australian Austin X6 (Tasman and Kimberley), Mark 2 models
YDO21	Australian Morris/Leyland Mini Clubman, with rubber cone suspension
YDO22	Australian Morris Mini Clubman with Hydrolastic suspension, later with rubber cone suspension
YDO23	Australian Morris Mini Clubman GT
YDO24	Australian Morris Marina
YDO25	Australian Leyland Marina
YDO26	Australian Leyland P76
YDO27	Australian Leyland Force 7V
YDO28	Australian Leyland P76 estate ('wagon')
YDO30	Australian Leyland Moke Californian
YY	Early stages of AR8/R8 programme
Zebu	Triumph 2000 (Mark I)
Zobo	Triumph Herald

APPENDIX III: BRITISH LEYLAND CAR ASSEMBLY PLANTS IN THE UK

British Leyland inherited a large number of assembly plants on its formation in 1968, and these assembly plants were fed by an even larger number of feeder and satellite plants dedicated to the manufacture of engines or sub-assemblies, both major and minor. In this book there is simply not enough room to list every one of them, so this Appendix is confined to the assembly plants – the car factories where all those sub-assemblies finally came together to make a complete car.

Abingdon

The Abingdon factory was opened in 1930 to build MG cars, and would always be seen as the spiritual home of MG, even though MGs had sometimes been built elsewhere and the Abingdon factory had built other marques as well when BMC, or its predecessors needed the space. Rileys were built there between 1949 and 1957, Morris Minors between 1960 and 1964, and Austin Healeys between 1957 and 1971.

During the BLMC and BL era, Abingdon remained the primary home of MGs, and its main products were the MGB and MG Midget sports cars. In 1979–80, the factory also built the Vanden Plas 1500 model that was based on the Allegro.

After the last MGBs had been built, the Abingdon factory was closed in October 1980 as part of the slimming-down process initiated under Michael Edwardes. Some of its buildings still survive as part of the Abingdon Business Park.

Browns Lane

Jaguar's headquarters had been at Browns Lane in Coventry since 1951, a factory that had started life as a government-owned 'shadow' plant managed by Daimler. Although the plant was modernized in the late 1970s, when a new paint shop was added, Jaguar had long since outgrown it and had relied for many years on feeder plants in the area: from 1960, the old Daimler works at Radford had become the engine build area and machine shops, and under British Leyland the former Pressed Steel Fisher plant at Castle Bromwich became the Jaguar body plant. In more recent years, Jaguar has moved all its major operations into Castle Bromwich.

Canley

The Triumph plant at Canley, also known as Fletchamstead because it fronted on to the Fletchamstead Highway, had been the main assembly plant for Standard cars in the inter-war years. After Standard bought Triumph, it became the Triumph assembly plant as well from 1946. A big new assembly hall was constructed on the site in 1960–61, and by the time of BLMC's formation in 1968 Canley was Triumph's headquarters.

After the Ryder Report, plans were drawn up to turn Canley into a large-scale component manufacturing centre that would feed other British Leyland factories. However, those plans had been overturned by 1978, when TR7 assembly was moved to Canley from the Speke (Liverpool no. 2) plant. As British Leyland restructured yet again under Sir Michael Edwardes, Canley was closed as a manufacturing plant, although it survived into the 1990s as an administrative, engineering and design headquarters.

Cowley

The Cowley plant was the traditional home of Morris, but by the time of British Leyland it had become a complex of factories that also incorporated the Pressed Steel Fisher body plant on the other side of the main road from the Morris works. The Morris plant had started life as the Oxford Military College, but William Morris had gradually developed it into a huge assembly plant after 1912. He had also helped establish the Pressed Steel plant to provide bodies for his factory from 1926, but from 1930 had pulled out to leave Pressed Steel independent and able to build for multiple car makers.

Under BMC, the Cowley plant had very much become the poor relation to Longbridge, the former Austin headquarters. That position remained unchanged under British Leyland after 1968, and in the mid-1970s the Ryder Report noted that much of its equipment was outdated and inefficient. Re-organization under Sir Michael Edwardes then saw Cowley become the main plant for the Light-Medium Cars division.

By the time of the Austin Rover Group in 1982, the bodies for the Ital, Acclaim, Ambassador and Rover SD1 were all being manufactured at the Body Plant (the former Pressed Steel works), and all except those for the Ital were painted there as well, using advanced new processes. Overhead conveyors took them across the main road (some crossed two roads) to the assembly lines on the other side.

From the early 1980s, Cowley assembled the non-identical Maestro and Montego twins, and it would also be chosen as the manufacturing and assembly location for the Rover 800 that was launched in 1986.

Liverpool No. 1

Triumph's Liverpool no. 1 factory originally belonged to Hall Engineering, who made office furniture and light pressings. Hall Engineering made body sections for the very early Heralds from 1959, and the following year Standard-Triumph took over the factory completely.

In subsequent years, Liverpool no. 1 was considerably expanded. It built the bodies for the TR4, TR4A, TR5/TR250 and TR6 sports cars throughout their life, and also those for the 1300s, 1500s and Dolomites. Pressings for the Stag and TR7/TR8 bodies, both assembled at the Liverpool no. 2 (Speke) factory, also originated here.

Longbridge

The Longbridge plant near Birmingham was the traditional home of the Austin marque, having been opened as a car factory in 1905 by Herbert Austin. Before that, it had been a printing works. It grew to become a major employer in the area, and by the time BLMC was formed in 1968 had a workforce of around 25,000 people.

In the early years of the Michael Edwardes regime at British Leyland, Longbridge was selected as the plant where the new Austin Metro would be built. To that end it was expanded with a New West Works where the bodyshells would be assembled with a great deal of robotic input – which represented a 'first' for British Leyland. Completed bodies were carried across a main road by an overhead conveyor to the assembly building, and this conveyor became a defining characteristic of the Longbridge plant in its later years.

Longbridge remained central to Metro production until it ended. It remained an important assembly location for Rover Group cars, and for that company's successors, MG Rover.

Solihull

When BLMC inherited the Rover factory at Solihull in 1968, it was assembling Rover P5B, P6 and P6B saloons, and Land Rovers.

This factory was built in 1939–40 by the Air Ministry as a 'shadow' factory to build Bristol Hercules radial engines. Its management was entrusted to Rover, whose headquarters were in Coventry at the time, and this was the second factory entrusted to them; the other was at Acocks Green, and was built in 1936.

When the war ended, Rover took up the option to buy the Solihull factory, and as their Coventry premises had been seriously damaged during the Blitz in 1940, relocated there. Every Rover from late 1945 to 1981 and every Land Rover from 1948 was built there, initially in the assembly hall built for aero engines.

Major expansion began with the opening of a new covered despatch area in early 1956 at the western end of the site. This was subsequently incorporated into the new North Works that was built to house Rover P6 assembly from 1963. After P6 assembly ended in 1977, the North Works was used for storage for a while, before being converted in the late 1970s to house engine assembly, and extended to take over Range Rover assembly.

A vast new assembly plant was built for the Rover SD1 in 1975–76, but that car never filled it. Between 1980 and 1981 Triumph TR7s were built there, but in 1982 Rover SD1 production was moved to Cowley, and Solihull became a Land Rover-only plant. There has been further expansion and extensive rebuilding in subsequent years as Land Rover production has expanded.

Speke

Triumph's Speke factory was also known as the Liverpool no. 2 plant, and was located about a mile from the Liverpool no. 1 plant. Standard-Triumph bought the site in 1960, but building work did not commence until 1966–67.

The Speke factory opened for business under British Leyland, beginning with the production of Triumph Toledo models and going on to build the bodies for the Triumph Stag. Toledo production was moved to Coventry at the end of 1974, and its former lines at Speke were refitted for production of the Triumph TR7. However, TR7 production at Speke was marred by industrial action and poor productivity, and a serious fourteen-week strike in 1977–78 was the last straw for British Leyland management. They closed the Speke plant in 1978.

INDEX